CW00537144

Nothing Not Giving Messages

OTHER BOOKS BY EDWIN MORGAN INCLUDE:

Poems of Thirty Years (Carcanet, 1982)
Grafts/Takes (Mariscat, 1983)
Sonnets from Scotland (Mariscat, 1984)
Selected Poems (Carcanet, 1985)
Tales from Limerick Zoo (Mariscat, 1988)
Themes on a Variation (Carcanet, 1988)
Crossing the Border: essays on Scottish Literature
(Carcanet, forthcoming 1990)
Collected Poems (Carcanet, forthcoming 1990)

OTHER BOOKS BY HAMISH WHYTE INCLUDE:

apple on an orange day: poems (Autolycus, 1973)
Rooms: poems (Aquila, 1986)

As editor:

Noise and Smoky Breath (Third Eye/Glasgow District Libraries,
1983; new edition forthcoming 1990)
The Scottish Cat (Aberdeen University Press, 1987)
Glasgow Observed (with Simon Berry) (John Donald, 1987)
Streets of Stone: Glasgow stories (with Moira Burgess)
(Salamander, 1985)
Streets of Gold (with Moira Burgess) (Mainstream, 1989)
About Edwin Morgan (with Robert Crawford)
(Edinburgh University Press, 1990)

Nothing Not Giving Messages

reflections on work and life

Edwin Morgan

edited by Hamish Whyte

Polygon
EDINBURGH

Copyright in the contributions by individual
interviewers remains with them.
First published in 1990 by Polygon
22 George Square, Edinburgh

Typeset in CRTronic Sabon by
Polyprint, Edinburgh
and printed and bound in Great Britain
by Bell and Bain Limited, Glasgow

British Library Cataloguing-in-Publication Data
is available for this book.

ISBN 0 7486 6077 1
ISBN 0 7486 6083 6 pbk

Acknowledgements
The publisher acknowledges subsidy
from the Scottish Arts Council towards
the publication of this volume.
Grateful acknowledgement is made to all
those who gave permission to reprint
material; to the interviewers; to Diana
Lee for translating the Turkish interview;
and to Robert Crawford, Peter Kravitz,
Kevin McCarra, David Neilson and
Winifred Whyte for advice and comment.
The drawing of Edwin Morgan by Alasdair Gray
originally appeared on the cover of
Grafts/Takes (Mariscat Press, 1983).
The cover design by Ann Ross Paterson incorporates
images from Edwin Morgan's scrapbooks, which are
held in the Special Collections department of
Glasgow University library.

Editor's Note

Nothing Not Giving Messages is a selection from Edwin Morgan's interviews, lectures, broadcasts, articles, statements, etc. over the past thirty years. The book is in two parts. The first consists of interviews given by Edwin Morgan on his life and work and dating from 1971 to 1988. They have been slightly edited to eliminate obvious repetitions, but not all repetitions, since similar questions are asked by different interviewers and the answers can differ in context or emphasis, as well as providing evidence of recurring themes and abiding concerns. The items in the second part span the years 1959 to 1989 and offer more considered statements by Edwin Morgan on his work — as poet, translator, critic and academic — including comment on specific poems, gleaned from a variety of sources. Plus a recent tour of Morganiana and a list of books read 1927–1940.

Edwin Morgan has followed the project closely as it has grown. He has corrected many a slip of tongue and pen and made valuable suggestions, without interfering in the general shape of the book. My special thanks to him for agreeing to the idea in the first place and for all his help. He has said that he would never write an autobiography; perhaps *Nothing Not Giving Messages* might be considered as notes instead of.

Hamish Whyte
October 1989
Glasgow

Contents

About the House
Whittingehame Court, 4 July 1989

Living Room

Ladderax bookshelves: top shelf has *The Works of the Ettrick Shepherd* (2 vols) next to *Babell* (Maitland Club; from Wemyss Castle library, shelf G7) next to *Beatles Complete* next to Robert Mapplethorpe and *Street Maps of British Towns* and the *Times Atlas of the Moon* ('more interesting than the *Times Atlas of the World*'); other shelves have largish books, arranged by genre, country then artist: Herbert Read's *Surrealism* (elastic band round it to keep in wad of cuttings and cards), *Pop Art*, Hockney, Malevich, Paolozzi, Caspar David Friedrich, Scottie Wilson (signed by George Melly), Velazquez; the *Pergamon World Atlas*; trilobites; a geode (actually ½ geode, 'better than nothing'); ebony figure from Malaysia with popping eyes and dice in his top hat (sent to EM's Aunt Myra by her ex-fiancé who had gone off to the East like a Somerset Maugham character); pile of videos: *Billy Connolly Bites Yer Bum, Deliverance, Predator, The Sharks, The Great Whales,* the complete *Star Wars* trilogy, *Ran, Battleship Potemkin, October*; blue tin of sewing stuff ('if a button comes off'); box of photographs from 1955 Russian trip; folders of Russian-interest cuttings.

On floor between bookshelves and mantelpiece: Japanese wooden toad. On mantelpiece: invites to art shows; Italian jar for pencils (present from Morven); brass Chinese dragon (Granny's); black origami house (from Christina).

At the television set (Tandberg — 'obsolete now'): on top: rivet from Forth Railway Bridge set in clear plastic; below: Philips video recorder without remote control ('good exercise'); more videotapes: *Goldfish* ('very soothing'), *Ian Hamilton Finlay, Max Headroom, Metropolis.*

Balcony and window boxes. Plants here and all over house.

Pictures: Joan Eardley, *Sweet Shop, Rotten Row, Glasgow*; Andrew Williams, *Achilles and Patroclus*; Pat Douthwaite, *Rhea*.

On sideboard: JVC midi system with CD; Penguin *Post-War Polish Poetry*; Kenneth White, *The Bird Path* (for article for *Books in Scotland*); pile of slim vols for review in *Cencrastus*; photograph of John Scott, cigarette in hand ('he was a very heavy smoker').

On small table in middle of room: Canon FC-3 portable photocopier.

Overflow box next to record cabinet includes: *Woodstock*, *Quadrophenia*, Early Medieval Music, Matt McGinn, Armenian liturgical chants, Yevtushenko and Voznesensky.

Dining table serving as work table (in preference to using study: 'I discovered I liked a view when writing'); tubular chair of chrome and black leather ('the chair in which . . .'); blue linen jacket draped over ordinary dining room chair. On table ('chaotic top'): Japanese calculator ('of course'); glass paperweight (debate as to what's embedded in it: coloured pieces of glass or scraps of material); the Morganspecs; sellotape in blue plastic dispenser; Magritte calendar (New Year present) showing *The Natural Phenomenon* for July; R. F. Mackenzie's *A Search for Scotland*; Scotland Diary for 1989; stampbook ('every conceivable denomination, for letters to New Zealand, Iraq, etc.'); sloping scratch pad; red W. H. Smith stapler sitting on pile of paper-clipped 'this and thats'; rack with notepaper and envelopes; clipboard with blank sheet of paper and pen and pencil ('I'm a great pencil man') waiting; correspondence weighted under paper-knife from kitchen (where opened in morning) showing letter from Neil Astley of Bloodaxe asking for blurb comment for a book and from me (bibliographic pestering); the libretto for *Valentine* (to be performed in 1990); *Beowulf and its Analogues* on top of folder marked 'Curriculum vitae etc. V'.

On chair in corner: Blue Bird manual typewriter, modified to include accents, square brackets, etc.; plastic bag used as cover (put on each night).

Globe lamp on chrome stand; black suite: vinyl Chesterfield and chair, leather chair. Mosaic-topped coffee table on which are: bits from *Nothing Not Giving Messages* in progress; Keith Bosley's translation of the *Kalevala*; two glasses of

Marks and Spencer's lemonade; Russian wooden cigarette box with hand-painted lid (filled with Superkings); box of Vulcan matches (EM doesn't smoke); cloisonné ('I'm very fond of cloisonné work') ashtray with floral decoration; sugar shaker (for strawberries long gone).

Kitchen

On shelf: B. Nilson, *Penguin Cookery Book*; Katharine Whitehorn, *How to Survive in the Kitchen* (a present); more sellotape in dispenser. Anda Paterson painting, *The Barras*; Colin Baxter Glasgow calendar on wall. Model Viking ship (made by Allan Shearer) on top of cupboard. On work-surface: small Hitachi ghettoblaster; two empty Japanese bowls; wooden fruit bowl with grapefruit and tomatoes; usual plants and a fuchsia rescued from the rubbish ('doing well against the odds'). On table: file box marked 'Concrete & Sound Poetry I'. Pulley (which EM had put in).

Hall

L-shaped, lined with books and pictures ('period'). Pictures include a Crosbie still life of fruit, *Silver and Satin* by David Warrillow and four Japanese theatre prints. Wall of Scottish books. Case of guidebooks, grammars and a set of *Writers and their Work* pamphlets. Hall cupboard: usual household items, boots and shoes; photograph of a Cedar of Lebanon (taken on Mount Lebanon) and a real hammer hanging on the wall.

Spare Bedroom

More pictures and books (in all rooms except bathroom). Books: most of Olson, Russian books again, Mailer, Pynchon (*The Grim Phoenix*), Saki; bag of books for donation to The Mitchell Library; plays, reference books, foreign poetry in translation, *Contemporary Poets*, Riding, Sinclair (Iain), Snyder, Stein ('it becomes alphabetical at one point'). Card table covered with Hungarian cloth. Top of chest of drawers: cloisonné ashtray; photograph of parents; photograph of

Mayakovsky and Lili Brik in still from film; pomander dated 1982; mother's brush and mirror set; brass four gospels bell (gleaming — 'my woman's mad for brass'). Alasdair Dunn cat on bedside table (memento of *Scottish Cat* reading).

Cloakroom

Old Penguins and Pelicans ('the world of the mind in paperback'); books on the novel, general lit. crit. Classics on top shelf: Vergil, Zukofsky's Catullus, Bob Dylan's *Lyrics*. *Handbook of Marxism* by Emile Burns next to Swedenborg's *Heaven and Hell* ('all you need'). Spare copies of own books. Low, dark shelf of books on Glasgow. Cupboard of wine bottles and cans. Coats on pegs and poet's cord cap. Victorian photograph of Whirling Dervishes.

Study

All walls, books: dictionaries; most of Kerouac; Kipling's *Plain Tales* next to Larry Kramer's *Faggots*, Jack London to *The Hoods* series by Vincente Torrio (Tony Lopez); Jules Verne, Gore Vidal, *Metropolis* by Thea von Harbou (paperback — Ace SF Classic). On shelf next to SF and Bibles (latter including Old Parish Church of Rutherglen Gift Bible 1945): yellow plastic moonwalker with detachable helmet, holding UN symbol. Granny's inlaid wooden box initialled J.McG.; brass hand sitting on top. Folders everywhere, cupboards full of box files. Small space on wall for pictures: Joan Eardley, *Stacks at Evening*; a James Morrison window ('the first picture I bought — £5'); a sketch by Mayakovsky ('from a bookseller's catalogue'). Photographs: the Bauhaus cat; Harry Robertson (dedicatee of *From Glasgow to Saturn*: 'a lorry driver — of no very fixed address — a happy-go-lucky character'); Malcolm Thomson (dedicatee of *Themes on a Variation*).

Three-legged teak desk (Lewis's). On top: glass paperweight; wire basket full of things half-done ('my *im*pending tray'); books by Calvino (for holiday reading). Chrome and black leather chair, with white piping trim.

Wooden chest with cupboard. On top: tankard for pens and pencils; sellotape in dispenser again; box containing every known size of paperclip; highlighter pen; more wire trays and folders.

Bedroom

Wardrobe: some clothes but mainly books: bigger art books; overflow Russian section; ghetto of Scottish poetry anthologies and Scottish drama; more box files; *New Writing Scotland*.

Library steps.

Ian Hamilton Finlay's *waverock* at window. Bookcase full of magazines. Small chest of drawers containing files of photographs — on top: button box (Russian peasant work like one in living room); Chinese cloisonné box containing odds and ends: cufflinks, RAMC badge, medallion of Ganesha ('very good luck').

A real wardrobe: clothes, pillows, sheets, etc.

Ship's chair (possibly from captain's cabin — acquired by father whose firm was involved in shipbreaking).

Pictures include Peter Howson, *Gallowgate Robin* and two interiors by Charles McCall.

Bed with brass headrail (polished once a week — cf. bell).

On bedside table: early model push button telephone bound in red leather; cloisonné bedside lamp.

Hanging from the door: a dressing gown, red.

HW

I

When poets get up into space

Hello. Happy New Year.

Happy New Year. Hello.

[With coffee and jaffa cake] Who do you think reads your poems? How wide an audience and what kind of audience do you think you have? It's commonly believed that poetry nowadays is for cliques and élites — English departments in universities, in fact. Steve Mulrine, for example, has now stopped writing poetry for this reason and is concentrating on both radio and television plays in order to reach a greater percentage of the population.

Every poet has times of despair but I am encouraged at the moment by the new movement towards poetry readings which I consider very important for getting out to the public in a more immediate way. The audiences there are usually young students, but there are poetry recitals which attract other kinds of audiences — the Saltire Society readings in Edinburgh bring in the older generation. Tom McGrath's idea of taking poetry to the people with readings in Royal Exchange Square which really did involve a great number of people who normally wouldn't bother with poetry. I go to a lot of schools as well to read my poems, and some of them are actually on the English courses. So I think there's a good audience there as well. This supposedly 'new' role of the poet as performer goes back to the concept of the bard — a return to the grass roots. A large section of the audience come along to see the poet in the flesh — the man behind the words. The poet becomes an entertainer again and his new position can have wide-ranging effects on his poetry. It's very difficult to break into the mass media

17

(mediums). Obviously it would be ideal to be able to address a national audience. Opportunities on radio are fairly limited — occasionally there are readings on Radio 3 and Radio 4 (Scotland). Television — almost impossible — the style of poetry readings just doesn't come across unless you have a marvellous producer and director — then you might be able to make a success of it.

That covers mainly people who listen to poetry. What about published books? The small circulation of poetry in Scotland is well known. Duncan Glen's Akros Publications are all editions of (at the most) 500 copies; MacLellan, the only real Glasgow literary publisher, has gone bankrupt. Your own works have been printed in mainly limited editions — and because of this prices of books have been high.

This is true. Some of my books of poetry have been limited editions because of their format. Prices are high because publishing poetry is hardly ever a profitable business. The only way to keep prices down is to publish books like the Penguin Modern Poets series, and to make a profit each issue has to sell in numbers of five figures and must include three poets in each volume. The demise of MacLellan's press has left a gap in Glasgow publishing — his 'Poetry Scotland' series was an excellent outlet at the time for even little known poets — and he could only print these 'literature' books because he carried out commercial printing like newspapers and hand-outs at the same time. At the moment the Midnight Press in Glasgow is publishing poetry at very low prices — booklets and pamphlets for 10p (2/-) and 'Poetry Glasgow' folded sheets for 5p (1/-), but there is still an emptiness in professional printing in Glasgow. The economics of publishing poetry are very difficult to overcome and obviously must limit the readership.

What would you like to see in poetry in Glasgow? Do you think that a poet can write in dialect without restricting his audience to one area?

There is a lot still to be done in Glasgow poetry. There has never been (as yet) a Glasgow school in poetry as there has been in

18

painting at the beginning of this century. So far Glasgow poetry has been as shapeless and indefinite as the city itself. This may change. I would like to see more poetry about Glasgow — reflecting the life of the city — though it does not have to be written in a grey naturalistic William Carlos Williams style. The city has so many aspects and so does the poetry — a very wide range is evident now. The dialect problem is a thorny one. I like to write in Glasgow dialect and try to be as natural as possible — true reproduction of speech is impossible unless you turn to phonetic spellings like Tom Leonard's set of poems or Steve Mulrine's 'Wee Malkies' which depends on a local mythology and background. The dialect problem may be connected with Scottish comedy. You see a dialect poem and somewhere in it you expect to see humour — a poet has to contend with Francie and Josie. It should be possible to break away from this kind of thing and write dialect poetry dealing with non-comic subjects. After all, the people who speak dialect don't go about laughing all day.

Do you think poetry in Glasgow is different from poetry in the 1950s and early 1960s? Do you think Lallans has any influence in poetry here?

Well, the main difference is that there is more poetry being written than ever before. Ten years ago, even at university, there weren't all that many people writing. Now there is plenty going on and it's finding outlets in the 'alternative press' magazines like *Ma Boheme* and *Onyx*. The influences in the late 1960s and the 1970s so far have been international and more particularly, American. The Lallans writers were mainly Edinburgh-based though some Glasgow poets like Tom Scott and even Alex Scott use the language. The idea of a common literary language, even although it is synthetic or 'plastic' is an excellent one in a country with so many regional dialects. MacDiarmid's early writing shows how viable it is — his imitators have usually failed through not progressing; the remarkable thing is that MacDiarmid keeps outstripping his disciples.

Is poetry an outmoded form? Gradually poetry has been losing most of its subject matter and function to prose or

other mediums (media). Nobody could write a long narrative
poem today without being laughed at. Poetry seems to be
more and more confined to the province of shades of meaning
and feeling.

I don't think the future of poetry is all that black. I think it will
be possible to write long poems again. The space age will
perhaps bring a kind of epic poetry back. When poets get up
into space, I don't think they'll be able to express the
immensity of their experience in a six-line lyric. You've heard
the astronauts fail to find words to describe their feelings and
complaining of their inadequacy in expressing the splendours
of the universe. The long poem may reappear in this fashion,
the myths may be the old ones (they still have a lot of life, eg
Prometheus) or perhaps new ones built on the figures and
heroes of early space exploration. Myth-making is happening
all the time. I think poetry is widening its subject matter nowadays — there is a new awareness of what you can say in
poetry — though in some cases I don't think Glasgow is ready
for the whole truth. I still maintain poetry has a lot to say and
it retains its relevance today — otherwise I wouldn't bother
writing any.

Is Scottish poetry necessarily parochial? Should it be striving
towards a new internationalism? Your experiments (if that is
the right word) in concrete poetry are, I suppose, international
— in as much as the form is not associated with any country in
particular.

To take this first point first — poetry is never parochial if it is
good enough — as I said before Glasgow poetry could still
produce a recognisable school which could have relevance
outside Glasgow. The internationalism of concrete poetry?
Well, its 'founders' were Swiss (Eugen Gomringer) and
Brazilian (de Campos) and when it emerged in the 1950s it was
a protest against sentimental and sugary poetry. I hope that in
the future it will be integrated into more conventional poetry
and that poets will use the formal advantages it offers. Perhaps
it will have a history something like imagism in its realign-
ment with mainstream poetry. To take both points together —
it's a strange fact that on the Continent Ian Hamilton Finlay

and myself are called the Scottish School of Concrete Poetry. The other poets claim that they can trace (especially isolating humour) a Scottish tradition in our work, so there must be unconscious influences somewhere.

Thank you. Cheerio.

Are you taking the lift down?

No, I'll

      walk

         down

            the

               stairs.

interview with David Smith (Glasgow, 20 January 1971)
Glasgow University Magazine 82:2
February 1971, pp. 24-26

Doing different things

You must be among the most varied of modern poets, working in concrete poetry, translations, line poems, and science fiction poems. Do you see a relationship between these various aspects of your writing?

I don't think that I personally do see those links. There must presumably be links since they all come from the same person, and the links must be there, but I've always tended to do quite different things, and I don't try very hard to see whether they all come from the same thing or are all to some extent related. I rather enjoy doing different things, you could put it that way, and I've got a large number of very different interests and I try to keep them all going. I think maybe some of these things are linked together by a kind of interest in language itself; the fact that I do translations and also got interested in concrete poetry which seemed quite unconnected perhaps, may be linked by a general interest in language, in what one can do with language, with the different kinds of linguistic effect and things of this sort. I remember even in that early book, *The Vision of Cathkin Braes*, there was a kind of sound poem, which was away back in 1952, before there was really a movement of that kind, I was interested in doing things like that obviously, and presumably there is something that you could trace back, but I don't very often or consciously try to see the links between the different things, and I suppose it means that I don't see the thing as having a settled, steady kind of development. I hope that things are developing but I allow it to go at its own pace, as it were, in different directions, in different ways, at the same time.

Does this tie in at all with your interest in giving readings? You've just finished a series of readings in America, I believe.

Yes, I like giving readings. I believe it often helps quite a lot in the communication of poetry to do this. I'm divided in fact to some extent between poetry on the printed page and spoken poetry or performed poetry. I think both are important and in some ways different things, and I know that some of the poems that I have been doing have probably been written with some kind of performance or speaking actually in mind, and this does involve slightly different approaches to the technique of writing poetry. But other poems have been written without any thought of this and are presumably meant just for the printed page or for performance if anyone cares to take them up. In America, it was interesting that I had been asked just to read my poetry but the people knew that I had written some kinds of concrete poetry and sound poetry, or various kinds of poetry which were not straightforward in the old sense, and almost everywhere I went they asked particularly for this kind of poetry to be read. And even poems which I had thought of as being more visual than aural, concrete poems, they asked me to perform in some kind of way, even if it involved various kinds of verbal acrobatics. But it was interesting doing this and just seeing what could be done with the actual speaking voice in perhaps transforming written poetry into something that could be spoken.

Did you find this attempting to recreate poems you had thought of as purely visual in verbal terms was crossing boundaries you felt in your own work?

Yes, I did feel this. But of course the Americans tend to be more open and flexible, I think, than we are as to what is suitable or what is the done thing, and it didn't worry them that one is reading what was primarily a visual poem. Strictly speaking it is mixing the categories and I was aware that I was mixing the categories, but not entirely, because visual poems, or concrete poems in that sense, the sense of being visual, nearly always do also involve some kind of word-play, play on sounds or play on forms of words or play on the order and juxtaposition of words, and if it's at all possible to perform this, then I don't see why one shouldn't really make the attempt, even though it was something that I hadn't myself thought of as being part of the poem. Once I had done it, although the poem lost something, to my mind, it also perhaps gained something else, just because I had never thought of trying this before, and I was just trying something new. It did work to some extent.

Would you like to elaborate on your relations to the general concrete poetry movement? I know you're thought of with Ian Hamilton Finlay as one of the two foremost Scottish concrete poets. Do you feel that your relations to concrete poetry are a particularly Scottish thing, or do they relate to the Brazilian movement, for example?

Well, in my case, the Brazilians were the first people that I really got to know and to like, and I presume there is some influence there. Theirs was the earliest concrete poetry I saw, and I liked them very much and then started to write, and presumably there's something that may have rubbed off from them. What I liked about their poetry was the kind of vivacious and witty quality about it which was sometimes in contradistinction to some of the European and perhaps especially to German or German language concrete poetry which didn't have quite this same kind of gaiety about it, because wit and humour and satirical effects, ironical effects, have been important to me in concrete poetry. Whether this is Scottish, I don't know. Some people writing about concrete poetry in other countries do claim to see what they call a Scottish kind of humour in both Finlay's work and my own, and they say that this does form something that is recognisable as belonging to one particular place or one particular country, and this may be true or it may just be that both he and I do enjoy producing effects that are playfully humorous in our concrete poetry. But I think there is a difference in that mine perhaps does tend sometimes to be making more literary kinds of points whereas his probably relies more on throwing back to certain things — perhaps in nature or in the world about us, fishing boats and windmills and so on, whereas mine will perhaps have references to things in the mental or intellectual or verbal world. So there is that kind of difference, although I like his work and there also may be connections that other people would see. But I don't feel that each of us has very much influenced the other. I think that we've both probably gone our own ways in concrete poetry.

24

Do you feel this last distinction made between your own work and Hamilton Finlay's ties in with the general trend in Hamilton Finlay towards a purely visual, abstract art, and the sense in your own later work that you're incorporating concrete poetry into line poetry?

Yes, probably so, probably so. I think Ian Hamilton Finlay has moved in a sense completely away from ordinary syntactic poetry. He's gone into concrete poetry first of all, and from there he's gone into the poem as object, the poem as three-dimensional object, so that you're left in the end with poems that have to be created in some other medium, whether it's wood or glass or literally concrete in some cases. The poem therefore becomes an object in the world. It still uses words; he still therefore calls it poetry; but it is an object more than anything else. In my case, I went on writing ordinary poetry at the same time as I was writing concrete poetry. It wasn't to me a step that was a complete break, a complete change, and perhaps because of that I have tended to want as it were to get concrete somehow related to ordinary poetry, perhaps filtered back in some kind of way. I have tried sometimes, I suppose, to do this, but other times it's perhaps happened quite unconsciously or subconsciously and it's interesting to see how this is possible with the feeling that it's not an entirely separated, isolated area by itself as it sometimes seems to be, floating in the void between art and poetry. Some concrete poetry certainly does seem to hive off almost completely from poetry in the old sense, but in my case there presumably have been more links between it and the older poetry.

In your first major book, The Second Life, *you present the two kinds of poetry, concrete poetry and line poetry, on different coloured paper, but in the same book. Was this a polemic attempt of some sort?*

I don't know if it was as conscious as all that, but it works in fact in that kind of way. Yes, I think at the back of my mind there was this idea. First of all, when I was discussing it with the publishers, they weren't sure, and I wasn't sure, whether it was right to include the two kinds, and we talked about this between us. I thought it probably would work if we did have the two kinds of poetry in the same book, but I also felt that you couldn't just say quite simply that this was poetry without making some kind of difference or without calling attention to it in some kind of way, and using a different colour of paper was simply an attempt to do that, a kind of compromise if you like between saying that it was poetry and saying that it was something quite different. We were saying really that it was a kind of poetry, perhaps, but we weren't very sure where it fitted in except that it bore some kind of relation and therefore could appear in the same kind of book.

One thing that struck me with The Second Life *in terms of your other work, were the emergent poems there, 'Message Clear' and 'Seven Headlines'. There are only these two poems of this kind in* The Second Life, *but you later published a series, all based on the same technique. Is there any sense, in particularly your concrete work, of starting out a way of writing within the genre and exploiting it later, and then moving on?*

Yes, I think so. I think in this case, that it is just what happened, moving on from the one poem which seemed to work not too badly and trying to use the same kind of technique to do others. I think you can only do that up to a certain point and then of course you realise that you're just repeating yourself and you stop, and you do something else. So in that sense you're exploiting a vein for a while; it does give some results, it yields diminishing returns, and then you have to find some other kind of thing. I suppose that what happens is that I maybe do this more frequently than other people do. I tend to do something like that, to cultivate some small area like that fairly intensively for a while and then perhaps just simply drop it and do something else altogether. The same thing is happening at the moment with what I call my Instamatic Poems. I began a while ago by writing short poems which were directly about events which I had either read about or seen in newspapers or on television. So it's a poetry which is very closely linked to real life in that sense, but I gave myself the kind of restriction that the poem must be presented in such a way as to give a visual picture of this event, whatever it was, as if somebody had been there with an Instamatic camera and had just very quickly snapped it, so the poem is a kind of snapshot and there are certain things you cannot do, you cannot talk about sound effects or people talking and things of this kind. It must be something *seen*, and it must be seen also in direct relation, in truthful relation to what actually was reported, and the reporting was important in the sense that although I could use my imagination to build up the scene as it might have been, if I had been there, it also had to be filtered through some intermediary such as a newspaper report or something I had seen on television. It was a double process before the poem actually occurred. Well, I began this by taking a number of events that happened on the same day, and just writing poems about these, and then I've been doing that since then, different dates, different parts of the world and different newspapers and so on; and just, I suppose, hopefully gradually building up a kind of picture of a certain period. So far it's a period of, I suppose, a few months but it probably will become a lot longer than that. But all presented using the same purely visual technique and using these deliberate limitations, because I think it often does help, it at first seems to hinder, but it probably does help to give yourself different limitations of this kind.

Do you see this particular process of Instamatic Poems as an attempt to introduce documentary into poetry in the material you're drawing from?

Yes, I suppose they are a kind of documentary poetry really, and maybe just taking up the challenge of documentary — whether one can really be documentary in poetry — because it seems to go against some of the things that poetry would claim to be, if poetry is a work of the imagination, if the imagination is very important in poetry, if vision is very important in poetry, then you're up against it if you're relying so much on something that has actually happened. You have to imagine something that has really happened, you have to imagine something that is actually there. You can do this, I think, if you are not there yourself. For example, I wouldn't write an Instamatic poem about something that I had myself seen. Supposing that some interesting or strange or violent event happened just at my own front door, and I was there and saw

27

it, or even there with a camera and photographed it, I wouldn't make a poem about that because I think there it would be going against this particular thing that I'm trying to do to get something interposing between the event and the poem which helps the imagination. But at the same time it would claim to be a kind of documentary poetry. It wouldn't be absolutely strictly documentary because I do use a certain amount of imagination, but it's documentary in a sense that all the poems relate to something that did happen at a certain place and time and the place and the date are mentioned in the title of the poem so that they could be checked. I wouldn't mind if the poems were checked by somebody who looked through the files of the papers to see whether in fact something like that had happened. But he wouldn't find that it was always a hundred per cent what had happened, but it's as close as I can make it, going along with the fact that imagination nevertheless to some extent must come in otherwise the poetic activity doesn't get going at all.

One aspect of The Second Life *is poems about Glasgow — the funeral of the gang leader, the encounter in a Glasgow café. Is Glasgow life one of the things you particularly draw upon for your writing?*

Yes, I have done to quite an extent really, and I think I probably would like to go on doing this, though it depends partly upon luck and circumstances. But I think it very often does help a poet to be rooted somewhere, without going completely into this line that it must be local, that it must be rooted very closely in the place where you live. I think it certainly is useful for some of one's poetry to be rooted in this kind of way. But it's not always easy to write about one's own place. It does often present peculiar problems and I suppose in the case of a place like Glasgow, the problems are fairly big and fairly obvious in the sense that the material is there, it's a place where things happen, it's a large place with a great variety of human experience going on in it. And yet on the other hand there's very little of a tradition of writing about Glasgow — it's very different, for example, from Edinburgh, where there is a tradition going back for centuries of writing about Edinburgh, and if you like you can relate yourself to this and perhaps even draw on it to some extent, you can feel you're a part of something, but in Glasgow, although there has been Glasgow poetry in the past, it has never on the whole been terribly good and it hasn't been a very continuous sort of process, so you really are starting from scratch and you have to see the best ways of doing this. But I certainly have enjoyed trying to write about the place and trying to make it manageable just by concentrating on small things, just perhaps one person or one encounter, just something happening that can hopefully focus something larger within the small sphere of the poem.

Do you think there's a characteristic tradition of Glasgow writing growing up now? I'm thinking of the work of people like Tom Leonard and Steve Mulrine who are, in a different way from you, using Glasgow dialect to recreate Glasgow situations.

Yes, I think this situation is very hopeful, and this is something that hadn't happened in the past. There is now, you could say, a sort of Glasgow group of writers, perhaps not a Glasgow school, in the sense that they don't all very easily relate to one another, but there is certainly a Glasgow group now, and this could change the whole situation because they are approaching it from different ways and they're gradually building up a feeling that it is quite possible to write about this place in poetry. You mentioned dialect: I have of course used Glasgow dialect on some occasions where dialogue is actually involved — the encounter with the drunk man on the bus in 'Good Friday', for example, and a more recent one I've done which isn't in print yet called 'Stobhill' which is about an abortion case and involves monologues by different people, and two or three of the monologues do involve, again, Glasgow dialect, because it's just the natural way these people would speak. So I would be quite happy to go along with this idea that a Glasgow poetry could still use some kind of Scots. In this case it wouldn't be the kind of Scots that Hugh Mac-Diarmid uses. It would be simply a local speech, a local dialect perhaps, if you can use that word. But I think that this can still very usefully be used — in fact almost perhaps has to be used if you want to build up a kind of Glasgow poetry, simply because so many people in Glasgow do speak something that is not really English in the ordinary sense of the term.

Do you feel that this kind of 'real urban dialect', if that's the word, is more hopeful that MacDiarmid's Lallans, which is created rather than actually used?

Yes, I think on the whole I do. I'm coming round to this feeling that if Scots is to be used at all at the moment, it's probably more profitable to use it as it's actually spoken. This may just be because I've got, and a lot of other people also have got, an interest in the relations between poetry and speech. This may be just a heresy that we're all passing through just now, that there should be this relationship, and perhaps it will die, I don't know, and we will revert to the older idea of a language which ought to be different from speech if it's going to be a poetic language. But at the moment there is this interest in speech, and if that interest is there, then it must, I think, have some relation to the speech that you actually hear round about you. There's not the same problem perhaps for an English poet as there is for a Scottish poet, because the Scots poet will hear greater variations from standard English than the English poet will normally hear, except in very few areas, and it would be surprising if he didn't still, I think, try to do something about this. Of course the argument against this is simply Hugh MacDiarmid's argument that to depend so much on local speech is to end up in provinciality of one kind or another. If you write Glasgow poetry, only Glasgow people will read it, and you know, one can see the force of this. His aim was to create, and if it wasn't there already, to create by hook or by crook, some kind of synthetic Scots, drawing on words from different periods, from different parts of the country, but hopefully building up a kind of Scots that would be gradually accepted as standard over all the country, and wouldn't be related just to one area. He comes from the Borders, but his own Scots is not particularly restricted to being a Border kind of Scots. And that argument is of course still in a sense valid; if you're trying to build up a national language for Scotland, which won't be English, then you will have to have a kind of national Scots. But this is so far from practicability that one tends to fall back on the other thing, that if you cannot have a national Scots tongue, then the next best thing is to use

30

English, but also to use whatever local speech there is available to be used, and I still think that you can get a good deal from using local varieties of the language.

Parochialism seems to bring up the next point which I would like to make, which is that your work certainly can't be accused of this as in many poems you draw on science fiction, which is probably the least parochial and most avant-garde, in one sense. What are your particular intentions in using science-fiction poems?

I don't know whether it begins by having any intentions. Probably intentions began to emerge, but it comes just out of an interest that goes back right into my schooldays. I can remember among some of the earliest things I read, there were fantastic and science-fiction stories, and some of the earliest films I can remember, too, were films that were either science fiction or on the borders of being science fiction. So it goes right back a long time, and I suppose it was natural that I should just, when I began to write poetry, try to bring some kind of science-fiction theme into it. I think that looking back at it, the early interest was probably just a liking for the strange and the fantastic almost by itself, a fondness for things like that, which is maybe hard for any one person to explain. But it went with, slightly later, an interest in science itself and in a number of sciences, I suppose, biology and astronomy particularly, which I know a little bit about. And I think eventually from that, I did develop the idea that it would be good if poetry could somehow bring scientific ideas into its sphere of operations. Of course others have tried to do this — it's never really worked well for obvious reasons, but I've always liked statements where poets do say that this ought to be able to be done, as in Wordsworth's *Preface*, where he says that the remotest discoveries of the mineralogist and the chemist and so on will eventually have to be brought into poetry, and I liked when MacDiarmid took this idea up also and said that it ought to be done. Well, I haven't exactly done that; I haven't really very much myself tried to literally bring into poetry scientific ideas and facts. And maybe when I'm writing the poetry what comes out more is just the sheer imaginative interest of events that take place in some strange

31

B

time, some strange place. But I think, looking at it in a general way, I would still hope that one could develop poetry that got away from the idea of having two cultures. I've never really believed that there are two cultures; I've always thought there's only one, and although it's very, very difficult and perhaps in some ways impossible, I would hope that poetry would at least keep nibbling at this problem and try to present in its words a world that includes science and scientific ideas. I think I would just put it like that. But in my own work, I would still hope that I could use some kind of science fiction, more in its way of presenting unusual situations in which human beings could find themselves, so that in the end it gets drawn up into a kind of extension, perhaps, of humanism. Taking a long view of the human species and its adventures and trying just to say something about the possibilities, the kind of things that could happen to men and women and how they would react to them. So that in poems like that, it's not so much the science or the scientific ideas that are important; these just set something off which really in the end is talking about human beings and how they would react.

You're still working on this line, I believe? One of your recent poems ['The First Men on Mercury'] was about the meeting between mankind and the alien, and crossed with this was your interest in language, in the intermingling of languages as the two characters speak.

Yes, I still do quite a few poems of this kind. Often just taking up a particular point like that and seeing what can be done with it. That was a poem, I suppose, about communication, about the difficulties that one would obviously get in communicating with some species that one hadn't met before — just what would actually happen. Of course this poem was a fairly light one in its actual presentation, but it is attempting to say something about this kind of difficulty.

Is there any sense in which a poem like 'The Death of Marilyn Monroe', where you're dealing with a Western culture hero, relates to your interest in science fiction as the modern mythological form?

Myth or mythology may be the significant term there. I think very often what science fiction is doing is building up a kind of mythology and maybe I like it for reasons which are linked to myth, just as I'm interested in figures who become figures of legend, like Marilyn Monroe or Hemingway and so on. It may be that many people in fact do feel the need for, or the lack of, a solid kind of mythology, and they are searching around in various directions for it and they may find it in popular culture heroes or anti-heroes or they may find it, of course, in science fiction, where man himself presumably is the hero, though there may also be individual heroes. And I think probably there are links there, although I had never particularly thought of them until you put the question, but I think there may well be. It may well be that someone like Marilyn Monroe does have a kind of science-fiction existence almost. You can almost take it that kind of way. There is something fantastic and unreal about it, although it is of course all too real on another level. But this whole area does interest me a good deal. It's the whole business of just what image of man you are interested in and trying to present, and part of it is bound to be ordinary — the poems about Glasgow, for example, are dealing with man as he appears in a big city — others are perhaps very extraordinary, as in the case of the extraordinary person like Marilyn Monroe, or the extraordinary incident, as in a poem like 'In Sobieski's Shield', where the people are perhaps ordinary, but they are thrown into a situation which is very extraordinary, and one is just seeing what their reactions would be to this. But certainly there is this interest in somehow trying to find a kind of web of myth that will draw various strands of one's reactions to humanity together, and I think that none of the existing myths by itself will really suffice fully, and therefore one has, to some extent, to create myth as one goes along, as so many modern poets of course have done. But I think this process is still going on. I think you still have somehow to create your myth, but in my case the myth is partly, to go back to your earlier point, a documentary myth. This is what makes it difficult for me to see everything together because I have this interest in something that is very far from ordinary experience, but I've an equally strong interest in what actually has happened, and maybe I am trying to somehow desperately bring these two things together, not presumably successfully yet, but hopefully — trying to do this!

If it's not too big a question, do you see yourself bringing them together eventually in some huge modern epic like Pound's Cantos?

Well, I suppose the answer should be 'God forbid', but I don't know, perhaps I am being pushed towards this! One mustn't have megalomaniac ambitions, I suppose there are so many awful warnings about this, long poems which never get finished, never get off the stocks. I've never written anything enormously long, but I have an interest in long poems, and would feel the interesting challenge of a fairly lengthy work. And presumably it would be difficult to do it because it would just have to somehow bring in these two apparently very opposite things of something that was very, very close to what has actually happened, a kind of poem of our times. I mean more close to what has actually happened than something like Pound's *Cantos*. Pound's *Cantos* are intermittently about things that have actually happened in history, and also to him in modern history, but very obliquely and very eccentrically, whereas if I was doing something like that, I would want it to be much more documentarily closer to what had actually happened, and yet at the same time to be also more imaginative, presumably, than the *Cantos* is. That's to say, relying less I think on earlier literature. I've the feeling of wanting to get away from that, I think; I'm a pretty strong anti-traditionalist in that sense. I really on the whole dislike history and tradition. I'm interested in what is happening, and I'm interested in what will happen, more than I'm interested in what has happened, I think, so that my long poem, if it ever comes out, will be rather different from the existing ones. It will perhaps be 'now' plus the future, rather than 'now' plus the past.

One of your projected poems is a dialogue which includes the cyberneticist W. Grey Walter. Do you see this perhaps as the area in which you could exploit the 'now' and the future? By dealing with a personality who is both contemporary and who is also creating the things which will influence us later?

Yes, probably so. I've always been attracted to people like that, inventors and innovators, very often, of course, in one of

34

the sciences, but also in the arts — Apollinare, Cocteau, who also comes into this sequence of poems [*The Whittrick*] — and a man like Grey Walter, who designs little machines which are meant to simulate human behaviour, and by doing this he hopes to throw light on human behaviour and perhaps also eventually to create maybe a series of robot-like creatures which could be android, would perhaps be somewhere between the machine and human beings. This, of course, is a well-worn theme in science fiction, but it's interesting that so much nowadays is going on in areas which used to be science fiction but which are now just quite simply science. And you've got again the interest in what is actually happening, but it also projects something which is perhaps going to happen and projects it interestingly because it raises various pretty wide-ranging questions which are partly ethical questions. You get a lot of people objecting to research like this because they say that there is this danger in man taking it on himself to actually eventually create life. Presumably these are all first steps towards creating something that could eventually be called life. They are already perhaps a kind of half-life. I suppose they are still in the main mechanical, they still involve mostly metal and electronic gadgetry, but they may be moving towards a closer kind of simulation of life if they eventually involve the use of some kind of organic material, as well as metal, so they come nearer and nearer to actual life-creation. This is of course the old dangerous Faustian dream presumably, or the Promethean dream if you like to give it a slightly higher term than Faust. I don't myself find this frightening or bad. It just is something that interests and attracts me, and I don't think really that there's much possibility of halting the process. I think man will go on attempting to create what is called life, and eventually will presumably do this, and he'll have a load of problems on his hands once he does this, obviously, of the first order, both ethical and religious problems, and political problems too, of course, will all be involved, but to me this is just something that I see eventually happening: it interests me, and I would perhaps like to write about it and be able to place it in some kind of context of art, some context of poetry.

You've written an article on the Russian poet Voznesensky, and your own poetry, of all kinds, seems to be concerned with transforming; the concrete poems transform words and shapes, your science-fiction poems, particularly 'In Sobieski's Shield', are concerned with the transformation of people and situations. Would you see this as a sort of ground-base of your poetry, or is this too academic a way of looking at it?

It probably is. I think I probably was attracted to Voznesensky because I sensed something like this, that there was something similar to what I have myself experienced and perhaps tried to write about. Yes, I'm very conscious, now that I think of it, of this whole business of change, transformation, and maybe even more positively I could say that I rather like this kind of thing. I think that whereas many people seem to want to find something solid that they can attach themselves to, I've always felt rather the opposite, rather a suspicion of something that is solid, and I've rather liked the idea that things are always upon a kind of knife edge, and can always change, and are always in danger, if you like to use the word danger, of being transformed into something else, and I just like the idea of transformation. It's maybe a kind of dislike or fear of the stable state, and I suppose there must always be a tension in every society, in every age, between change and some kind of settled state or order, and it's just that I tend rather to like the idea of things changing than the idea of things being settled, though obviously there must be some kind of order in society, at every stage, at every period, that you can't avoid order. But I would tend to be more suspicious of the periods when there is a great deal of order and I would tend rather to like and to be attracted by the obvious hazards that there are in the periods of even quite violent change. It links up, too, with various ideas, I think, about revolution, which I think are probably important. Voznesensky of course is not a terribly political writer in the Russian sense. He has been criticised in Russia for not being political enough. But his approach to language and to poetry is of course in a kind of state of permanent revolution, and this interests me a great deal, because I think that any kind of revolution has got to face the central problem of how it is going to keep being revolutionary, and again if you believe the revolution is important, you must find some means of keeping it active. All these ideas certainly interest me a good deal. They keep interesting me although they obviously do open out a lot of problems, the problems of, for example, people perhaps asking you 'What do you believe?' and I always find this kind of question very, very hard to answer — you can ask me if you like, but you won't get much of an answer I'm afraid! Because I often just quite don't know what I believe, or maybe what I believe in 1970 won't be the same as what I believe in 1971. To me, the question of belief is a very, very difficult one, and one which is active. It's not something to my mind that is passive or can be simply and immediately answered. It's a question that interests me, but it's not one that can be answered just by a simple form of words I'm afraid.

You wrote a poem in The Second Life, *'What is "Paradise Lost" really about?', in which you seem to give a metaphor — that people usually seem to find in* Paradise Lost *some set of beliefs, but you change this into the fox and the hunter and the duck metaphor, in which belief is something which is gained and devoured, and can't be passed on. Would this be a sort of attempt to answer when somebody asked you what you believed?*

Well, I suppose perhaps it is. I should perhaps just refer them to that poem and let them work it out for themselves! Yes, it's a curious thing that, well, Milton was a man himself who did probably feel that he did have very strong beliefs. I think if you had asked him, he would have told you, and in a fairly confident way, what his beliefs were, but when you're writing poetry or creating any work of art, the whole thing is thrown into the melting pot right away and what you think you believe is not necessarily what you actually do believe, and you may not even really believe as much as you think you believe, or even say in speech or in prose, that you actually believe. So that belief, the more you look at it, the more it fragments itself or dissolves or transforms itself into something else. You may in fact believe quite strongly in something that is not quite the same as what you say you believe in. You may be a man who likes belief as Milton did, but your actual belief may be something rather different. For example, I think Milton was more of a humanist than he thought he was. I think he thought of himself as being a very religious man, but I don't think he was as religious as he thought he was. I think he had strong humanist beliefs which we see now rather differently from the way he would see them in the seventeenth century.

You mentioned earlier your interest in revolutionary situations. Most of your translations seem to be not so much of political writers as of writers who are involved in revolutionary situations — originally the Russians, and now East Europeans and Hungarians. Would it be fair to say that these are the sort of writers that you are interested in translating, or is it that the writers you are interested in happen to be involved in situations like this?

I don't know exactly about that. It may be the second. I think I am and always have been interested in writers who have been thrown into a revolutionary situation; this is a thing that does fascinate me a great deal. But it also does just so happen that I think some of the most interesting modern poets have been in this situation and one is attracted by their works for two reasons, partly because of a situation — someone especially in Russia, say, after 1917 — but partly also because in this particular revolution in 1917, the state of literature was very interesting and active, so you get two things, you get a political revolution, and you get also a kind of revolution of language, a revolution of literature going on at the same time, and naturally what is being done is of the greatest interest, both aesthetically and linguistically, and politically, so that a man like Mayakovsky is bound to be able to interest people from different points of view. In the case of the Hungarian writers, it's probably more strongly the feeling of writers being presented with problems which are the problems of a small country. It's partly problems of a national culture which impinge on and perhaps try to dominate the small national culture. And I think I got very interested in Hungary because I saw it as a sort of parallel to the Scottish situation. It's obviously different in many ways but I think one can see it as a sort of parallel where you have to somehow and maybe at all costs try to preserve something that you feel is distinct to yourself in your own place, your own country, whether it's Scotland or Hungary, when strong pressures are being put on from outside, whether it's from English in our case or from

Russian in the case of the Hungarian, and the artist there, the writer there, is presented with these very difficult problems which he can't quite escape. He may try to or even want to escape from them, but he can't quite do it. They are always at the back of his mind somewhere. And the writer in a very large and confident country like Russia or America doesn't have this problem. So the two things are different, but I find both things important, both the general revolutionary problem of modern society, and the particular, more national cultural orientated problem, and I think a Scottish writer would naturally be drawn towards both ways of looking at things.

Could we discuss your reactions to Scottish culture and to Scottish writers? You say that Scottish writers would be drawn towards this. I think it's very true that there seems to be a predominant interest in translation in Scotland. Robin Fulton, for instance, translating Italian . . . I can't think of anyone else off-hand. . . . Well, Alan Bold editing an anthology of revolutionary verse, drawn from cultures like this. Do you think this is a keynote of modern Scottish writing now? A cosmopolitanism almost?

Well, I think I'd like to see more of it than there actually is. The fact that you sort of gradually had to pluck your examples out of the air maybe shows that there isn't as much of this as there ought to be. It's a bit patchy, but I think there is a good deal of interest, and of course there has been in the early twentieth century too. It's something that I'd like to see more of than there is, just because there's so much of the opposite as well. There are also quite a number of people in Scotland, in the literary situation in Scotland, who are not very willing to look outside at all, and who would lay far more stress on the native traditions, and try to keep drawing on that, and of course I'm more, myself, drawn to what one can get from elsewhere, from outside, because it seems to me that it's important that one should be able to put the one thing up against the other and to see what the differences and the similarities may be.

Would it be too crude to say then that you're not a Scottish Nationalist?

I think I am, actually. I think I would probably call myself that, though I don't very much feel attracted to the SNP. I'm not a member of any of the political parties, but I think in a sense that I feel Scottish and not English, and feel also that there is still a meaningful sense in which you could call yourself a Scottish writer, even though it's very hard to define this. In that sense I would still feel that there is enough that is distinct for it to be defined and developed and, if possible, carried forward as a kind of tradition. I think there must obviously be a good deal of overlapping, both with English and with foreign international cultures — this is inevitable. But I would still feel quite strongly enough conscious of Scotland as an entity or the Scots person as being different from the Englishman, to want to keep this. In that sense I think I would call myself a Scottish nationalist. I also think that even in the political sense, that although it's very hard to see how the thing is moving and obviously the Scottish National Party is in the doldrums and hasn't had very much success with the electorate in Scotland, there's a good deal of floating nationalism quite clearly in Scotland, which hasn't been properly channelled by any party which appeals to the majority. It may very well be that this could still happen, that there still could be a fairly widespread movement for separation from England. I don't think this at all impossible. I still think, you see, that the political history of the United Kingdom is open. I don't regard it really as being closed; I think the English tend to assume, in their marvellously bland way, that it is finished; but I think that politically, constitutionally, changes will probably happen yet. I think it'll probably happen first of all in Ireland — changes will obviously have to happen there — but I don't think that either Wales or Scotland can be ruled out in this, and I wouldn't be surprised if eventually you would have some kind of federal system at least, if not some kind of separation of the non-English parts of the United Kingdom. I think I would probably go along with this; I think I would accept the situation where Scotland was quite simply a separate country.

In contemporary Scottish writing, do you feel that today's writers justify this? That they're at once good enough and non-English enough to be establishing and carrying on a distinctive culture?

I think that this is a bit on the edge. I think there is a good deal going on; a lot of it is not what you might say very obviously relatable to Scottish traditions simply because there has been so much influence from elsewhere, from America for example, and the thing does become internationalised in that sense, to quite a degree. But on the other hand there is a good deal going on that is Scottish. The writers in Glasgow, for example, or someone like Alan Jackson in Edinburgh. These are people who are doing something which is recognisably not English and they continue to do it and presumably to feel that it's worth doing. Alan Jackson's position is very interesting and intriguing simply because he's a kind of anti-Scottish Nationalist really; and yet I would say that his own writing can be quite clearly labelled Scottish and not English. So what one actually says about oneself, what one actually states one's beliefs to be, this is not necessarily the last word in the matter. It's a nice irony about his situation. But I think that although if you had to ask all the writers in Scotland whether they were believers in a viable Scottish culture, a non-English Scottish culture at the present time, you might not get a majority saying that they did believe this, you could still look at the writing itself and you might nevertheless very well feel that there was something there that could be described as distinct and having its own values. But the overlap is certainly there, there's no getting away from the fact that there is Anglo-Scottish and Americo-Scottish writing going on. This is in addition to a much more vehemently Scotto-Scottish writing which is also there. The three things are certainly present and it's an awful melting pot, but I would just think that the whole situation is still very much a fluid and open one, and things could jump in different directions, and they could jump still even yet in a Scottish direction — I would certainly feel that.

Do you think that this Scottishness would necessarily be accompanied by a Lallans/Scottish Language development, or as at the moment it seems to me with, as you mentioned, Alan Jackson, Scottish trends coming out in an English language medium?

Yes, I think it wouldn't necessarily be a Lallans or Scottish language thing, largely because, I suppose, so many of the younger poets are just not doing this: they are writing in English. Some of course do use either a Lallans type of Scots or, say, a Glasgow dialect type of Scots, but I suppose the majority are nevertheless using English and presumably English would still go on being used as the main language medium. But poets are still using different kinds of Scots, they are still using Gaelic and of course they are using English, and it's very hard, I think, to lay down any kind of law about this and to say that the future for a Scottish literature must be this or that, it must be Lallans, it must be English, or it must be Gaelic. Until Gaelic dies out completely, if it ever does, until people stop using any kind of Scots, you just can't really pre-empt the whole situation. I think you have to go on allowing people to write as they feel they must do, and therefore it is an untidy situation. I think one has to just frankly admit this, and I don't see how it can be tidied up except by something being laid down from above. If independence was ever gained, you would then have a kind of Israel or Eire situation, you see. You would then have to make decisions about the language, and it might be that a Scottish parliament would decide that the national language must be this or that, it must be Scots or it must be Gaelic. But if this did happen, you'd be up against the problem of human nature, and just what people decided to speak wouldn't necessarily be what by government decree they were supposed to speak. It's a very difficult situation, and writers, of course, can try to change their language, and they can try to write in ways that are not perhaps natural to them. Sydney Goodsir Smith, I suppose, wasn't born speaking Scots, and yet he has written almost all his poetry in Scots, and some of it is good, so it can be done, quite clearly. My feeling about the whole thing is just that it's one of those open situations which haven't been settled yet and won't be settled for a long time. One simply must really keep the options open.

Do you think this is a peculiarly Scottish thing? I was thinking of your paper on Dunbar where you describe this 'fouth of language', where even as far back as that, you had one poet who could effectively manipulate various linguistic areas.

It's not *only* Scottish, but it is a Scottish thing, I think. Partly just because of the historical situation, where you had a number of different races and languages being brought together, and although English in the end became the dominant thing, the other things lingered on for quite a while and obviously had to be accepted as part of the situation. And I think where you get this, you do very often get a kind of linguistic awareness, and writers very often do quite naturally show this. They don't always necessarily show this: in Switzerland, for example, they don't particularly show it, as far as I know, and yet you would expect them to show it even more there; but in Switzerland it's slightly different because people tend to be bi- or tri-lingual, and just as a matter of what they have to do, from schooldays onwards, they do learn two or three languages, and even four sometimes. But in Scotland it's never been quite like that. People have just had the interesting situation of feeling that one culture or language has been the dominant thing, but others are uneasily in the background, and you're uneasily aware of this. And this seems to sharpen the linguistic situation in some kind of way, and you get a great deal of experimentation perhaps going on, in Dunbar and in Burns and in Fergusson and MacDiarmid, trying to produce unusual and different kinds of linguistic effects, just because of the extraordinary fluidity of the language situation. This is still present perhaps to some extent, though it's not quite so acute as it was in earlier periods.

Would you like to say something about your translation of Beowulf?

Well, I suppose this was a kind of byproduct of the university. When I took the English course, I liked, as most people didn't, the Anglo-Saxon part of the course, and I got greatly enthusiastic about Old English as a language, but particularly as a language in poetry, and got to like *Beowulf* particularly, and just thought I would have a shot at translating it. It attracted me I think as a language in poetry partly because of the rather unusual mixture, of apparently a great freedom and flexibility and even roughness in its rhythmical effects, and yet underlying that, quite a complex actual metrical system. You got a strong feeling of very marked but rather rough rhythms, and yet once you looked at it more closely, you began to see there was a great deal of art in this, and it was a combination of roughness and art that attracted me, because very often when you get strict metrical systems, you get a certain kind of resulting smoothness which was the very opposite of what you get in Anglo-Saxon poetry, and I liked the effects you can get from something which wasn't smooth. But I also like the tone of Anglo-Saxon poetry. I liked the kind of brooding melancholy tone. The mixture of brooding melancholy and something heroic and stoical attracted me a lot, and still does attract me in any poetry, but especially in Anglo-Saxon poetry. How that fits in with being interested in cybernetics and Grey Walter, I don't know, but it's another facet.

Would you see the period of culture in which Beowulf *was written as almost a revolutionary one, where you've got an emerging Christian culture in a pagan environment?*

Now that probably is the key to it. Yes, it was a very mixed, difficult, transitional kind of culture which I think wasn't sure of its values, and *Beowulf* is particularly interesting in this respect because it's so very largely a pagan poem although it has quite strongly felt Christian elements in it, and it also has a very, very strong kind of pagan undertow, and it gets its values very often, its poetic or aesthetic values, from the clash between the two, though I think in the end that maybe the stronger things do come from the pagan part of it. It does have parallels with later situations, perhaps with our own situation today, and maybe subconsciously I felt that this was what it was all about, and perhaps it attracted me because of this. But I still think that it's a very good poem; I'm quite prepared to defend it!

Did you also translate The Wanderer *and* The Seafarer?

Yes, I have done quite a few of the shorter poems as well.

Have they been republished anywhere?

No, they've just been published in magazines here and there, but there's never been any collection of them. I've done quite a few of them, including the very marvellous fragment called 'The Ruin', which was published in the old days of *Horizon*. It's a very fine poem which has all the old sense of the immanent decay of all things, which perhaps is on us again, in the twentieth century!

Part of this interview with Robin Hamilton (Glasgow, 5 August 1971) appeared in Eboracum *(York)* 11½, (1972). *A copy of the transcript of the whole interview is in the Edwin Morgan Collection, Mitchell Library, Glasgow (*MS.220/16).

Look outwards

When did you first start publishing?

Nothing in book form until 1952, that was the little *Vision of Cathkin Braes.*

What was that meant to be?

It always seemed a bit odd, this book, because it was meant, in fact, to be one of a pair. At the same time as I was getting that one published there was supposed to be a book of more serious poems [*Dies Irae*] being brought out by a different publisher. He went bankrupt and the poems never appeared. So it was meant to be a half of the coin, as it were.

Has the funny, spoofing element stayed with you, or was that just an early phase?

It has stayed with me, yes. I've always liked comedy and the comic mode, and I probably take comedy seriously, I believe you can do serious things with it. I've often found that in the way my poetry's gone. After a bout of perhaps very serious poems, some kind of reaction, a kind of comic phase comes after that. It's happened again and again, a very curious thing.

Then there was The Cape of Good Hope *in 1955. Was that based on your wartime experiences?*

Only, I think, as regards imagery, and the idea of the voyage itself. I was on a troopship going round the Cape up to Egypt, and I was remembering how I had been impressed by the extraordinary seascape at the Cape — pretty stormy of course, a very jagged and remarkable coast; although it wasn't about South Africa particularly.

What was the poem about? It seemed to be a journey of alienation, for instance, 'I chose emptiness when fullness appalled me'.

It was a very desperate phase I went through, a very unhappy phase. As you say, alienation was the keynote of the poem, solitude and the alienation of solitude, the difficulty of social adjustment. In that sense it's a very personal poem which I had to get out of my system. I think it probably doesn't work as well as I thought it was working at the time.

Were there a lot of young intellectuals fed up in the early 1950s?

I think it probably was a widespread feeling, but I can only see it looking back. At the time I thought it was just my own personal problems. I didn't realise there were others dotted around having their solitary problems. It probably did amount to something that was quite widespread, but I saw it in terms of myself and my own unhappiness.

Is it the most serious thing you've ever done?

It depends on how you take the word 'serious'. It was the most intense in that it came very existentially out of me, out of myself and out of my own life. It has that kind of personal seriousness, even if it's not a great success as a work of art.

Then there is a period of foreign translations, and you went to the USSR in 1955. What did that do for you poetically?

Not very much for me creatively. I remember being surprised by the great variety of Russian personalities. It seemed to be just as full of eccentrics as it must have been in Dostoevsky's time. The image you get from reading about Russia is that everyone is very regimented and they're all thinking alike; but in actual fact, this is obviously very far from the truth. There are difficulties about getting published, but in the actual way in which people talk and behave, they really are in some ways very free and permissive.

Was this behind your translations of Mayakovsky, Neruda and Brecht, to prove they were human after all?

Yes, these translations do relate to having been in Russia to some extent. But I have been interested in languages for a long time, and these poets have always interested me for linguistic as well as political or humanist reasons. At that time, too, it seemed terribly important to have their sort of direct and engaged, committed kind of expression.

What about political and social messages? You've written some very bitter poems, like 'Flowers of Scotland' — but not many.

I'm not often a direct social commentator, and I sometimes wish I did more of this. Perhaps I should do more; often I do feel very strongly about these things, but it's partly the famous difficulty of doing this in poetry. There are problems to overcome about intractable material. It may be that these things are not burningly or centrally important to me. If I was being pushed into a more direct political situation, I would write more about it, but that kind of sharp stage hasn't been reached yet.

You once said 'poetry has no ulterior motive' — do you still believe that?

Sometimes poetry does have ulterior motives. There is a direct poetry, one has to admit this — Brecht I've always liked, and Brecht can be absolutely naked and direct. It can be more effective through irony, metaphor, imagery — and may not be directly committed at all, as in Pete Morgan's poems. Some are fairly direct, others are very indirect; I like the way he goes about it very much. It may be that there is a kind of inhibition about writing fully committed political things in Scotland, because of the complexity of the situation. You've got to

48

decide between, say, left, centre and right in UK terms, but you've also got to think in terms of nationalism, within Scotland, versus something that again concerns the whole of the UK. You have a Scottish National Party which is obviously very far from being radical, and only recently there was a proposal for a national party which will be aiming to be left wing. A party like that might bring together things which haven't been brought together before. It certainly is a possibility that you might be split between feeling something about socialism, and something about nationalism, and knowing that the two haven't clicked together much in the past in Scotland.

Are those your politics, nationalist and socialist?

I'm not a political animal really, except I have now and again very strong feelings about things, but they're more feelings than thought-out intellectual positions. I would rather use the word radical than socialist.

If you are so nationalist, why are most of your poems in English?

It's more natural for me to speak English than Scots, because of my background and education. It doesn't mean that I wouldn't want to use Scots, but I use it for special purposes, in things like translating some poet who happens to go better in Scots than in English.

Yes, why did you put Mayakovsky into Scots?

Because I felt it was working much better in Scots than in English. I tried both, and it seemed to come across with a much greater vigour and fluency into Scots. I also tend to use Scots where it would be used naturally in a poem, in speech. I'm very much aware that this leaves the whole position in the air — whether one should use Scots as a deliberate political act — this is clearly a possibility.

Is Scots to be used for political purposes only?

It doesn't amount to a complete national language, and that is the difficulty. I think that Scots could be revived. That's what the Israelis have done with Hebrew, deliberately revived it as an act of national policy, and it has worked; something like this could happen with Scots. This really depends upon the political situation; I don't think you can start, as Hugh MacDiarmid wanted to do, from using Scots and then move from that into politics. I think that the politics have got to happen and then you decide what language you are going to have in a new, independent Scotland.

Which brings us to Scottish International. *What was the idea behind it?*

A desire for a literary quarterly which wouldn't be entirely literary, but would also deal with society in a wider sense; and would also look outwards a bit, at what was going on elsewhere. Our tendency in Scotland is very much to look inside, because we want to preserve what we have as something that is besieged from somewhere else. We therefore tend to look very hard at, for example, our own history, perhaps too hard. As a reaction against this we felt there should be a magazine that would include translations of foreign writers and discuss foreign as well as Scottish material.

How successful has it been in these two objectives?

The reactions of readers are difficult to gauge, because you don't get much feedback in a quarterly. One of the reasons we've gone monthly is to answer your question, because it's something you get from the readership. The magazine has begun to do something new; Bob Tait especially has this aim of trying to map out what life in Scotland is actually like, what people's jobs are like, what they think of them, and in this way to build up a picture of Scotland, as distinct from the myths and legends, which are very thick on the ground. What we haven't done enough of is serious literary articles; literary criticism is still very weak in Scotland. This is a slow and fairly difficult process. You can't draw critics out of the air, you have to encourage and nurture them. In going monthly, we also believe that there is a wider readership available. If you want to cover the cultural scene it's very hard unless you become monthly, preferably weekly.

Would you like to go weekly?

The idea crosses one's mind occasionally. Quite seriously, there is a place for a Scottish weekly, like the many English ones — *Tribune, Spectator, New Statesman* — all orientated towards what's going on in London. You feel irritated that so much is happening here which is not reflected by them. Whether or not such a weekly journal would get off the ground here, whether we've got enough top-grade journalists, I'm not sure, but I would like to see somebody trying this.

What are the good points about Scottish literary culture? What makes it tick? Its nationalism, presumably . . .

That has got something to do with it, yes. The feeling you're out on some kind of edge probably keeps you on your toes. It has bad effects too, of course. We're also lucky in that the last decade has been fairly lively. The decade before that wasn't so good; but the 1960s have been pretty lively, especially in poetry. The problem is to keep people in Scotland — if they could feel they could get published in Scotland. As soon as you go to a London publisher, as a novelist virtually has to do, then you've begun the drift south. If we had one or two good publishers who were concerned to foster native literature, not just best-sellers, this would make a big difference.

Would you describe yourself as a romantic?

With the usual disclaimer about labels, yes. I'm not very fond of the eighteenth century, whereas I do like the romantic movement.

Do you think there's a place for romanticism in poetry today?

I think we are in a very romantic period, yes. The 1960s have shown that this is a new wave. It can be escapist, some of it is; things like beat poetry, flower power movement and parts of the hippie cult do have a strong escapist element, but at the same time they are romantic. There is a good deal of political romanticism around. There are those who believe in action, in doing it, and those who want to withdraw, and meditate.

Which one are you? Are you a meditator or a doer?

Ah, you've caught me there — I suppose I am a meditator. I have great potential do-it aspects. It's like the question, what would you do if the barricades were actually there. . . No one can say what they would do, but I am capable of action, even if I don't go around with placards or joining societies.

The Second Life (1968) showed an enormous range of types, including concrete poetry. Have you progressed in any direction since?

Yes, in several directions. People often find it difficult to see the central line in what I'm doing, and I find it difficult myself to say what this is. One of the things I've been doing more of is what I call a news poem — really a sort of collage poetry which consists of things that are cut out of newspapers and magazines in such a way that a message not intended in the original context suddenly appears. The other kind are what I call Instamatic poems, which are based upon actual things which have happened as reported in the newspapers or on television. I try to imagine somebody had been there with an instamatic camera, and quickly taken a photograph. The whole thing is presented directly in economic, visual terms. I try not to add comment, but there's a very careful presentation which very often does include a kind of invisible comment.

What about concrete poetry? Is this a serious art-form to you?

It is, though I use it for comic purposes. At times it moves towards being trivial, I agree, because of the enormous temptation of word-play. It can also be used seriously as in the *Emergent Poems* like 'I am the Resurrection and the Life'. You have to adjust to this particular genre. People do feel suspicious of it because they don't like thinking in direct, visual terms. They feel that if poetry is to be poetry at all it must have certain spoken and rhythmical effects which can in fact be read and spoken and do have a phonetic as well as a visual aspect.

You lecture on another visual medium, film. How does film grab you?

Enormously, I'm a great film fan, even more than the theatre. I think I belong to what was a film-going generation. Certain films obviously have made a tremendous impression on me, because I still remember them almost as experiences, there in the romantic flux in my mind.

Do you have a philosophy? Loves or hates?

Injustice is a thing that I react most strongly to: I have a very strong feeling for fairness. I tend not to have a great bank of hates; rather to be an acceptor than a hater. I like to join things together rather than split them apart. I try very often to find values in things that are not particularly valuable, even perversely sometimes, seizing on things which are undervalued or rejected and try to bring them forward. I'm an anti-Leavisite in that sense. I don't like singling out the best always and laying stress on that; I like to go for the small things, to see what is valuable. I tend to push that too far, and say that everything is valuable, into the Blakean position of saying 'everything that lives is holy', which has its dangers, obviously.

Thank you very much.

interview with John Schofield (Edinburgh, 26 February 1972) in New Edinburgh Review *19, 1972, pp. 12-14*

Let's go

*You once provided the reader with a useful fix on your own
writing when you said you were interested in a poetry that
acknowledges its environment, in your case Glasgow and
beyond that Scotland, but that you were also drawn to
something that may seem the opposite, a highly imaginative
poetry exploring time and space as in science fiction. These
two interests are clearly brought together in the volume* From
Glasgow to Saturn. *Does this imply that these two kinds of
poetry are somehow one thing for you?*

I suppose the title of the book might suggest there is some kind
of link, though that is perhaps only the title of a book. Looking
back I think the more imaginative side of it came first and
getting down to the local part of the environment came later.
There has been an attempt, perhaps, to bring the two together
but it may be that I don't *try* to bring things together in that
particular kind of way, that I rather like to keep things in fairly
separate categories. It's true that the local and Glasgow poems
are relatively late — most came after 1960. When I look back
to the earlier period when I began to write, both before and
after the Second World War, it was partly a question of the
kind of influences that I saw around me, the books I read, and
at that time, of course, it was probably Dylan Thomas and that
kind of poetry which was being most discussed and which
excited me most at the end of the 1930s. That was not a poetry
of environment, although Dylan Thomas, for instance, wrote
very good *prose* of environment, but it was his poetry that
excited me and it was very different. Surrealism excited me: I
read David Gascoyne and Sydney Graham was a friend of
mine at that time, so that there was a great deal of discussion
of a poetry that enjoyed calling up irrational elements. But
there wasn't very much attempt on my part at that time to

write a realistic poetry though I think I had a hankering after it even then.

Would you regard the exploring of time and space as a function of your concrete poems?

Maybe an interest in space is more obvious than an interest in time because concrete poetry as a visual poetry interests me and that, of course, involves the exploration of space. I'm not quite sure what you mean by the time part of it.

Well, in a concrete poem the normal relations of the word to time and space are completely reshuffled. You have, as it were, a series of simultaneities rather than a gradual movement through sense down the line.

That was the ideal of concrete poetry, to be able to present something that was instantaneous. It doesn't always do this, of course, and perhaps in the nature of language it's extremely hard to do this. Quite a number of my concrete poems are a kind of compromise in that you can read them. The 'Emergent Poems' have to be read from top to bottom in the old way although they also present an image that has to be seen with the eye instantaneously. I think I wanted to see what concrete poetry was up to in relation to poetry in general. It wasn't that I just switched over to concrete poetry as a means of producing instantaneous images — that was part of it — but I think I also wanted to see if there was some kind of common ground between it and linear poetry. Quite a number of my poems are exploring the half-way house, not strictly concrete and not strictly linear but mixing the two forms.

Your concrete poems are very much part of your general and intense interest in the modern world.

I do like the idea of contemporaneity. I was never greatly attracted by the idea of tradition. I positively enjoy the contemporary world and have a sense of it, I think. I want, if possible, to reflect that in poetry, taking great risks, of course in doing this.

55

It is also a way of aligning yourself with a world *which is continually taking risks.*

Yes, and continually changing and changing fast. I think it's the speed with which things seem to be moving — maybe it's an illusion — we're sometimes told this is not true, but it *seems* to be true and this is one thing that I do enjoy reflecting. It probably must influence the way you write, the kinds of poems you write, even the kind of subject you take up. It also affects things like the length of a poem, the feeling which is fairly general that it is extremely hard to write a long poem nowadays but nevertheless there's a hankering after doing it somehow, and it is a question of just seeing how you can bring together the idea of a lengthy work and the idea of quickness or simultaneity or modernity or something of that kind. This is one problem that, like many other writers, I have thought about a good deal.

I suppose the series or the sequence is one possibility.

That is the usual solution, I suppose. I am still thinking about a sequence myself in 'The New Divan' which is a hundred short poems very loosely linked together. It is supposed to be some sort of whole, though not one that is easily analysed and they don't form a sequence in a very strict sense of the term. It is just an attempt to explore what one can do at some length and this is still a great problem. I've also tried to solve the problem in a long poem called 'Memories of Earth' which has a narrative structure and uses a continuous blank verse medium.

In your essay on concrete poetry, 'Into the Constellation', you quote a cryptic poem of Josef Albers which says, 'Calm down/ most of what happens/happens without you'. This is a very anti-expressive position, suggesting that the organising will of the poet attempts a rather futile interference in poetic occurrence.

This is quite a difficult point and concrete poetry is quite divided as to exactly what the authorial process amounts to and how obvious it should be. I think the main point is that although the authorial hand can be seen often quite strongly it is meant to be a cool hand, a hand that is not deliberately baring its soul or its nerves or expressing something that gets at you emotionally. If the process *is* seen, it should be seen as something more in the nature of a controlled experiment, something more scientific than expressive. As you said it is an anti-expressive poetry. You give yourself certain fairly admitted and definite limitations — there are certain things you could not do in concrete poetry, but it is trying deliberately to do certain things which poetry has not very often done and it is perhaps, in a sense, very nearly but not quite self-defeating as poetry because what it is doing is limited in various ways. It may be trying to present what Ian Hamilton Finlay often refers to as a *beautiful* object — he's very fond of using the word beauty — something which appeals to you as an object of contemplation which has some point. There must always be a point in it and the point either may be that it is merely interesting or perhaps interesting and beautiful, or it may be more beautiful than intellectually interesting. The more complex the concrete poem gets the more some of the theorists shake their heads over it because they feel this may be going against the basic spirit of laconism or economy. The first concrete poems were on the whole short, they have become longer as the movement developed and this has not always been regarded as a good thing. Perhaps concrete poetry inevitably had to develop as different ideas and ambitions were coming into it and using it as a technique, though it wasn't meant to be so much a technique as an entirely new method of writing and producing works of art. But this is almost inevitable as a movement grows and gathers momentum.

Of course there are several kinds of poem that may be called, more or less, concrete. For instance your poem, 'French Persian Cats Having a Ball' is high on concrete. A very precise quotient of meaning is expressed through typographical presentation and everything that appears to happen in the poem is thrown up by the typographical as well as verbal punning between 'chat' and 'shah'. This seems to me to fulfil the requirements of a concrete poem:

chat
shah shah
   chat
      chat shah cha ha
      shah chat cha ha
  shah
  chat
cha
cha

              ha
            chat
            chat
           chatshahchat
        chachacha   chachacha
          shahchatshah
           shah
           shah
            ha

cha
cha
chatcha
  cha
  shahcha
    cha
   chatcha
     cha
    shahcha
      cha
cha

                sh   ch
               aha
              ch   sh

Doesn't it also suggest to you that this is working in the way of the definition in that it is not something that is meant to say 'Look at the author!', but rather 'Look at that!' Here is a thing on the page which is meant to interest you in a certain kind of way, but it's not saying you should look behind it to the writer and his feelings when he wrote. In this way it is a very non-egotistical, non-expressive kind of poem.

Except that for most people the shock of this form is so great

*that the orthodoxies still tremble and one is quite naturally
prompted to speculate about the reasons for it and hence
about the kind of writer behind it all.*

Yes, but really this is irrelevant. Given that kind of poem you
are meant just to enjoy it. You're meant to look at it and get
something from it without asking the further question, but I
agree that many people do find these questions troublesome.
But as you say 'French Persian Cats Having a Ball' is a kind of
central concrete poem which goes along with the main,
original definitions of concrete poetry. It would be different,
presumably, from some other poems like 'Message Clear'
which can be read from top to bottom in the old linear style
and which presumably is also in some sense expressive since it
is supposed to be a monologue spoken by Christ on the Cross.
In that sense, I daresay, it's a less pure, less *good* concrete
poem.

'Message Clear' is one of a group to which you gave the title
Emergent Poems, *which is presumably intended to suggest
that they belong to a sub-form within the general area of
concrete poetry. These poems seem to me quite definitely
emotional works — the poem, for example, taken from the*
Communist Manifesto *would be a case in point.*

Yes, though in my own mind 'Message Clear' is more
emotional than the others because of the actual circumstances.
The others were done as more deliberate experiments with
making the poems emerge from various quotations until I
thought I had done enough. 'Message Clear' really forced itself
on me as an experience. It was almost written involuntarily.
That is most unlike the usual method of writing a concrete
poem. It came to me in the old sense in which poems were said
to be inspired.

*There's a paradox there surely. The fact that the poem
happened to you would make it, in some ways, even more of a
concrete poem if the essence of a concrete poem is that it
should be so much more a happening — as in the little
injunction from Albers that we mentioned earlier.*

59

But it should not be so much of an *emotional* happening as that poem was. This poem was written when my father was very ill, dying of cancer, and I was coming home from the hospital. Suddenly this line 'I am the resurrection and the life' came into my head and then the poem began to emerge from the line. I think about half of it was in my head going home on the bus and I had to come in and write down as much of it as I could right away before it disappeared. That is what I meant by being very much against the theory of concrete poetry, just like any 'ordinary' poem might come to be. But it still is very interesting to think that a poem of that kind comes out as an actual concrete poem yet is related to ordinary human experience in this way.

There seems to be a great range of possibilities under the general heading of concrete poetry. If we take the poems 'The Computer's First Christmas Card', 'Message Clear', 'Centaur' and then 'The Loch Ness Monster's Song' the range is very obvious. At the same time 'Message Clear' is exceptional because the others all have a strong quality of play about them, they are game poems, words having a binge. 'The Loch Ness Monster's Song' strikes one right away as a joke poem, and I hope, at least in the first impression, that's being fair to it. 'Centaur' occupies an interesting sort of middle position:

```
          i   am,  horse
          unhorse,  me
          i   am,  horse
          unhorse,  me
          i   am,  horse
          unhorse,  me
          i   am,  horse
          unhorse,  me
          i   am,  horse
          unhorse,  me
          i   am,  horse
          unhorse,  me
          i   am,  horse
          unhorse,  me
          i   am  horse:
          unhorse   me!
```

*Within its limits this strikes me as perfect. There is a real
development through the repetition, and the punning and
palindromic effects within the words dramatise a mounting
frustration and anger. When the centaur gets to the end and
says, 'unhorse me!' one is positively moved. It's interesting to
find this quality here when one's response is purely
intellectual.*

This may be partly an overlapping with linear poetry. That
poem, 'Centaur', is a kind of dramatic monologue, like
'Message Clear', it's 'Thoughts of a Centaur', if you like.
Basically, perhaps, it's just that these thoughts would be
paradoxical. It would be hard to sort them out, but there could
very well also be a kind of agony and I think you're right that
this does come in the end where perhaps it moves towards
being more a statement or cry from the human part of the
centaur. Possibly it's a man who is partly horse more than a
horse which is partly man, because the man would be more
conscious of the animal part of him, even more worried by it,
and therefore he says at the end, 'unhorse me!' but at the same
time the two things are joined together and there is no escape
from the situation. But it is an attempt to produce a concrete
poem which is carefully controlled and economical in its use of
words and yet does also give you, hopefully, some kind of
insight into the feelings of such a creature as a centaur,
assuming that it did exist.

*You agree, then, that this poem is something of an exception
—at least that it is possibly a less pure concrete poem. Would
you agree that when it comes to the pure concrete poem or the
sound-poem the element of game often makes a pre-emptive
bid for our response. 'Siesta of a Hungarian Snake' for
example:*

s   sz   sz   SZ   sz   SZ   sz   ZS   zs   ZS   zs   zs   z

Yes, although that would be a fairly basic example of what
would be generally agreed to be concrete poetry because it has
the iconic quality, the economy, and it is a basic enacting of the
idea of the poem by means of the typography using no words
but only letters and the space between them. It shows forth its

subject. Certainly it has the element of play in the title, I suppose, because the title makes you prick up your ears and wonder what this could be and whether the poem represents it in any recognisable kind of way: the element of play is clearly there, but it is also a poem which is true to its title in the sense that it shows you the sleeping snake stretched out on the ground. It has had its midday meal, so it's fatter in the middle than at the two ends, and this is why it's having its siesta. Also the combination of letters is meant to give you something of the visual impression of the zig-zag markings you might get on the snake and it is a Hungarian snake because these are frequent combinations of letters in the Hungarian language. The poem is making a series of little entertaining points and seeing how many of these points it can put into a very economical form. It is true that this kind of poetry, because it rearranges elements and makes a habit of using permutations of the elements of words, almost inevitably seems to be playful because you are in fact playing with the blocks of language in such a way as you hope will give pleasure to other people. You enjoy doing it yourself and you hope this joy will get across. I like to defend the play element because it is part of joy and a concrete poem often comes out of a kind of surplus not exactly of feeling but a surplus of activity. The joyful energy that goes into this is to me probably the most important part of it.

In the essay 'Into the Constellation' there's a very interesting quotation from Eugen Gomringer: 'The aim of the new poetry is to give poetry an organic function in society again, and in doing so to restate the position of poet in society. . . . The constellation is an invitation.' How do you think concrete poetry could bring back to poetry some kind of organic social function?

It's a two-way process. If people don't accept the joy, don't accept the invitation, it clearly won't work in this social kind of way. When they read this in Gomringer many people thought of it as a paradox since it seemed that the last thing this kind of poetry would do would be to give a poet a place in society again, but I think he sees it arising from the *sign* aspect of poetry, the poem as sign, first of all — something there visibly not necessarily on the page at all but in some other form, perhaps in an actual neon sign or on the wall of a building or perhaps in a three-dimensional object like a piece of sculpture that you look at in the world 'outside'. This is getting away from the page in the book and getting into the world and it would become a part of the environment. Whether you would still call it a poem could obviously be argued, but that would be his way of taking it and I think that Ian Hamilton Finlay agrees with this and would also go along with this idea that if only people can *accept* something that they don't find easy to define, if they will just quite simply react to a thing like that, say a three-dimensional poem that they might see in a garden or a town-square or a field where they are not expecting to find a poem — if they can just accept the joy of it without worrying very much about category, then this would perhaps eventually produce a new kind of environmental poetry where a poem is part of the common cultural environment that we see round about us. It would still involve letters, words, it would still be verbal but perhaps minimally so from the point of view of a theorist who wanted to insist that poetry must be readable in a sense that wouldn't always apply to three-dimensional objects which you would walk round and take in in ways that are more than verbal. They involve the eye, feelings of space and distance, and mental activity too in ways that are surprising and might require quite an agility of mind. The element of play again. I think it is just the idea of getting the poem out into the world again that Gomringer had in mind. Ian Hamilton Finlay has done this to a considerable extent. He has training as an artist, he has painted, he makes toys and perhaps he is already more oriented towards the business of making things, whereas I have possibly a more literal kind of background, and am perhaps more thirled to the page than he is and so haven't made this further step of casting out into the object.

The first of your Essays *presents an argument in favour of greater sensitivity on the part of the poet towards man in his whole environment, particularly recognising that this is now a very technological thing. It seems to me that the chief difficulty is to determine the degree to which technological aspects of the environment have moved into the arena of the common sensibility to such an extent that the omission of a very full response to them is an actual deficiency on the poet's part.*

It is difficult to decide this — it's a difficulty that has been recognised for a long time. Wordsworth is taking up the point when he says in his 'Preface' that the remotest discoveries of the mineralogist and chemist ought to become a part of poetry, but qualifies this by saying that this will be true when they do become a part of general experience and so on, but I think it's a question of acknowledging the difficulty of the situation but nevertheless hoping that something can be done about it even if it's just nibbling away at the problem. What interests me in someone like MacDiarmid who has written a lot of poetry trying to deal with this problem which many people regard as unsuccessful, not poetry at all, but the effort to do this seems to me in itself to be important if only because the environment does contain these things. I think an artist ought to be reacting to as much of his whole environment as he genuinely can feel for and encompass, but it's partly a question of the desire and good will of the poet to meet his environment rather than just waiting until it impinges with a loud ping on something he's doing or something he experiences. I think the poet ought to be a bit more active in *pursuing* his environment, after all he can see it all round him, it's there, it's a *plenum*, very rich and full and becomes increasingly so with every decade of the twentieth century. The tendency of many modern poets has been to retreat in horror from this environment and to defend their retreat as loudly as possible. It was my annoyance at this attitude towards the environment that set me off on this track. The problem is real and hard to solve, but I feel that something has to be done to bring more things in the environment into poetry.

Do you concede that there are a good many things in today's environment that are repellent, that technology has its horrors?

This is seldom my first reaction. I tend not to emphasise this side of it because I think that many of the things that are said to be horrible or repellent are perhaps phases of a long-term process that is not going to be horrible in the end. This may be a somewhat Olympian view of things.

Would you say that this recoil from technology by the artist involves a continuation of man's spiritual flinch from the human consequences of the industrial revolution?

I think a lot of it derived from that. But it has had a second wind in recent years in the 1960s and 1970s when there has been a second wave of talk about ecology — Friends of the Earth, the Back to Nature movement — which has expressed itself in doing things like forming communes, not just people writing about it in books. It is obviously felt by many people that there is something particularly dangerous about the spread of technology at the present time and one has to acknowledge these fears, but I still feel that this is some kind of retreat or escape from things which are not to be escaped from, that they have somehow to be faced up to, that the solution is not to as it were go back into the organic world of nature and to forget about the machine but to do something about the aspects of machines that displease you and in order to do this you have to use science and technology. Science is a cure for science, technology is a cure for technology. The computer causes problems, but it also cures many of the older industrial ills that are still with us.

Hence your criticism of Edwin Muir for wanting to take man back into a pre-atomic Eden.

Yes, I do feel this. It's one of the reasons why I'm more drawn to MacDiarmid. The two are interesting opposites.

So you invite us to disapprove of Muir's archaism and to extol MacDiarmid's rising to the level of what is happening to man technologically. At the same time you admit that there is in MacDiarmid a lack of warmth.

Yes, you want to put the two together. I agree that Muir has a very taking humanity that MacDiarmid doesn't have. There is a great deal in MacDiarmid's work that shows a particular kind of ruthlessness and dehumanisation which can be disliked strongly. I would like to see both the warmth and contemporaneity combined, though there's no poet quite doing it — perhaps Voznesensky. He is very interested in the

65

scientific transformation of the world — this is a constant theme in his work. He does also express doubts about science and technology, but these doubts are from a sympathetic point of view which is not the usual attitude of poets. I would like to see a poet who could somehow put the machine in its full human context, but not just keep saying 'Down with the machine' as so many poets have done.

Do you think it is quite fair to write disapprovingly of the Yeats-Eliot-Stevens axis in terms of their failure to respond to technological revolution and to seem to imply that this was in some deep sense an evasion of the real?

If I were writing a different kind of essay on these poets I would say different things. I do get a lot from these writers. But I was using them as outstanding figures who have been regarded as the main poets of their time and almost without exception have taken up this attitude. I was only writing about this one aspect of their work, only saying that in this one thing they all seem to turn their backs. I'm not saying that what they do write about is bad or unreal. I agree with you that a lot of Eliot's early poetry has a considerable reality about it. 'Preludes' even more than 'The Waste Land' gives me a very pungent feeling even today. But even in 'The Waste Land' I find I have a very double reaction: as a person who uses words I obviously get a lot from it, admire and like it considerably, but taking it as a whole I do find a considerable element of repulsion in the view of life taken in the poem. It does not jell into one face that it always presents to me. I keep going back to it because there's so much in it that is there to be admired and learned from if you are a poet yourself and at the same time it is something that I cannot accept or like. This is true even more of the view of life I detect in Yeats.

In your own critical writing revelation often comes in the form of sharp metaphor. In the flow of writing the technological allusion is often very telling and natural, e.g. when you mention Wordsworth's ' "auxiliar light" that like an endless servomechanism between optic nerve and sunset kept a round of glory going in the act of perception'. But I think one has to

66

be very careful about advocating a forced attention to technological matters. Very little of the actual language of the procedure and hardware of space exploration, for instance, will become part of common experience. It's all right to insist that art must interlock with life, but isn't it dangerous to suggest that the poet must make himself unnaturally vulnerable to the whole gamut of technological vocabulary?

I think I am entitled to express disappointment that more poets do not respond to the kind of things that attract Voznesensky, for example. There's a great deal poets are just not drawing on, even just from the point of view of metaphor. A great deal depends on the poet, and on his temperament and what his interests are. If the right man came along and was able to be knowledgeable about such things and was interested in trying to see how they could be brought into poetry then it might be quite a revelation to people who don't see how it can be done. You couldn't give a tremendously faithful account of the experience of one of the astronauts unless you were thinking in these terms because it is a technological experience, there's no other way of talking about it. Human beings do go up in rockets; they are highly trained men and very specialised and they're *not* poets but they are undergoing human experiences, of landing on the moon, of docking, linking one vehicle to another in space — and these things could be expressed in cold technological language in prose, but somehow you feel that there must be a way of using these experiences in poetry. Maybe all I'm saying is that there could be different kinds of poetry. It may be that there could be a simple, even perhaps romantic kind of poetry of space exploration where things would not be described in technical terms but where something of the epic adventure of exploration would come into it — a kind of carry-over from an earlier poetry; but there might also be a different kind of poetry which was more willing to use the specifics in the situation as far as possible and therefore to have to use technological language, although such terms don't always survive, especially nowadays when things are moving so fast that technical terms become obsolete. Things do perhaps survive in a different kind of way if they are taken into art. The artist is partly there like the shaman of the tribe to record what is happening, telling the tribe's history.

This point of view arises, I suspect, partly because you happen to find this a very exciting time to be alive yourself — you want it to go down, you want man to say that he was here in precisely this sort of way at this time.

Yes, I agree with this.

You wrote a very interesting essay ['Three Views of Brooklyn Bridge'] about the responses of Hart Crane, Mayakovsky and Lorca to the phenomenon of Brooklyn Bridge. You say that politics were of minimal concern to Crane. There is the suggestion that it is permissible to find politics of minimal concern but much less permissible to be inadequately moved by the technological feat.

That's a bit below the belt! The essay wasn't about politics but about the use of material objects in poetry. My main point here was that although the three men have very different reactions there is no escape from the physical reality. Mayakovsky added something from his background where politics and industrialisation went together hand in hand very closely in the 1920s — he almost had to be politically orientated and I'm not praising him especially for that. Crane might perhaps have been slightly more interested in politics than he was, but I wasn't complaining about that: I was just saying that in his case the thing that interested me particularly about his reaction to this actual bridge is that he is not just making something of it as a spanning mechanism or a symbol of love, but saying it is actually Brooklyn Bridge he is going to talk about. He wants you to think about this actual bridge and if possible to know what it looks like: this taking an actual thing in this way is a part of the poem. It's the very opposite of Eliot's unreal city. What an extraordinary thing to say that London is an unreal city! This is the kind of thing that really riles me about Eliot! Crane gives us a very real bridge in the city of New York but Eliot looks at the crowds going over London Bridge and finds it unreal! Can you believe it? Can you believe that a man like that existed? Did he actually walk in these crowds? Was he reading Dante . . . or did those feet in ancient time . . . extraordinary!

In all your most recent poetry as well as in the volume of Essays *published last year the emphasis is on the* real *in the life that is lived modernly as well as in the life that was lived actually in Wordsworth's time. The pull of your writing is clearly away from escapist poetry which evades real situations or runs off into some bolt-hole of the poet's mind and you are in favour of a poetry which is in some deep sense socially responsible. The ground of the preface to* Sovpoems *in which you discuss Soviet artistic policy is this sense of art being news of life rather than exercises in aesthetics. This seems to have developed in you rather than having been there from the beginning. Your long poem of* 1955, *'The Cape of Good Hope', was about the need for all artists to avoid, like Stephen Dedalus, being caught in the nets of involvement; the sea in that poem — and perhaps this was giving Eliot his come-uppance — was at once a very real, violent and mastering sea, the very sea itself, and at the same time a metaphor for the unknown, a Melvillean sea. The prescription implicit in the poem and accorded artists of various kinds would seem to be that they must take risks in complete freedom. They are to be questers. But for the artist the time comes when he feels his isolation, so that Leonardo must descend from the height of his creativity to humanity and pain, Michelangelo must decline into his desolation, Newton realises that 'before woman I loved light' and that he has lost the key of peace, for Melville solitude returns and Mayakovsky's sacrifice of self ironically and tragically results also in a terrible solitude. All these men, however, find that they have to try to return from the chosen emptiness and become 'trussed in the common human chains', even if it is only to find despair in captivity. I would like to know what this poem says about yourself, because having reached that point in* 1955 *where you seem to be saying, like the Beatles, 'Get back', one must be involved in the human community, silence falls. This poem comes out in* 1955 *and the next substantial publication is ten years later with* Starryveldt *in* 1965. *During this period you translate, most notably Montale whose poetry, rich and extraordinary as it is, does not seem to belong to the kind of writing that is going to occupy you in your own creative work characteristically from about* 1960. *When your creative writing begins to be very active, you are especially prolific in a poetry that does not seem to square with the position you appear to reach in 'The*

Cape of Good Hope'. You are writing concrete poems which are not really involved poems although they may build up to a body of poetry which is intended to be involved in the cultural life in a special way. They are very different from the sort of involvement of Glasgow Sonnets *which come much later.*

I was writing the first of the Glasgow poems about the same time as I was doing the concrete poems. These both come together about the same time, about 1962 or 1963. These things began almost simultaneously. It is a general impulse, not an impulse towards one thing. But I think that the realistic kind, the Glasgow thing, did really come first in 1962. Then almost immediately after that came the interest in concrete poetry.

Could you comment on this gap of about ten years?

I think 'The Cape of Good Hope' did come at a crisis point. Probably the thing I learned in writing it was that I wasn't going to go on writing that kind of poem as I had perhaps thought I was. It's a poem, I suppose, that expresses a certain kind of dissatisfaction and worry about creative direction. It is aware of the dilemma of the perhaps necessarily solitary creator and his equally necessary involvement with humanity and it is acknowledging that I haven't managed to solve this very satisfactorily in myself, that I was worried by it. The problem *seemed* to be best solved by not allowing the voyage just to go out but also returning. I was tempted to make it a voyage that just went out and didn't come back, but I decided at one point that this wouldn't do: you've got to get back into the common life at the end. But although it expresses hope that this would happen it is not terribly convinced about it. It's still bsically a poem about solitude, I think, and perhaps against itself making a case for the great solitaries — almost, as someone said afterwards, a sentimental case that all the great people have been solitaries, which isn't really true if you look at it closely. I was only dimly aware of that at the time but I wasn't able then to write more directly about experience: that only came about after 1960, something that happened very unexpectedly in a very sudden way. I just suddenly discovered that I *could* write about simple things happening in Glasgow to me or other people or about things I read about in the paper. I found I could write about these things without necessarily metaphorising them and I hadn't written a direct, realistic poetry like this before, apart from a few things here and there. When it suddenly happened that I was able to do so about 1962 I realised that this was what I had in a sense been telling myself I ought to do further back and had not been able to do. Probably 'The Cape of Good Hope' is about that: it's struggling towards the position that I couldn't creatively reach at that time, and couldn't reach for six or seven years. How this happens I can't tell you.

Can you tell why the switch went off?

I wasn't exactly aware of it as a switch going off probably because I was still active doing many things such as translation. I was very worried that it wasn't the creative stuff but unable to do anything about it because you can't basically do anything about these things. You have to wait and hope that a new phase will be reached and this phase did come in after 1960 but *how* it came about I don't know. It must have been a general phase in my life. That's why I called my book *The Second Life,* because it did seem to be a general thing in my whole life not just that I was writing better. I had often felt pessimistic about the way my writing was going, wondering in fact whether I *could* do anything about it and of course usually coming to the conclusion that there is nothing one can do except be patient and hope that things will change in oneself. I think probably if you are going to write well at all at any time you have to have this kind of patience or even *belief* more than patience. It probably goes back to some kind of underlying persistent belief that you have in yourself that you don't advertise, that you have got something and it will come out some time if you just manage to hang on and hope. The next phase will come round and you will be able to write. I didn't find I was able to do much about it until after about 1960.

During this fallow period did you actually take pen in hand and try *to write? Did you* try *to produce poems?*

Yes, I've always tried to. It just didn't work. There was a lot of activity of that kind which just didn't come to very much in the way of finished poems. There was one long poem which I did finish called 'The Whittrick', but this wasn't published as a whole until 1973. I knew there was something wrong. If you are in a period like that when you are not happy about your progress, working with words in some kind of way probably is helpful and I suppose that the translation even of Montale was helpful.

The work of Montale seems more like a kind of throw-back to a sort of poetry that you were really trying to escape, rich, verbal, aesthetic.

I don't know that it was really. Montale is more concerned with the real than you suggest. There's an anguish in Montale which is the anguish of Italy under Fascism — he doesn't write about Fascism very much but it is there and I think this gives a tenseness and an edge to a lot of his writing that is not immediately obvious. You can feel this when you get to know it and in a sense it is about the real, not an escapist poetry. I agree that it is oblique, but it is very full of detailed and vivid images from life, full of realistic detail of actual places he has been to. It is very real in that sense and it is full of the kind of images that I have always liked — the revolving doors of hotels, for instance. Why do more poets not talk about the revolving doors of hotels which are a part of everyday experience? He makes this into a marvellous image and yet it is also something that is part of our own and not earlier experience. I reacted to Montale very strongly and I am sure I learned from him.

Between The Second Life *and* From Glasgow to Saturn *there's the volume called* Instamatic Poems. *These poems, a world away from Montale, are extremely cryptic, apparently based on the press photograph or report, usually something tangential to the mainstream of events, not headline news but something quirky, ironic, terrible, always with a very clear, limited but strong impact. This is possibly due in part to there being a strange quality of irony in the very fact that no matter how vivid or shocking these situations are they remain at a tangent to the headlines. It is rather like Auden or Brueghel's point about suffering always taking place in a corner. They follow many of the recommendations you make for the contemporary poet in that technically they are very much of their time, in a thoroughly modern mode. They are as immediate as a poem could be: the book is a tube with the poems pumped directly through at the reader. They are exercises in an immediate response to the data of the life that is going on round us, yet there are often small, crisp judgements implicit in these poems. There is often a sting in the poem's tail that gives that judgement. The poem, 'Glasgow 5 March 1971', describes the moment after a violent scene in a court room in which a knife has been thrown at the magistrate. You end the poem with the delicate observation:*

> One feature
> of this picture of the Central Police Court
> is the striking absence of consternation.

That is at least an assessment, if judgement is too big a word, and it goes beyond the strict objective recording of data.

I think this kind of thing may sometimes have crept in against what I thought the poems were doing. It's probably something extremely hard to cut out even if you want to. The aim behind the poem was to have the camera-eye and to present just a picture of something that happened without comment, but I think you're quite right that this kind of comment is sometimes there. There are other poems which are much more clearly just a picture, but the more violent or cruel or apparently calling for comment the thing is then the harder it is to cut comment out, though, certainly, it was meant to be as minimal as possible. In writing something that is to be a poem the mere selection and placing of detail, even if it isn't a general comment at the end, in itself very often does give a kind of direction to the reader which he has to follow. It's partly again an interest in the recording part of the poet's job. Here were a number of strange, sometimes funny, sometimes frightening events which really happened, if one can believe the papers. They appear in the papers, and are quickly forgotten, yet they do say something about the environment and what human beings do to themselves and to others. Why should the poet not do something about this if he possibly can? Some people describing the book have said it's very macabre, but there are other kinds of instamatics there. The macabre is strong, certainly, but this comes from the fact that these poems reflect something that is itself a reflection: they come from the media. The media don't give good news, they give bad news usually, so inevitably the poems reflect that.

I think I would agree with readers who find the book's emphasis to be on the dark or the macabre. There are humorous clippings to be culled from the papers, after all. Of course there is often a macabre humour arising from the swiftness with which the images are presented and also from the irony inherent in the laconic manner when what is happening is so momentous or monstrous. Isn't this dark tone rather at odds with a quality of optimism which, I think, runs through your work as a whole?

I think there is a quality of optimism in general and it may be that this book is a compensation for that. Here is a book saying that everything is not quite as rosy as one might be inclined to think. It did seem to be being done quite naturally in the sense that I collected a fair hive of cuttings over a period of weeks and months without picking them out and writing about them and just seeing which ones seemed to survive as being still interesting, worth writing about a few months later or even almost a year later, I threw away a lot of the cuttings. These just happened to be the ones that still seemed to be worth doing something with. I wasn't particularly aware of it as being a collection of specially macabre or cruel or frightening cuttings but these seem to have been the ones that have made the most impact. This may be partly accidental and I think I didn't consciously and deliberately look for items of this kind but these were certainly the things that caught my eye. It may just be that they would have caught anybody's eye, like the extraordinary one of the man with his Black and Decker drill which is so extraordinary in itself that one doesn't have to choose it, one only reads it and notices it ['Shrewsbury February 1971']. I don't think it shows any special macabre quality in *me* to pick it out. It was there in several papers:

A company director on the point of retirement
is sitting on the concrete floor of a garage
with his back against the wall. The flash
reveals the blood pouring from several neat holes
in his head, but most of all it shows
a monstrous shadow cast on the white wall
where both his arms are raised above his skull
driving a rapidly revolving Black and Decker
power drill steadily into the eighth hole
which is to be the last.
The drill gleams with oil
above his conscious eyes.

There's no comment here — unless you count 'on the point of retirement'! Any other comment would be impossible.

This particular poem does catch the essence of the whole book — it has all the ingredients: it's got the bizarre, or bizarrely humorous, the macabre and the absolute economy of presentation.

And it was also something that could be presented as a picture. I had to throw away many of the cuttings I'd collected because I couldn't get them into one camera shot. A newspaper story is narrative, often involving people in different situations at different times, and I couldn't use that kind of thing. It had to be something that could be fixed at one particular moment, so this also restricted the actual choice of things that I took and perhaps, from that point of view, it often tended to be an event and quite often a violent one. Again, this is to suggest that it wasn't always *my* choice that finally came through. But then 'London June 1971' is not violent, neither is 'Nice 5 March 1971'.

The final poem in the book, 'Heaven September 1971 AD', was not taken from any newspaper generally available:

God is lying on a cloud
watching the teleprinter.
He is killing himself.
The new version of the Lord's Prayer

75

has come through from earth
and fills the large white screen.
HOLY BE YOUR NAME YOUR
KINGDOM COME. He points at it
as he rolls about, and his son in blue
smiles tightly, shrugs politely.
DO NOT says the screen
BRING US TO THE TEST. Behind them
the little holy ghost
chokes on his hubble-bubble. YOURS NOW
AND FOR EVER. A dragonfly
covers AMEN.

There is a suggestion here of cynical superiority to the world presented in the foregoing poems, a touch of 'As flies to wanton boys'. It reads as a single overriding comment which in a sense demotes the often very acute human experience implicit in the poems. So the effect is really to knock human values.

I see what you mean, but that wasn't intentional. God can afford to laugh at it all, although I think I also meant the Trinity to be themselves the object of a certain mockery. Certainly the son and the holy ghost are and I would have thought that possibly God the Father might also come into this.

I wondered if the Trinity were laughing at the incongruity of the people who inhabit the world of the Instamatics making this pitifully comical attempt to get closer to God. What an antic, especially when God is like this!

By implication perhaps, but it was just meant to be about that particular version of The Lord's Prayer and its inadequacies as prose. It is more a comment on that. It was not meant to be an overriding comment on the book, just a poem that stood out from the others as being unverifiable. It was basically an imaginary Instamatic poem about God reading the new version of The Lord's Prayer.

Your feeling for animals is interesting in view of the fact that you are so much a city man.

I have a great solidarity with the animals! I feel that animals have had rather a raw deal in the scheme of things. I like animals. I learned a good deal about biology and especially about zoology when I was at school. Animals are also a part of the environment: they are there and why should the poet not try to give them a voice, as it were. I think a lot of my poetry is in either a straight or in some disguised form dramatic mono-logue, and I quite often do try to give an animal a voice just as I might give an object a voice as in 'The Apple's Song', just to get *everything* speaking, as it were. An animating process, making the world articulate. I think I feel that the whole world is able to express something, so that when I write about the hyena or the heron or the timber-wolf it is just as far as possible trying to get into the life of these creatures, not to stand outside and look *at* them as a man might see them, but also to feel along their lives. This may be only an imaginative exercise but it's something that I try to do, something that one would like to be able to do because animals have a secret that we have no real access to. They have something that goes further back than we do and I like to keep in touch with this if I can.

You talk of giving the world a voice. I think sound is important to you in several ways. You write sound-poems like 'Chinese Cat' and 'The Loch Ness Monster's Song' and I feel that there is in the collection called Twelve Songs, *for instance, a very definite influence of music, especially pop music. There's a very neat sort of quasi-haiku called 'Oban Girl':*

> A girl in a window eating a melon
> eating a melon and painting a picture
> painting a picture and humming Hey Jude
> humming Hey Jude as the light was fading
>
> In the autumn she'll be married

This almost teases you into reading it into the rhythm and beat of the song itself, as well as having the rather wistful throw-away quality of the song.

That is probably there because I was fond of that song. On the general point, yes, probably there is an influence from popular songs, although I couldn't exactly trace it. The whole pop song thing burst on me very strongly in the 1960s — the Beatles, particularly, but many other groups as well. I daresay much of this does get into one's poetry in various ways. The poem called 'Strawberry Fields Forever' would be an obvious example.

You ask in your essay on 'The Resources of Scotland', what guarantee have we got that what we are doing is distinctive and could not have been produced anywhere else?' Looking around the Scottish writing that we have today, do you feel that this is distinctively Scottish?

It's always very hard to define something like Scottishness — I suppose that emerges from the essay itself. I think in a certain context if it's felt to be important to try to establish identity then people will do this even although they won't always convince people outside. You will find various ways of talking about Scottishness which do claim to make it fairly clear-cut, though this often means talking about Scotland as a place or talking about the Scottish people and making use of very obviously Scottish qualities. You could claim on the other hand that simply to be born and brought up in Scotland is to write as a Scottish writer and that this Scottishness will come through in some way but once you take up that line it is very hard to define it and you get different books and different authors that put forward definitions of this that just cancel each other out in the end. But I think it's partly a question of just what people feel at any given time. If they feel as they probably have been feeling in the last five years or so that it's more important to try to get Scotland defined, or defined again, they will do this, whatever the difficulties. And you will get someone like, for instance, George MacBeth who always claims to be a Scottish writer, who feels he wants to be taken as a Scottish writer even though he doesn't live in Scotland.

In the same essay you say that it's time that writers in Scotland reasserted the ear and tongue of their country. Do you think that the failure to do that adequately is confined to Scottish regional writers — if it is in fact a failure. Isn't it something that we would find in Welsh writers, in a writer from Yorkshire?

It is perhaps a regional problem but it's more acute in Scotland which has a historical identity in any case and is a place where there are already traditions in existence, and these issues are not being served by the present situation. It is partly also the purely practical situation of having publishers almost entirely in London who perhaps can't be expected to be very interested in the exact expression of Scottish language or Scottish feeling and who would become impatient with this, whereas were there a system of well-established Scottish publishers this would be the natural situation.

Do you think this would give rise to a body of work which would uninhibitedly express the local flavours of life to a significant extent?

I think it certainly would. It doesn't mean all books would be of this kind, but many novelists and short story writers would be encouraged to reflect in a more precise way than they do at the moment people who speak and behave in a Scottish fashion.

In your essay 'The Beatnik in the Kailyaird' you say that the problem of Scottishness has proved something of an incubus. Have you found this to be a particular problem? Being a Scot and a poet?

I think it's something that's impossible to avoid altogether. If you are a Scot you are a Scot and you have certain problems that come with the territory and you can't entirely solve these no matter what you do. I think it has in the past — not so much now — been an incubus in the sense that writers have often had to keep trying to prove in some kind of way that they are Scottish writers and have not written as freely and naturally as they ought to have been able to write. I think it's only in recent years that we have gradually been able to get out from under this thing.

The obligation to prove that you're a Scottish writer surely is the incubus.

You may feel this yourself quite strongly or you may feel that you are part of a community of writers that is *telling* you to be Scottish. This can be damaging in itself. Or you may genuinely feel that you *want* to show that you are Scottish, that you are very different from an English or American writer and you may therefore write as overtly Scottish as you can, either using Scottish language or writing about Scottish places or Scottish experience, Scottish history, perhaps making your whole work devolve round matters of this kind. But no matter how strongly you feel it, this may be damaging from the artistic point of view. It's a very natural feeling and one understands it, but you may be preventing yourself from saying things that could be expressed if you weren't narrowing yourself down so much in this kind of way. I think the tendency in the past has been for this to be felt strongly, that we must be Scottish, we must show this. Possibly this goes back to Scott and Burns or even further. It depends partly on the whole situation of Scotland with its unfinished political history, loose ends all over the place — devolution in the air now, of course. It goes well with this feeling of a dissatisfaction with the *status quo*, not quite knowing where to turn but feeling that you don't want to lose such identity as you have, however hard it may be to define. The Welsh feel this, so obviously do the Irish, but the English don't, they don't have this problem, so it is a very real political problem within the United Kingdom. Somehow a writer has got to find his own solution which may be in some cases very Scottish, but in other cases he must examine himself and see whether he has to be as Scottish as all that, and whether he is better less worried about place, about the national identity.

Your own poetry does not strike the reader as suffering from the pressure of this kind of feeling. I'm not forgetting that you chose to translate Mayakovsky into Scots or that you make play with Scottish placenames in concrete poetry. It doesn't seem to me that this has been part of a conscious drive to prove yourself a Scottish poet rather than any other kind of poet. You might have translated Burns into Polish had you been a Pole, just because that is your temperament.

Yes, I think this is generally true though I think that, like most

Scottish writers, you do certain things because you are Scottish. It's a mixed thing. The actual decisions you make as to what you're going to write about or what technique you are going to use are not always recoverable afterwards. I'm not *quite* sure why I translated Mayakovsky into Scots. I do give reasons in the book itself and I'm sure these are true, but I'm not sure whether they're the whole truth. It's very hard to get at the whole truth in these matters and I think that probably there's a mixture of artistic and national or patriotic motives at work. There was the challenge of the difficulty of doing it: is it possible to translate into Scots a poet like Mayakovsky who is a very inventive, accomplished, unusual user of his own language, extending it in all sorts of directions into great sophistication but also into demotic and slang and so on? The challenge of doing that was a large part of it, certainly, but this is itself a kind of patriotic thing, even to feel that challenge and to take it up, quite apart from the temperamental thing of liking and sympathising with Mayakovsky as a poet and as a person and feeling that I was on his wavelength and therefore could write about his poetry or translate it whether into English or Scots. It's a mixture of things, but the patriotic thing is there to some extent. It's mixed up with other things, of course, the local as opposed to the national. I feel very strongly about the *immediate* environment of Glasgow, you see, and have written often about that. I suppose this is partly natural because I live there, but there is probably also a little slice of the deliberate about that too, to let people in London or wherever know that here is someone living in and writing about Glasgow of all places! It is very hard to disentangle these things in your mind looking back on what you've done. That is perhaps Scottishness too, perhaps people in Scotland or Wales would feel more apt to do that. A Londoner would probably not feel the same mixture of feelings about whether he should or should not write about London, put it, as it were, to other people: 'Here is London!' There is in fact surprisingly little poetry about London, yet it is a great place, but someone who is living in an unsatisfactory unfinished environment will feel pressure within himself to keep writing about it in some kind of way, but hopefully not in ways that *force* him to write against his own grain. My own grain is much more open and flexible.

I think most readers would regard you — or on the basis of your work ought to regard you — as a European rather than a Scottish writer.

This is my nature and therefore the Scottish thing in me is combined with that somehow. I feel that I'm a Scottish writer and I would always describe myself as such. I feel the natural annoyance that Scots writers feel when they are talked about as English writers, as they very often are outside the country, but it doesn't mean that everything I do has got to be overtly Scottish. I have wanted this to be one of my aims: to widen the horizon by translating. Although I use translations for my own purposes in keeping my hand in when I'm not writing creatively, I've also got a kind of missionary aim too. I do want to bring this range of other European writers into the Scottish awareness. Something like Mayakovsky, which can be done in the Scottish medium, makes it a very Scottish act but in other cases it's not, it's done obliquely through English and one hopes it too will be part of the air in Scotland, that people will be aware of what's going on elsewhere and that they will find this useful.

Do you think the global village has arrived?

It's a patchy affair, a kind of broken balloon!

There are times when your optimism seems qualified. One of your greatest interests is in the way in which science and technology have changed man's total environment and this is something you enjoy and write about in various ways. One of the ways involves the kind of fantasy that appears in a poem like 'From the Domain of Arnheim' or 'In Sobieski's Shield'. Is there not something dark in these poems' treatment of the future? There's something stern, of course, about 'The First Men on Mercury', but that is part of a beautiful turning of tables on the assumption of the earthmen, but there's something dark there too.

There is, yes, and in the other two poems you mention there is something dark. I would regard 'In Sobieski's Shield' as not being dark finally. It deals with an experience that has a lot of terror and horror about it since it is an attempt to imagine the feelings of a man who has been sent to a distant world by this method of being dematerialised at source and rematerialised at the other end. What would the feelings of such a man be when he woke up? Would he feel that he was the same person? He has obviously had some kind of tremendous shock to his whole system so would he feel he was and would he *be* in fact the same person? What would his reactions be? Would he have his own life and how would he react to other people who were there with him in the same situation? It was meant to be a poem about shock — the shock of reaction to what I regard as a possible method in some distant future when rockets are no longer sufficient to cover the huge distances involved — a very distant but maybe possible method, submitting the human being to an extraordinarily traumatic experience — really *using* the word 'trauma' — but trying to say as it goes on that despite the trauma, despite the man's worries about whether he is still human or not, he *is* still human in fact and shows that he is by his reaction and by his continuing sense of a job to be done as the poem says at the end, 'Let's go'. The last words are acceptance of the environment and going out into it, into further dangers — and a kind of acceptance of the unknown. So it's meant to be hopeful. It's also meant to be hopeful in the sense of showing a kind of continuity: the bit where you have a kind of flashback to the First World War is meant to show this kind of continuing resilience of the human race through its various tragedies, the First World War being a huge shock of a different kind involving millions of people, far more terrible than the Second World War in some ways. Here it is being brought into the life of one man and his friends and wife. It's a different kind of shock, but in both cases you are meant to have the feeling of a kind of continuance through terrible circumstances and the final thing the poem is saying is something about hope, I auppose, more than anything else. In the case of 'From the Domain of Arnheim', again it's the shock to a superior race which goes to a world that is in an early stage of development and is surprised by what it finds there. What it's surprised by is the sense of a very buoyant race of people who are going to do great things in the future. They are going to survive, not frightened by what to them appear to be alien spirits, gods. They have no gods: in a sense they are going to make or be themselves the gods. It's this sense of man being aware of great dangers and going through great shocks but coming through and having hope for the future. To me they appear to be poems of hope, though people possibly read them in different ways.

Do you anticipate hope sustained? You have projected imaginatively into the future. There is buoyancy, this rejoicing in your century. Do you anticipate the sustaining of that in the future?

I think I do. It's more a question of feelings rather than any intellectual projection. Obviously any kind of disaster could happen and clearly there are many chances of great disaster in the offing but I think maybe my feeling has something to do with something other than disasters. It's something about what happens after the disasters, the ability of the human race to do something about its disasters that has always impressed me. The survival instinct is something that is basic to all life but in man is fully conscious that he is himself putting obstacles in the way of survival by developments like the hydrogen bomb. But he is capable of creating new ways of overcoming even very great disasters. This may be in itself only partly a rational faith, just something that I feel, but I don't think it's entirely that. I think it would come out of an objective reading of history. At its time the Black Death was a serious danger in Europe which nevertheless was got through, and there have been other things like that, tremendous disasters in their time. It seems to me that it's built into us to be very determined in overcoming disasters of that kind. This is part of our species and I don't think it's entirely irrational that one can have a hopeful or even a *very* hopeful long-term view of the possibilities of the human race. I think it's because we're so flexible. The species that died out were very rigid. The great Saurians were very impressive creatures but they hadn't the kind of flexibility to master changes in the environment that man has. It seems to me that is the great thing about the human species, it now knows how flexible it is and how much power it can eventually have over a wide range of environments including non-terrestrial environments. I think it goes without saying that we shall go to other environments and adapt to other environments and adapt to them perhaps even physiologically like in Stapledon's *Last and First Men*. I think this is something one must envisage happening in the long term and so I do quite often think of these long-term processes. I'm quite convinced that we do have a very distant future ahead of us.

So you will continue to say, 'Let's go'?

I'll continue to say, 'Let's go'.

interview with Marshall Walker (Glasgow, 25 August 1975) in Akros 11:32, *December 1976, pp. 3-23. Published separately by Akros Publications, Preston, 1977*

A poem doesn't need a subject

Let us first get to know you a little. What have you done up till now?

I was born in 1920, in Glasgow. Except during the Second World War, I have spent all my life in this city. During the war years I was in Mediterranean countries like Lebanon, Palestine and Egypt while doing my military service. Afterwards I returned to my native town and entered the university. I got a good degree, and I qualified to be a lecturer. At present, I give lectures on the novel and the theatre at Glasgow University. Because I write poetry I prefer not to give lectures on poetry or related to my own poetry. I have six books of poems published. Add on the pamphlets to these, we can call it twelve little books in all.

Our readers do not know you yet. What are the subjects of your poems and what do you aim to do with poetry?

I like to write about the people who live in my native city and their everyday lives. Nature and nature-man relationships and the effects of industrial life on man are often the subjects of my poems. Apart from this, I try my hand at science fiction. For example, the situation of a creature coming from Mars to our world and a human being who has gone from our world to Mars are often the subjects of my poems nowadays.

Why science fiction?

Because our age is the Space Age. Also I find it interesting to write such surrealist poems. And again, as I see it, for a poem to be a poem it does not need to have a subject. For example, a poem can be created just by sounds. That is also possible.

Such poems which have no meaning when the words are read, gain meaning by sound.

The Western world, especially since the Second World War, has not produced new young poets. What do you think of this?

I don't agree with that. For example, in my country, there are many young and able poets. The Western world does have such poets. Maybe you don't know them.

In that case I will ask you another question. What percentage of people are interested in poetry in your country?

All kinds of poetry are written and read in my country. Especially people where I live are very keen on this branch of art. There are people who gather in various centres to read poetry and to discuss what is read. In recent years, poetry has become more widespread through recordings. Nowadays quite lot of people buy these records.

What did you know about Turkish literature before you came to Turkey? How is Turkish literary life seen from abroad?

I don't really know, because we don't have many of your works translated into our language. But recently an anthology of Turkish poetry, compiled by Mrs Menemencioğlu, was published in England. I did see it but since I could only get hold of a copy just before I came, I only had a quick look. Of course I also know Nazim Hikmet. Nazim Hikmet is probably the only Turkish poet well known in the West. His poetry is very very fine. I read Nazim in the translation of Taner Baybars into English. Nazim takes his place among the greats of the twentieth century in living and reflecting his life and his country into his poetry and all he writes, or this is the way we evaluate him.

Can you tell us which of the international poets you like best?

I know Aragon and Yannos Ritsos very well. But one of the poets I love best is Neruda. Neruda puts his country and its problems into poetry very beautifully, so that his poetry has influenced me most. Neruda's sensuous impressions are also strong in his poetry and he uses his talent in such an amazing way.

Can we talk a little about the interaction of art and politics?

As in England in the 1930s when politics influenced the man in the street, art and politics are inevitably intermeshed, because the greatest source of inspiration for an artist is the day he lives in. During the Spanish Civil War, English poets, like many others, wrote poetry against Spanish fascism. For example, Auden has such poems. As you know, there was a similar situation in France in the 1960s. On the other hand, these days, we the Scots don't deal only with the right and the left in our political poetry, we have an important problem which we try to pour into our poetry and that is our independence. Inevitably, the prospect of an independent free country for Scotland, its independence on its own soil becomes the subject of our poetry. These efforts will go on until an independent or a federal Scotland is founded.

In the university, what do you lecture on most?

Very varied. From the classics to the romantics, to contemporary writers. We deal with them all, Joyce, Eliot, etc.

Did you know that Eliot has been translated into Turkish by our present Prime Minister?

Yes, I know that your Prime Minister, Bülent Ecevit, is a poet and a translator. Our Prime Minister is not a man of letters. I believe Ecevit translated Eliot's *Cocktail Party* into Turkish.

I trust you will leave Turkey with good impressions. Thank you for this interview.

I thank you.

interview with Cüneyt Ayral (Ankara, 10 April 1979) in Dünya, *22 April 1979*
English translation by Diana Lee

Your jack london bit

What impressions of your childhood in Glasgow can you still remember?

Well, I was born in Hyndland, but I don't remember that! A bit of the city we were only in for the first two years or so, and what I remember were places like Pollokshields — I was there for quite a while. More than that I think, Rutherglen and Burnside, Rutherglen especially, where I was living for most of my early schooldays. So I remember these parts and I only came back to the West End of Glasgow recently — that's where I actually come from. My memories of the 1920s are of a fairly conventional middle-class upbringing, at that time. I remember the later 1920s, particularly — of course my own dates coincide with the decades so it's easy to remember them as decades. I remember the late 1920s and the beginning of the 1930s as a time when things were not so good. Although I was only vaguely aware of economic troubles, I remember this as a time when we moved to a smaller house. My father was in business, in a firm of iron and steel scrap merchants and business fell away badly towards the end of the 1920s. I remember it, I suppose, as something — just in the background. I didn't really understand it, wasn't really terribly conscious of what was happening in society until the 1930s.

Presumably, at this time, you were at school?

Yes, at Rutherglen Academy — I think it's Stonelaw now — almost all the time except the last three years when I was at the High School, from fourteen to seventeen.

Your early schooling, was it a mixture of goodies and gorgons? What can you remember about it?

I didn't like it. I remember that. I did not like school! It wasn't that I wasn't doing well. I was doing well enough except when I disliked certain subjects but I didn't feel at all happy about it. It wasn't quite so bad in the later years; a bit more freedom, and I began to enjoy it a little. But, no, I just didn't like it!

Have you any memories of English at school?

Of English? Some, but not very many sharp memories, though I do remember one teacher at Rutherglen Academy. I recall him as someone who was enthusiastic about the subject and that's the kind of thing I probably do tend to remember about that time and he was probably interested in the fact that I was writing a lot; essays, poems, and although he didn't do very much in the way of helping with my writing, he did talk to me, and I remember that as being probably the first time I felt there was some kind of interest in the act of writing. I didn't think about English as a subject I either liked or disliked. I felt that if it had any kind of importance, it got me off on to my own imaginative line. I enjoyed especially being given some imagination-stirring subject to write about — fire at sea, something like that. I always felt really stimulated by things like that which weren't really part of the lessons as such, not part of the instruction. The instruction I don't remember with any particular kindness at all.

Were you encouraged by anyone to write or did it just happen?

It just seemed to happen in the sense that I always liked writing but maybe there's a two-way process all the time. Perhaps if you do start to write, even very short essays, marked well at school, and someone says they're interesting or unusual, then it sets something going in your mind and you want to do more . . . and you do more, and it carries on from there. So there is a kind of feedback, just by writing essays which means something to the person marking them, not necessarily correctness, but something interesting. I wrote a lot of very long essays; there were complaints that they were far too long. I did spend a lot of time on them as there must have been something there that I really enjoyed doing. My parents would tell me to go out and kick a ball instead of writing in a jotter but I was hopeless, absolutely, at kicking a ball, and most other games, too, except tennis. As far back as I can remember actually writing things, I must have enjoyed it.

Sometimes showbiz personalities are asked if they have a tradition of it in the family. Did you come from a literary family?

No, no, not at all! Neither of my parents was greatly interested in what you would call the arts. There were a few books in the house, certainly, but nothing like the books of a literary house. There's really no connection I can trace except, when my father was a young man he was very interested in the theatre but more a question of theatre-going than interest in drama itself. He kept a book of pasted-in programmes, things he'd seen when young. I was much interested in this later on. I didn't know about it very early but he showed me it and I understood more of it later on. He'd been to a great variety of things in Glasgow but he wouldn't, say, read a play himself. I don't remember him ever doing that. If he read books they'd tend to be war or spy stories; stories with a sense of adventure about them. I think he had the kind of view that literature was at its best when it had a close relationship with something which actually happened. He'd often quote a novel that he'd read: 'Did you know that the Russians were doing such and such . . .?' He took it as if it was actually a true thing. There was no talk about cultural things at home. Father was a business-man and most of our friends were also in business and the talk tended to be about business matters or money or events of the time or the most popular records we'd play on the gramo-phone — the immediate things of the day — but not much discussion of cultural affairs. I've never thought of that as being part of the background at all. It was only when they saw that I was interested in really all the arts; art, painting, writing — I took Higher art at school — that they got interested them-selves. I talked about these things and they had to come to terms with the fact. One result of all this was that I very nearly left school, about fourteen, I think. Because of the interest in drawing, painting, at school, they thought I might get a job where I could use this. Both they and I had no thoughts of an academic career at that stage, at all, but they knew I was good at drawing and painting. There was a chance of a job at Templeton's carpet factory. I would have been a kind of apprentice designer, I suppose. I was attracted by this idea. I don't quite know why it fell through. I was very nearly fixed up but perhaps in the end they thought that it was a risky thing to do and wouldn't lead to much in the end; even if you became chief designer at Templeton's, it's perhaps not the greatest thing in the world. If they were ambitious for me they probably decided in the end not to take this up. However, it's an example of the kind of thing I was so fascinated by, that I would be quite happy to go and design carpets for the rest of my life, at that stage, at fourteen or fifteen.

Is this an interest you've passed in later life?

Yes, I don't do very much but I've done all sorts of things, now and again. I haven't, though, kept it up as a strong thing. I think it comes out in things like concrete poetry where I like to do my own concrete poems, to actually draw them with fibre pens and so on. I might do Christmas cards but to my regret I've never really carried it forward.

Was there a conscious decision you made, at any time, that you were going to university and you were going to study English?

It came out of the art thing, I think. Towards the end of my time at school, obviously, people had to make decisions about what I was going to do. I was going to go to the School of Art in Glasgow. That was the general plan, I think. My mother and father weren't very sure about this, like the carpet thing. They didn't know much about that whole side of life at all. They didn't know how good I was, you see, and what it could lead to. They knew I did a lot of it — as I've said I got my Higher Art at school and so on, but they also knew I was writing a lot and thought there might be something I could do with it. I think that's what led them into thinking I might do English at university. But it was decided really by all my drawings and paintings being shown to someone who was teaching at the School of Art. He came round to the house, had a look at them, and I think my parents thought they'd just leave it in his hands to decide whether I showed enough promise to carry on doing it and he frankly thought not. He said I was a very good drawer, that I could represent things very well but he didn't think there was enough there to make a career out of it or, if there was, it would be a risky thing, and he read my stories and essays and thought they were very much better. So in a sense it was more his decision than either mine or my parents. I think this is just the way things happen sometimes when your parents don't know much about what you're doing, or what interests you and they get outside help. I think he was the man who decided more than anything else. I was quite happy to go and do English because obviously I liked it. I liked drawing and writing just about equally at that time. When I went to university it was not with any thought of careers. I took English amongst other subjects. I was swayed, I suppose, by the Adviser of Studies to put down the Civil Service as the kind of thing I might do, not that I had any hope, desire, wish or longing. I just couldn't think of anything else and that was what he put on the form so that was why he advised me to take things like history, French, political economy and so on, to which I added a few others, like Russian, off my own bat.

What were the sweet delights you experienced there, at university?

Sweet delights? Oh Baudelaire, T. S. Eliot, James Joyce. I'd not much knowledge of 'modern' literature. I'd read a tiny little bit of T. S. Eliot and that was about all, but even at the High School they didn't do much of recent literature. It all rushed on me really, at university, especially the French class because it was much more geared to recent things than the English class, at that time. We did the French Symbolists; I took a great interest in people like Rimbaud and Mallarmé. A lot of earlier French literature too. In the Russian class, it took me a while to get into the language well enough to be able to read it, slowly and painfully. Again it was a series of revelations,

Mayakovsky especially. It was a series of kinds of writing I'd never been aware of before. Of course, at that age you're very impressionable and they made a big impact on me, as well as reading more of my own near contemporaries like Dylan Thomas, Gascoyne, surrealism and things of that kind. I have a very strong interest in the Surrealist School of painting.

Why Russian?

Almost accidental, really. I had a friend taking the class and I thought I would, too. But I think there was probably more to it than that. At the back of my mind there was something I remember, someone coming to the house who must have been very left wing, although my parents were very conservative. This person came and left some magazines which, looking back on it now, I realise must have been early Soviet propaganda magazines with marvellous visual effects, really stunning photography, all concerned with building up the new Soviet state through technology. I remember, about twelve or thirteen when I saw these things and they made a huge impact on me. I don't know what happened to them, possibly thrown out as being subversive, I don't know, but they gave a kind of feeling that something extraordinary was happening, over there, in Russia, and I remember hearing about the suicide of Mayakovsky in 1930 when I was ten — it must have been widely reported — and I remember this making an impact linking up with these strange things happening over there. It sank down into my mind by the later 1930s but it must, I think, have been there, possibly somewhere the seed was sown that made me decide, along with this other chap deciding to do it, that I would do it too.

Were you political at that time?

Not very, really, no! My friend was. He was a communist. I was left wing. I think in the late 1930s, just before the war, politics, whether left or right, were terribly strongly bound up with the peace movement. The Peace Pledge Union and pacifism was talked about, as I remember it, possibly more than fascism, communism or socialism. There was a stronger sense of war and peace and what one should do to avoid war. There was a strong desire not to have war and it was this I was interested in more than politics itself. I think I was a socialist but not a member of any political party.

Do you detect parallels between the 1930s and the 1980s?

Yes I do. In fact as I said that there, I felt it odd that this is so. Possibilities for destruction are of course greater now, more awful, than they were then, but the mass movements are similar. Perhaps our feeling for other countries is different. I was in Germany for example, not long before the war. A school trip to Germany in 1937. We were given our instructions before we went because we were going to be to some extent the guest of the *Hitlerjugend*, the Hitler Youth Movement. We were warned what to do and not to do. Always to shake hands, never to give the raised arm salute. In fact, we all enjoyed the trip tremendously and at that stage it's curious, how, being in a country which I suppose we must have known had already done some pretty terrible things during the 1930s; yet the schools arranged trips which went off very well and we had friendly relations with our contemporaries of the same age in German schools. We went to Bonn and Koblenz and sailed up the Rhine and the only thing that was indicative of potential strain was an incident which involved my camera. I took lots of photographs. I went for a walk into a field alongside the Rhine and came to a field with an aeroplane in it not far away in the corner. I took the photograph, realising, I think, that this was just a bit daring, a bit improper to do. I had no sooner taken it than figures came flying from all directions. They marched us off to the camp, and they took us into a little room and started speaking to us in German, which, of course, we didn't understand, but we answered a few words, not very much, but they made their feelings perfectly clear. Well, what they did was, they didn't harm us at all, but they confiscated my camera and they indicated that I was to come back the next day and I would possibly get my camera back. So I went back the next day. I found my way to the camp, I got my camera back — minus the film. So I never got my photo of the aircraft. So there's a slight warning there that everyone wasn't friendly!

When things blew up in Europe, where were you?

Well, I was studying at university. That was in 1939, and I was doing English and various other subjects at university.

Was it much different then from what it is now?

University itself, you mean? I don't know. It's very hard to make these comparisons really, because so much happens in the interim. It's very difficult to suddenly get right back into what the past was like. The classes were big and noisy, probably noisier then than they are now. A lot of interruptions. Some of the lecturers had a very bad time. I've seen one woman who was actually reduced to tears and leaving the room because she couldn't take any more. I think maybe there was more of *that*. That was very much the Glasgow tradition and it goes much further back than my time. I used to hear from my seniors much worse things from their days. I don't know how much one can really trust these tales, but I certainly remember it as being so bad at times, it was really impossible to hear what the lecturer was saying. But this depends very much on who the lecturer was. Some would get silence, some of them would just not. It depended very much on you and so, possibly the lecturer, whoever he or she was, had to make more of a thing personally out of the situation to make sure what he was going to say was going to be listened to.

Did you make a decision at any time — 'I will now become a lecturer'?

No, not really. Of course, the whole thing was interrupted by the war. My degree was interrupted by going away and coming back. I did three years, went away, came back and finished the last year. Well, I took my third year again actually, when I came back at the end of the war. No, it wasn't so much a conscious decision. I was doing well in the last year and I thought at first there might be a possibility of a university job, but I wasn't really aiming towards it in any terribly conscious sense. When I got my result at the end, it so happened that there was a choice. Either I could get a scholarship to go to Oxford or the chance of just joining a department as an assistant, at that time, in 1947. I think because I was twenty-seven at the time, I didn't fancy any more studying. Especially after being away for five or six years. I thought it would be better really to take the job, and I, in that sense, just became a lecturer because it seemed the better of the two alternatives. *Now,* of course, if you got a similar choice, you'd probably feel you'd want to get the other degree, because I've only got the one degree and nowadays you'd have a very poor chance of getting a university job unless you had a PhD. A first MA would not be regarded as anything like sufficient. At the time, I wasn't really thinking in terms of career in that sense. I just thought — well, here's the chance of a job. I felt I'd like to get started and do something. So I took the job.

During the time you were away from university, did any other profession attract you? Presumably you saw much more of life than you would have done had you stayed at university.

Yes, but not in the sense that I was attracted to anything else. War was more of a very unsettling experience. I knew less when I came back what I wanted to do, I think. It also took me a while to pick up the threads. It was very, very hard, starting again after being away doing completely non-intellectual things for such a long time, and I didn't do well at all, to begin with, when I came back. I wondered, in fact, whether I should go on with university work. In my final year, things suddenly picked up and I got, in fact, a very good result. No, I wasn't positively attracted towards anything except that that kind of experience of being away — I was abroad almost the whole time in the Middle East — gives you strong feelings about other places and I felt that I would, probably, if I'd have liked to have gone away again to some other foreign country. I thought of doing this, but it wasn't linked to any specific job. I just had this terrible restlessness and not knowing whether I wanted to settle or not at any one job. And that restlessness carried on for quite a while, towards the end of the 1940s certainly. My first two years when I was teaching at university, I still felt extremely restless and not knowing whether I'd made the right choice or not, and wondering what I should do. So I think just the war experience itself has a very strong effect on you, quite apart from anything that might happen to you — and nothing very much happened to me — in the physical sense, I wasn't wounded or anything, but it has a very strongly unsettling effect on many people.

Has it affected you as a writer?

Well, it was a great block. It affected me badly, I suppose you could say. It took a long time to get back into writing poetry. I didn't write during the war. I tried, but I didn't write anything of any consequence whatsoever. It took quite a few years after that to get back into writing. So, from that point of view, it didn't help me at all and I felt it to be a bad thing, creatively, for a long time. I think eventually, just because these are experiences that are hitting you at a young age, your very early twenties, that they're bound to have an impact on you. Later on, they were experiences which could be used and to me 'The New Divan', as a sequence of poems, is something which relates strongly to the war years. I mean, that was many years later. A lot of it was coming back to my mind in the 1970s and I began writing about it then. It's not always directly about the war. It's a poem which goes back and forward in time and space a lot, but to me it's focused in the Middle East, where I was during almost the whole of the war. But that's a very delayed action kind of thing, and it all comes through a process of memory and recreation of the war, which is not at all like writing about the war in any ordinary sense of the word.

This is a fairly common thing.

Yes, I think it very often happens actually. You never know what you're going to do with experiences, but especially a thing like war experience. You may write about it quickly, like Hamish Henderson — *Elegies for the Dead in Cyrenaica*, which I like. It's a very good book. That was written fairly soon after it, and it can happen that way. But in my case, it just seemed just to have had this immediate blocking bad effect and it took a long time to get out of this. Gradually, I found I was able to use some of these things.

If I can bring you back to university times. In the last interview we had in our magazine, Willie McIlvanney talked of 'gangs who spoke by the hour for money when they didn't care about what they were saying'. He was talking there about university lecturers. Have you any comment on this, either then or now?

Yes, well it is a job in one sense where you are getting paid to do that job. This is something that's bound to vary from lecturer to lecturer, I would have thought. I mean, some that I listen to and some that I came to know as colleagues, certainly did care a great deal about what they were lecturing on. I think it would depend . . . I don't think you can take an entirely cynical view of these things. Some certainly, especially when they came to the great expansion of universities in the 1950s and 1960s, would feel drawn to something that was more of a career structure thing than a vocation. That is true. Maybe that was, in a sense, what he was aware of when he was there, and as the departments got bigger and bigger, and of course, English departments did become pretty big with a great number of students. We expanded fairly rapidly and it's certainly true that when there is a very large department, there are some who are dedicated and some who are not. So in that sense, he is right, that there were some who were not dedicated. But it's not generally true. Even the majority, by any means.

You yourself are in the position of being both an academic and a writer. How do you see the development of creative writing in universities and, if I can add a supplementary to that, is there any scope for an optional Honours paper in Creative Writing?

A whole paper in creative writing or do you mean a time spent writing something in the final examination?

No, an examinable Creative Writing Paper.

Well, we did discuss this off and on, and there's a certain kind of case for it. In the end we decided to make it an optional thing, in the sense that you can submit creative writing when it comes to the finals for English, and many have done this as

99

an extra. They can submit poems, or a play, or a novel, or short stories or anything at all, and it's read by at least two people — usually by myself and Philip Hobsbaum. It's not marked but we both write reports on it and this is there at the final examiners' meeting and the idea is that it can't bring you down, but it can help your chances; it can add to your chances, raise you by a class, or by half a class, give you a better grade than you would have had otherwise. But this is something that's not, in that sense, fully written into the system. It's not something in any sense taught. Was your question 'should it be taught' or 'should it just be something which could be an alternative paper to one of the papers at the end'?

I think so. Having accepted that it is taught, and that there are facilities now for improving your creative writing, should it be examinable? For example, in CSYS in school at the moment, there's a whole paper devoted to creative writing, and as a teacher, I think it's valid.

Yes, I agree so, though I think there would be opposition to it. I think some people would say that it would be very, very hard to judge. People do say that even about our present system, that it's hard to judge, and I think they only allowed it because there were at least two people on the staff who had written themselves and who would have been in a position therefore to judge it. I don't think that's necessarily a good argument but I think a lot of people would feel this. In some ways it would be good and this again has been done now and again on a small scale, but to get them to encourage students to try out some sort of insight into the formal structure of poetry and how difficult it is, in fact, to write a good sonnet. Something like that is not terribly creative but it is something that would be a very useful sort of thing.

Would you have a kind of paper with questions about creative writing?

No, let's say a folio of creative writing in any form, either specified forms or unspecified forms.

Not as an extra, but as an alternative you mean?

I think either way. As it is at the moment it is simply an optional addition to what you do. You don't get anything off the official paper by doing this, but it could be, I think very possibly, an alternative to one of the papers. Whether then there would be an argument for actually teaching more than we tend to, I'm not sure, except maybe more to the American system where it's much more highly organised in that kind of way. They do believe, and practise it, too, but they do believe that you can teach most aspects of creative writing. They don't have any inhibitions about doing that and they believe that you are all the more a professional writer if you've been through such a process. Most of the best-known recent American poets have been through such a process and have themselves taught. I'm not entirely happy with this myself in the end. I think it can lead to certain kinds of over-conscious writing and it would, I think, depend on the writer. I think he'd have to be able, in a sense, to get what he could out of such a course, but at the same time, have another life outside the course from which he was drawing sustenance. I think if you were only doing creative writing courses and pleasing your examiners, you might write a very good minor poetry, or a very good imitation even of major poetry but I don't think it would be necessarily expected that you would write poetry that would really have something original and unexpected and powerful about it, because that might not come from anything that anyone might have taught you at all. No one knows, perhaps, where the greatest things in poetry came from and I'm not sure they can be taught. You might get it more from something quite outside any university or even intellectual circle whatsoever. But I think, on the level of craft, there's a lot of badly written poetry around just now and it may well be — I know that because I've been judging this National Poetry Competition, reading 20,000 poems over the last five months — so I know a lot of it, the majority of it in fact, is very badly written and it may well be that you may well be able to help a great number of people to write better than they are doing at the moment. Whether that should be in the university context, I'm not sure. In Russia, for example, they have literary institutes in Moscow, where if you're interested in writing, you go there. It's not exactly a university but it does have a high level of teaching and that's one way of doing it. It's like becoming a doctor, you can go to some medical institute, or if you want to become a composer, you can go to a conservatory. So if you want to become a writer, you go to a writer's institute. That's one possible way of doing it. But I think myself with all these things, there's also something writers should be very wary of.

Is this an appeal for the preservation of the soul, of the muse or the inspiration or something?

Preservation of yourself, of your openness, liberty if you like. Openness to experience. Your Jack London bit, if you like. We're not all Jack Londons, but Jack London had something.

Who did you think are the major writers in Scotland today? You've been judging a poetry competition. Obviously, there are established writers in Scotland, are there any up-and-coming writers that you can see?

Well, I think that of the younger people, Ron Butlin and Andrew Greig I think are two of the most interesting. Tom Leonard, of course, is moving more into the middle range now. He's a man of great power, I think. I think some of the younger people like Robert Crawford who graduated at Glasgow just last year, are very promising. Liz Lochhead is, I think her second book — *The Grimm Sisters* — was very good stuff indeed. I'm not sure whether there are enough — all very hard to quantify this — enough very young writers that have made an impact but this is very hard to know because they rely obviously on magazine editors and whether their work is getting across to any kind of public. I think the magazine situation is not as bad at all as it might be. It's reasonably good, but it sometimes takes a while for people just to get their names across to those who would be interested to see their work. Certainly *Lines* and *Akros* do what they can in this respect and other magazines too.

This is maybe a difficult question, but are there writers in

Scotland today who you would say are of international stature?

Well, I think Sorley MacLean would be one. He's had a good deal of international recognition in recent years I think; it took quite a while, as it did MacDiarmid before him, for this to happen. I mean, it was true of MacDiarmid before he died. In his last decade certainly he was getting much more widely recognised in other places.

Is this because of what Sorley MacLean has to say, or the way he says it, or is it a combination of the two?

It's a mysterious thing, because no one knows exactly how these things happen. Suddenly you realise that someone is well known abroad and he's being invited to other countries to read his work and so on. In his case, it is partly the interest of a major writer using a minority language which people fear is dying out. There's a strangeness and a fascination about this that attracts a lot of people in other countries where they also have a minority language like that. Especially a man of great power deciding to use this language instead of English or Scots, is a very interesting spectacle I think, in other places; it's not surprising that he would have this kind of reputation.

When you mention him, I find that he's depressingly badly known in this country, even now. I sometimes wonder if this is a feature of Scotland or a picture of everywhere, that you are not recognised in your own country?

It may well be true. I would have thought that when his collection became available in paperback, he would become better known but I don't know for sure.

Part of your writing obviously deals with Glasgow, with Scotland, yet you've done much in the way of exploring the international scene. How do you reconcile the two?

I don't suppose I do try to reconcile them, I just do these things.

It's something which just must come from your own nature and things you feel attracted to. I've always been equally attracted by something that's intensely local and things that are international. I don't know how far back this goes, but it must presumably go pretty far back. I can always remember even at school, of having a very wide range of interests. I would suddenly get interested in, well, Egyptology, astronomy, things like that, which weren't required learning at all but which I got thoroughly fascinated in and which would take me to things which were either distant in time or space. I think that process has always gone on. An interest in science as well as the arts for example. I never thought there should be a split between the famous two cultures. I think if you think in that kind of way, you don't find dilemma or split or paradox really in writing sometime about your own native place, which in my case is Glasgow, and something which perhaps is science ˙fiction or relates to some other country or culture altogether. It just seems to come naturally to me and I just go on doing it. I don't have a kind of theory about it and it's just something I find myself doing.

What then was the point of translating Mayakovsky into Lallans as opposed to English? There are those who would say Lallans was unreal, manufactured and it's obviously not your natural way of speaking.

No, that's true. I did it as something . . . well, I tried doing Mayakovsky in English as well as in Scots, but it didn't seem to be getting very far in English and I tried Scots and it seemed to be, immediately, a much more comfortable way of doing it. It seems to be able to meet a lot of the effects that he was getting in Russian. I think it was partly that the Scottish tradition, so long as it still existed, was able to produce effects in poetry that were rather like what Mayakovsky was doing, especially the way he mixes satire on a great range of social and political matters. I do think this goes back through MacDiarmid and Burns right to Dunbar. There's a great deal of it in the Scottish tradition and I think if you wanted to translate Mayakovsky, you could tap that tradition more readily than you could trap anything else in English. I think, from that point of view, it seemed that there was a kind of continuity almost with Mayakovsky even though he came from another country. There's also the challenge aspect of it, that MacDiarmid had been doing various things in Scots. Was it impossible to build on this, to accept the challenge of doing something difficult in Scots? The only way of getting Mayakovsky into Scots is by being, to some extent, eclectic. You have to, because of his very wide vocabulary, and also because of the fact that he's creating language as he goes along to some extent. You have to use the MacDiarmid method rather than a method which would be strictly following some local dialect, whether Glasgow or Aberdeenshire or wherever. You have to use a national Scots, or synthetic or plastic Scots (various people use different terms to describe the 'full canon of Scots' as MacDiarmid would say). So you have to go to dictionaries as well or speech as far as it survives. And I think I enjoyed just the challenge of doing that and the fact that it does seem to be working in some strange kind of way, because the test is if you have to read aloud. So there's something in there of the speaking voice as well as something that comes from dictionaries and it just seemed, in the process of doing it, to gather momentum and I was enjoying doing it a great deal and I suppose it is a test in itself if what you're doing is worth trying.

Professor, what did Mayakovsky say to you?

He said a lot of things to me. It's not a simple thing. It was partly the poetry, the language, the extraordinary vivid language he uses. It really is a striking use of language all the way through. Very, very fresh. And it was partly the life, I suppose, the background of his life, and the fact that, in a way, it was a kind of tragic life, in that he did eventually kill himself. The struggle that he had to try to get into poetry, ideas that he believed in, because he wasn't what nowadays people would call a dissident. He believed in the Soviet State. He was trying to get, I suppose, a new kind of poetry into existence which would be a Soviet poetry, Communist poetry, and yet would have every kind of aesthetic interest as well. It wasn't going to be a tub-thumping poetry. He knew that was a danger all the way along and he tried to avoid that as far as possible. So he's got this extraordinary struggle with the material of his art to produce what he would regard as really a new kind of political poetry, a good political poetry in which he was thoroughly involved himself and which would have all sorts of striking poetic effects that would please other people than those concerned mainly with politics and society. He was helped in this to some extent by his background in his early years before the revolution, his interest in futurism, and avant-garde poetry, but not helped the whole way because he naturally began to clash with Soviet ideas as the 1920s went through to the end of that decade. Of course, this led to all sorts of problems in the way in which he thought of developing his poetry. So just the sense of this man struggling at this extraordinary moment in history makes him, I think, a kind of legendary heroic figure and I found him very attractive from that point of view. So it was a complex of things I think, although people say his life was a tragic life because he killed himself relatively young, he was, in a deeper sense, optimistic, and I think that was one of the things which drew me to him, in the sense that I had read people like T. S. Eliot whom I admire but didn't really like from the point of view of what he was saying; the pessimism, the very deep-rooted pessimism of Eliot and also the sense of, whatever he was doing in being avant-garde as regards the form of poetry, he was extremely conservatively traditional in other parts of his mind. Whereas, in Russian futurism, perhaps especially in Mayakovsky, there's a sense that the experiments in art — the modernistic experiment in art — is to be linked up with the future, not with the past and I'm drawn more, in that sense, to European modernism, especially Russian modernism, than to the modernism of Eliot and Pound although, obviously one learns, couldn't help learning, from what they've done about matters of technique.

If I can return to something you said earlier on, you talked about the 'speaking voice' and concrete images in poetry. That automatically makes me think of a question that I have jotted down here about Burns and Dunbar. You've acknowledged what you call a 'spooky, underground debt' to Burns and Dunbar [see p. 192], or to certain aspects of their work and what do you mean by 'spooky', or don't you know?

I don't know! I've no idea! Did I write that?

This is what happens when you meet critics.

I think it's maybe in the sense that in poetry of the past like that, you don't know what it is really that does get you from a poetry of earlier poets. It's hard to define, I think, especially the further back you go. I like Burns and Dunbar equally. I wouldn't like to say one is better than the other. The further back you go, the stranger are the shocks of going back you get from them and Dunbar is harder to understand than Burns. We know much less about him. We know very little about him actually, because most of the arguments about Dunbar and what kind of man he was are circular and come from the poetry. So you don't quite know what he is, what he's doing, but you have the work itself. In the extraordinary mixture of moods in Dunbar — one would like to think he was a moody man in an interesting kind of way — are things that can be very attractive. But what was spooky (was that the word I used?) was, in a sense, that you can't quite place him in relation to yourself. You read early Scottish poetry, you are Scottish, you are brought up in Scotland and in my case I've lived there and haven't gone elsewhere, apart from the war years. So I feel in that sense very Scottish. I don't think it's a question of consciously trying to relate myself to earlier poetry, because I don't really do much of it. I'm not a great one for tradition at all, but maybe that's why I used the word 'spooky' because I don't see it as a great succession of Scottish poets and then I come in to a certain phase and carry on the chain. Possibly that's what does happen but I don't on the whole think of it like that, I tend to pounce on things that I find interesting and I don't quite know why I find them interesting.

I wondered maybe if it was a sort of very difficult to define sensation, something like a literary déjà-vu?

Yes, maybe something like that. Yes, I think maybe so. Or even the sense that you discover you're doing something in poetry for a reason that you can't think of, really, which is like something that maybe MacDiarmid or Burns or Dunbar had done before, and, suddenly, there it is. It's like Shelley's idea of all the poets building up one poem. We're all part of it in one sense. Some great Web of Poetry and we're all part of it. That would be a spooky idea. So maybe it's true.

How about the editing of the anthology Scottish Satirical Verse. *Did this teach you anything about the Scots as satirists?*

Well, I discovered how much of it there was, that's the most obvious thing about it, the great amount of satire, shading off in various ways towards just fun or high spirits, or on the other side towards invective. Yes, I did discover some poets and discovered aspects of other poets which had not on the whole been very much emphasised in the past. It put things into a slightly new perspective. I always had the feeling that there was a good deal of satire around and I wanted just to collect it together and see how much of it there really was.

Are we a snappy lot do you think?

Well, we seem to be, in some ways, an unamiable lot, if you take that as being typical, but of course it's not the whole picture by any means.

You've mentioned elsewhere when you were young, you had a liking for Verne and Rice Burroughs and your writing of 'huge, fantastic narratives' [see p. 192]. *Did you never latterly want to attack the novel or, let's say, the play? Was it always poetry with you?*

It was always poetry really, except for those days at school that you mentioned there. At school, I probably wrote more prose than poetry. I did write these very long stories. They all disappeared but I spent a lot of time doing that and they were influenced by people like Burroughs and Verne. But later . . . no I never even began. As far as I remember I tried some short stories. They weren't good. I just sort of stopped doing that. Plays. I regret not having done more, too. But I'm not sure I would have made much of those. I love plays, I love theatre, I love drama but maybe my drama just gets into the poems. I think many of the poems I write are dramatic but they're not like writing plays. I think writing a play is a different thing. Whether or not I would have done it I don't know but I certainly regret never having done more of that, in the sense of trying to write plays a long time ago.

Your favourite novel?

My favourite novel? Well, then, *Wuthering Heights, Moby Dick*. These are the two that just flew into my mind anyway. I like a good deal of Dostoevsky. I like quite a bit of Tolstoy. Joyce, I suppose, I don't know whether he's in any sense just a novelist but whatever he is, he made a big impact on me. Many others because I have always read a great deal of novels and poetry. Well, that's just some names, the very first ones that come into my head. *Moby Dick* certainly made a great impression and all Melville's work — I've been right through it.

Why Moby Dick *in particular? What did you see in* Moby Dick *that appealed to you?*

It maybe showed . . . perhaps it's not the best novel . . . perhaps it showed what you could do with a novel. It maybe showed that the novel is an extendable form that you can put poetry into. You can make it a great poem because it is a kind of poem in a way. It does so much. It's a bit like Milton, isn't it, and I think Melville has basic, extraordinary effects where sometimes he's very detailed and down to earth and scientific, when he's describing parts of the whale, and so on, or how a whale is caught, and others are practically allegory, although he didn't like the term himself. I think it's just the feeling that he can stretch the form. *Wuthering Heights* also stretched the form I think.

In your own writing, would you say you had a particular philosophy or point of view to convey?

I think a writer finds it very hard to say this. I think it's more for other people to say what they find in what you write. I don't start out at all consciously, maybe except in some individual poem here and there, there will be something you feel you must utter. It might be something just translatable into fairly recognisable terms of philosophy or politics or whatever. I don't, as a general thing, regard myself as being somebody who has a philosophy put into poetry, as it were, and I would probably find it very hard to say what any such philosophy was. I think it's more a question of individual poems, I think, as they come up and eventually perhaps they do all fit into place somehow. I don't think it's the poet's job particularly to see what he's up to in that sense. I think the more self-conscious you become about that sort of thing, the more dangerous it is for you. Unless you *have* a political . . . unless you're a political poet. Unless you're a Dryden or a Pope and you have a message of that kind to put forward, you'll do it and it'll be fully conscious and it can be good poetry too. But I don't think the present age is one where it's easy to do that, even if you do have a very strong political message. I think it's very hard to find the means of doing that in poetry. Even Brecht, who was the greatest in that sense — I always loved Brecht's work and he's a great poet — one of the greatest modern poets — found it difficult and yet always managed to do it successfully.

As a kind of corollary to that do you embark on specific writing projects or do you write as the mood takes you or as the occasion presents itself?

I suppose it's usually as the occasion presents itself or as the mood takes me. Except if it's a long thing. It depends on the length of the poem really. I think the longer the poem is or seems to be going to be, the more you think about it as something you have to plan to some extent. 'The New Divan' is something on a large scale. Although it's a short poem, it's also meant to be something that is more than that in itself and I suppose things like 'Memories of Earth' which is relatively long or a series of poems like 'The New Divan', which to some extent was planned also, and thought about as well as just written. So I think it's a mixture. I think the kind of running basis of the whole thing as it comes up, for most poets anyway, especially nowadays, when people don't write very long poems, is that you wait for something to either move you or hit you in some kind of way and you write about it, rather than having great plans for poems. I think probably most poets do have plans, even great plans, for poems, but they get a bit suspicious, too, because the more you plan poetry I think the more you tend to scare it off unless you're very lucky. Even in

'The New Divan' I kept it as a fluent plan. It wasn't something I wanted to make too specific.

Suppose we imagine for a minute or two that you have become Robinson Crusoe or you have become Roy Plomley's guest, can you think of half a dozen poems you would take to your desert island. We'll let you include one of your own.

I might not want that! I suppose if you're going to be a long time, they'd better be long! I think *Paradise Lost* would have to come into it and I think Wordsworth's *Prelude* would have to come into it. I would want Hopkins's book but I don't know if I'd want to take 'The Wreck of the *Deutschland*'. Mull Hopkins over and I think he would stand a lot of re-reading. I think that would be a good thing. I wonder, now, who would be best? I think I would probably like to take some of Mayakovsky because he's just one of the people that I've made a special thing of and I never seem to tire of his work. How many is that? Four I think. My own poem would be 'Trio'.

What are the differences between Professor Morgan and Edwin Morgan, poet?

Well, I'm only titular professor so I wasn't burdened with the full panoply of administration and I preferred it that way. They are separate in as far as I could enjoy university teaching, doing my job well and benefiting from the social and corporate side of it whereas poetry is done alone. I don't know what the connections are. University provides an intellectual stimulus which helps counterbalance the angst in writing half-decent poetry. Writing is physiological in the sense that it affects your whole body; if your poem's in a transitional state you're unhappy, moody. So writing is different from the university environment but not entirely different because giving a good lecture provides a kind of satisfaction; the class contact. A bad lecture makes you brood, you ask yourself continually how you could have improved it. A bad poem affects you similarly. So, different, and yet, the same. However, I suppose a good poem, in the end, is more satisfying because there is more store set by it. Some people are remembered by one poem. To be remembered by twelve, twenty is marvellous. But in both areas it is dangerous to be complacent. T. S. Eliot felt that writing poems drained him; he was always afraid he wouldn't write another.

Finally, Professor, what plans do you have for the year?

Well, I have an idea for a longish poem in sections. I'm making a translation of a Dutch medieval play, *The Apple Tree*, with help, for a group called The Medieval Players. I'm not writing a pastiche of Early English but trying to find a medium which is contemporary yet suggests the medieval. I'm trying to find the language to suit. There is also, although I can't say much about it, the possibility of a programme on the new fourth TV channel.

Professor, thanks for your time and help and all our best wishes.

interview with William 'Buzz' Barr (Glasgow, 6 January 1982). Barr commented that the interview was conducted on a cold night 'in a spirit of bonhomie, which was due in some measure to Glenlivet, but largely due to [EM's] inherent courtesy'. English Ayr 7, [March 1982], pp. 22-39

Poetry about anything

It seems to me your work posits certain questions about the nature of poetry and its relationship to fact; that those questions are set outside the British mainstream, and against an American/European background: is that accurate?

This is a hard question to start off with, because it's so big and moves out into so many areas. My first reaction is to recognise some general truth in what you say; my second reaction is to feel complexities stirring around the word 'fact'. It is true that since adolescence I have found much American and European literature (and architecture and cinema) absorbing and challenging, but was it because of 'relationship to fact'? I certainly enjoyed Upton Sinclair's *The Jungle*, Whitman's 'poetry of fact and science', the sense of a real urban Paris in Baudelaire. But I also devoured Alain-Fournier's *Le Grand Meaulnes*, Thea von Harbou's *Metropolis*, Frederic Prokosch's *The Asiatics*, and that's a very different world! No doubt teenage turbulence fed on both. Perhaps the authors (as distinct from individual books) I first felt particularly drawn to — Poe, London, Verne, Wells — showed a mixture of fact and imagination that could be found in Britain but was more freely and adventurously developed elsewhere. One last 'fact': I remember the death of Mayakovsky, shortly before my tenth birthday. It must have been widely reported in the newspapers. I don't recall anything about it, except that somehow it was a 'public' event, a writer in history, of interest all over the world. The impression must have been strong, to remain with me over fifty years. The writer as himself a 'fact': that is very much the European spirit — from Pushkin to Brecht, from Dostoevsky to Lorca — and I admire it.

Let's turn to America and the Beats; you have a strong affection, don't you, for the freedom won by Ginsberg and his contemporaries; are you attracted to their freedom of spirit or form?

Yes I have. In Ginsberg it was equally a freedom of spirit and of form. I am thinking of 'Howl' in particular, which was the first poem of his I read. The long swinging lines, the extraordinary juxtapositions of imagery, the sexual explicitness — all these things appealed, not separately but as part of a new amalgam of liberation towards the end of the 1950s. The Beats came as I was struggling out of a rather bleak and tight phase of my own poetry, but whether I liked them because I had begun to loosen up and liberate myself, or began to loosen up and liberate myself because I liked them, I shall never know.

Ginsberg demands a dimension of social responsibility, of direct comment: does that appeal?

Yes — even if it is only his claim (in 'America') that he's putting his queer shoulder to the wheel. It is probably the 'direct comment' that guards and guarantees the 'social responsibility'. That is what the Americans have to give to us, peculiarly. From the Beats I got into Williams, and Creeley, and Bukowski. I learned, really learned for the first time, however much I may have thought I believed it intellectually, that you can write poetry about anything. You really can! The world, history, society, everything in it, pleads to become a voice, voices. More and more of 'the world' came into my poetry from that time. By 'that time' I mean that from 1956 to 1961 I was throbbing like a chrysalis but not quite out. In 1962 a new phase began.

Turning from this liberation of voices to the strictures of translation; in Rites of Passage *you distinguish between translating known and unknown languages, and in Miklós Vajda's* Modern Hungarian Poetry, *for which your services were employed. You don't read Hungarian, do you?*

I don't read Hungarian in the sense that I could read a Hungarian poem and then proceed to translate it, unless it were very simple. But I do know something of the language, partly from visits to Hungary and partly through the activity of translating. I have a good dictionary, and a grammar, and although I am supplied with literal translations I always check through the original text to get the feel of it, and on two or three occasions I have been able to point out omissions or mistakes in the literal versions.

Well, Vajda describes sending his translators cribs, but receiving poems. How does translation in general, and that anthology in particular, relate to your poetics?

Bilingual Hungarians have assured me that I have been particularly successful in translating Hungarian poetry. If this is so, I don't quite know what the reason is, but it may be a combination of two factors: I share the Hungarians' own preference for a fairly close translation which will make at least some effort to deal with form as well as content, and I found I had a great enthusiasm for Hungarian poetry and wanted to make it better known in the English-speaking world. Before I had any contact with the Hungarians at all, I discovered Attila József in Italian translation, and made my own translations from that, out of sheer excitement and delight at coming across a poetry of such deep urban pathos and concern — it was almost like finding a kind of poetry I had been half-searching for (in Baudelaire, in 'B.V.' Thomson, in early Eliot) but never truly experienced till then. Budapest and Glasgow! That too was in my chrysalis days of the late 1950s. Later I found kinship with an entirely different poet, Sándor Weöres, virtuosic, a master of sound-effects, a real thaumaturge, and my versions of these two poets are probably the best of what I have done from Hungarian. Although they are so different, I am sure they appeal to different aspects of myself, and translation nearly always works best when one can get that sort of projection.

Your latest book, Grafts/Takes, *stems from that world outwith the poet's self:* Grafts *from Michael Schmidt's abandoned lines;* Takes *from newspapers is it? Now Douglas Dunn says of it in the* TLS: *'Does it matter where lines come from?' For him it does; are you rejecting that Romantic stance?*

Since the idea, in *Grafts*, was to make Michael Schmidt's fragments merge or interlock completely into the contexts I created for them, I did not even keep his snippets after I had finished the poems, so that now, already, I am not always sure where his contribution fits in. On the other hand, one reviewer did identify correctly a line he guessed was inorganic, un-Morganic, so the web is not seamless! I think my attitude is not one of theory or belief so much as one of practice. I have found, on occasion, that material outwith my own experience, including 'found' lines or phrases, has set off or been incorporated into poems which overall have worked well. What I don't like is Eliot's use of resounding, major earlier writing, whether poetic or religious. The found material should be minor, and preferably prose, so that there is a challenge to engage in some sturdy or subtle metamorphosis. Is this really, as you suggest, a non-Romantic stance? I don't feel non-Romantic! What is more Romantic than 'The Rime of the Ancient Mariner', and we know where that came from. Or what more Romantic *avant la lettre* than Enobarbus's description of Cleopatra's barge, and we know where that came from. Surely the *result* is what counts. (I think I see what you mean, in that some users of found material like Ian Hamilton Finlay and Thomas A. Clark, are cool, classical. But my approach is different.)

All this reminds me of what you said about MacDiarmid, his later poetry's voracious appetite for other people's writings: you spoke of 'a text outside the text, a sort of dark doppelgänger' — does that apply to you?

I used that phrase with reference to Stephen Fender's argument, in *The American Long Poem*, that Pound's quotations from historical-biographical works required, for proper understanding, a knowledge of the contexts he had taken his passages from. I don't think this applies to me to any great extent. The actual newspaper reports have no surviving importance in *Takes*. I suppose it would help in a poem like 'Tarkovsky in Glasgow' if the reader had seen Tarkovsky's films, especially *Stalker*, but I don't regard *Stalker* as a companion text to the poem in Stephen Fender's sense. Even in my recent 26-poem sequence *An Alphabet of Goddesses* (individual poems have appeared in magazines, but the sequence has not yet been published as a whole), which was triggered off by an exhibition of Pat Douthwaite's drawings in Edinburgh, I would not see the drawings as being a necessary accompaniment to the poems —

in fact, it would be misleading to publish them together, as we are doing quite different things, and the poems do not 'illustrate' the pictures, or *vice versa*.

We can't end without touching on Scots: in the Shakespeare translation, the 'haill voice' of Mayakovsky, you seem to use it as a kind of Volkslied, *but in 'The Beatnik in the Kailyaird' you said 'the Scottish Renaissance has begun to loosen its hold on life'. And there's no 'original' poems — do you feel Scots has a role left?*

In that article I wasn't saying there should be no more use of Scots; I was making a plea for openness and awareness, rather than tradition and precedent. I thought a flexible attitude to language, rather than rigid or polarised stances, was what was wanted. I had begun my own poetry in English, at school and university, and felt impelled to continue and develop that as far as I could. I started using Scots in translations in the late 1940s and through the 1950s — perhaps this was sparked off by the Lallans controversies of that post-war period — and applied it deliberately to a range of very different poets and poetry: Platen, Tuscan folk-songs, Shakespeare, *Beowulf*, Mayakovsky, Guillevic, Heine. There would be nothing strange about using Scots for Heine, or for Italian folk-song, since there are natural links and parallels. But there was a real, dialectical challenge in remaking, even in short passages, such English classics as Shakespeare and *Beowulf*, or a mystical Marxist materialist from Britanny, or a Russian futurist Communist who was remaking *his* language. I still think remarkable things can and will be done in Scots, as well as in local *patois* like Glaswegian, but I am content to keep the split in my own work between English-based original poetry and translations which may be in English or Scots.

interview with W. N. Herbert (April 1984). Conducted by post but EM tried to make his replies as spontaneous as possible. Published under the heading 'An Alphabet of Morgan' in Gairfish *1:2, Autumn 1984, pp. 57-71*

Nothing is not giving messages

Does your childhood matter a lot to you?

It doesn't seem, on the face of it anyway, to mean all that much to me, really. It seems to be something that was just there. Reasonably happy, except with the kind of problems, perhaps, that any *only* child has. I think that if I was married and was wanting to have a family, I'd want to have more than one child. I think there are always some problems about that. But I never felt that it was something that I particularly wanted to write about, and I don't think it comes into my poetry to any great extent at all. I read everything. I was very voracious. I read the kind of standard things in the sense that there would be collections of legends or fairytales or children's classics like *Alice in Wonderland* — I remember reading that. But as soon as I was able to choose at all I read a lot of adventure stories of various kinds. Perhaps some of the names are not very well known now. G. A. Henty, I don't know whether you know G. A. Henty's novels? Edgar Rice Burroughs, and, later on, H. G. Wells, Jules Verne, Edgar Allan Poe. Tending to be either adventurous or a mixture of adventure and imagination — Jack London, that was another one I read pretty early — adventure plus strong imagination, shading off towards fantasy and science fiction. Also standard school stories. And annuals, annual collections that would be perhaps in the house. P. G. Wodehouse I enjoyed; I read most of his stories. I tended to pick up some author like Edgar Rice Burroughs or Jules Verne or P. G. Wodehouse — and Dickens also I read very widely when I was in my early teens — and just pretty well go through them, trying to get their books out of libraries, often being disappointed once I'd got hold of the two or three I really liked and found the rest weren't nearly as interesting.

Were you attracted to informational books — encyclopaedias and the like?

Yes, indeed so. I was thinking just now in terms of fiction — but, yes, very much so. I often in fact pestered either my parents or grandparents to allow me to get encyclopaedia-type books which were coming out in weekly parts. That was a great thing in the early 1930s especially when I was getting interested in that sort of thing. Almost any subject really. Some were just general encyclopaedias. Others were about, say, nature or astronomy. I loved these, yes, and I enjoyed very much the more general kind where in each weekly part you would get the story being carried on from about a dozen subjects and you'd be flipping from one page of archaeology to the next page of marine life or something of that kind. And I liked the juxtaposition, the idea of great variety of knowledge and I was never somehow put off by this. It always seemed to feed in somehow to what I wanted to get from reading.

Did that feed in to scrapbooks that you kept at the time?

It must have done, because I started the scrapbooks pretty early — about eleven; eleven or twelve. That was just collecting cuttings from all sorts of places and pasting them into these books — little exercise books to begin with, and then they were later collected into larger books. That again was just a collection of pretty well, you might say, anything that caught my eye, caught my interest. There was no selection of subject whatsoever. Just everything that seemed to be of interest to me — in it went.

What sort of speech did you hear as a child — standard English, Scots, or what?

Well, it was a middle-class Glasgow childhood. Both my parents were Scottish — grandparents, the whole family was Scottish and they tended to come from the Glasgow area, so that the speech was what you would call educated Glasgow speech, but with a good many Scottish phrases and words and idioms being used, and I certainly remember these and used them a lot. I've got a poem or a collection of poems called *The Whittrick*. That is a childhood memory of a favourite family word. Both my grandparents were very fond of using the phrase 'As quick as a whittrick'. It just means a weasel, but a weasel of course moves so quickly it's almost like a flash — you don't know whether you've seen it or not. It was a very common phrase. It may not be so common now. There were lots of words like that used in the family without any thought that they were strange, or even Scottish; they were just the way people spoke. In Glasgow itself, of course, moving around — we always used public transport because there was no car (my father didn't drive — we just used trams and buses and trains) — so obviously living in Glasgow your ear is attuned to the broadest kind of Glasgow speech as well as what you're using yourself. I always liked listening to what I heard being spoken in the streets, in buses, and so on.

Do you think that collage of speeches fed into your writing?

I think it may have done, though I didn't think of *using* Glasgow speech until much later. I certainly enjoyed it. I enjoyed different kinds of speech, and I think I was probably thinking about that fairly early. I'm not quite sure how early; perhaps I was collecting different accents and making something of it. I liked speech and language in general, pretty well as far back as I can remember.

When you were an undergraduate at Glasgow University you concentrated on English but also studied Russian. Was that an unusual combination?

Yes, I suppose it was. I took two languages. I took French and Russian, and other subjects like history and political economy. But I'd only done French at school; I was good at it and liked it and I thought I'd better do that and another language as well. And the Russian was something that — it was partly political, I suppose, really; but partly also just a purely personal thing. I had a close friend who was doing Russian and who was very far left. He was a Communist. We were talking so much about Russia, I think, that it just came to both our minds at about the same time that we would like to take the Russian class, and I enjoyed it very much.

Was there any tie-up with the literature of the 1930s in that decision?

Yes, I think so. Because to me at that time starting to — well, I was writing of course even further back (in fact I started at school when I was about ten or eleven) — but at university when I was beginning to write more seriously (about seventeen or eighteen) — yes, the thirties, the so-called thirties poets (everyone always thinks of Spender, Auden, and Day Lewis as being the main names) — yes, these were very interesting at the time and I devoured their books as they came out. Also Dylan Thomas, just perhaps a little bit later, and David Gascoyne and people like that. Yes, there was that thirties thing of a political poetry which was strong. Though I remember enjoying Auden best because there was more than politics in what he was doing. I loved the obscure menace of his early poetry and still do. To me that still is the most powerful part of his work though the shift in critical opinion has gone towards his later work to a large extent. But I'm still haunted by that early poetry because I liked it a lot.

I suppose there's an Old English presence in some at least of early Auden. I've heard both poets and professional medievalists admire your version of Beowulf. *What interested you there? Did that come out of what you were doing in that period?*

Auden was very much influenced by Old English poetry, that's true. But, no, it came out more from my own English course, I think. I was one of the few who positively liked Anglo-Saxon. It was generally thought to be a hard part of the course and wasn't very popular. But I liked it and fairly soon I suppose got into the way of being able to read the language and to enjoy it. The poetry appealed to me very, very strongly. I liked both the melancholy side of it, the elegiac side of it which is pretty strong, but also the heroic side of it. It was the first really convincing heroic poetry that I read as a student and I thought I would like to have a shot at it. I had read various translations, and it didn't seem to me that any of them really met the case, and I thought I would just go through the whole thing, and do it. I did quite a few other Anglo-Saxon poems at the same time, or later.

Were you affected at all by MacDiarmid's slogan about getting 'back to Dunbar'?

No, I don't really think so. I suppose I was getting back to Dunbar in a way, but it wasn't really because of that. I think it was more an interest that I myself had in that general medieval and especially early medieval period, because I was just as interested in, say, *Gawain and the Green Knight* and *Piers Plowman* and *Pearl*. I loved that poetry very much; still do, in fact, admire it tremendously. And that in a way abuts on the Anglo-Saxon poetry, and I got into that when I was — but I think it was more as a study of English, what I had just read and learned as part of my English course than something that came to me from what other people said I should be doing.

When did you first read MacDiarmid's work?

That's something I'm not sure. It's a funny thing, you can't always remember a thing like that exactly. I must, I'm sure, have come across some of his poems here and there in magazines and anthologies before the war, but not to any great extent. He was a name that I hadn't really associated very closely with ideas about poetry. Then, during the war when I was away in the army, people sent me various things and I got into his poetry a bit more then, but it was really after the war I began to discover his poetry more and more. Before the war it was actually quite hard to get hold of, you know. Most of it was out of print. He published with small — 'fugitive' I think is the word — publishers, and the books were very hard to come across. You tended to come across his work in a piecemeal sort of way and not to get the whole picture of what the man had done. It didn't make really a strong impact on me until after the war.

What kind of impact did it make then? How did you react to it?

Well, it was first of all the Scottish poetry. I think the fact that I was away from Scotland during the whole of the war — abroad — gave me stronger feelings about Scotland (looking back towards it) than I might have had otherwise. That was certainly sharpened. I remember writing to people who were still at home and asking them 'Please send me books which had Scottish poetry or Scottish language in them'. I got a very good anthology of medieval Scottish poetry by M. M. Gray sent to me, and that was a kind of revelation; so that immediately after the war I was still thinking in those terms. I don't think I had quite come to accept the idea that what MacDiarmid had done was something that was bound to lead to a wholesale revival of Scots. I don't think that that was an idea that had really either sunk in or, if had sunk in, had conquered me, because (as you know) the earliest poet probably that I'd got to know well was Sydney Graham; and that was not a Scottish Renaissance thing. That was different altogether. So in my mind what MacDiarmid was doing, when I began to get into it in the late 1940s, was *one* thing, but I had also other things in my mind, and the Graham thing was still very strong of course. From that start, Graham's poetry always impressed me as being so much the real thing. I could argue with him. As you probably know from the *Edinburgh Review* number [75] where I quote from his letters we argued a great deal about this, but I always felt that there was a great energy, a great power in Graham that I went out to, and even if I didn't always like what he did and said so, I always thought there was something very powerful there. It was a *verbal* energy. When I didn't like it, I felt it was too uncontrolled, but when it was controlled I thought it was as good as what anybody was doing at that time. I knew the man of course. It was partly a personal thing. I knew him and liked him and I was impressed by the force of his character, whereas I didn't *know* MacDiarmid at that time, you see. I hadn't met him. So Graham was a powerful personal presence as well as a writer. Knowing someone well like that when you're in your teens and you're both beginning to write, it is a strong bond in any case, whatever you think of the other person's poetry. He was interested in mine, I was interested in his, and we talked a lot about it.

Though it was another Edwin Morgan who published a small book on Baudelaire in the early 1940s, was Baudelaire's work important to you?

It wasn't just Baudelaire. It was the whole of the French Symbolist movement that really got under my skin when I was a student, Baudelaire and Rimbaud, but Verlaine too, and others. Baudelaire particularly. I think to me it was a kind of revelation. I particularly admired what Baudelaire was doing because it was classical. If you want a classical poetry, that's it. He had an extraordinary command of regular modes of writing, and yet at the same time he's got a very deep infusion of something you could only call Romantic, even decadently so. And I thought that was wonderful. It made a great impression on me because there was nothing like that in English as far as I know. The great satisfaction of formal elements in Baudelaire coupled with deeply strange, often bizarre subject matter led me on to other French writers who were pre-Romantic, like Racine. We *had* to do Racine. We did *Andromaque*, I remember, and various other plays too in the French class and I surprised myself by liking this. It still didn't make me like Dryden, Pope and Johnson, but I admired what they were doing in the French neoclassical style. And even in Rimbaud where you're moving even further from Baudelaire into the modern period — a poet who makes himself a Modernist or an apostle of Modernism — even there there's an extraordinary concern with form that I liked. Except for his prose poems where it's a special genre. But when he's writing in a kind of classical style he also is able to combine that formal control with the most extraordinary adventurousness of ideas and language.

Were you attracted to Baudelaire as a city poet?

Yes. That's another thing which would be a part of it. As in the case of Eliot. It was Eliot's early city poetry that I really liked. The 'Preludes' in particular made a very strong impression. But, yes, Baudelaire and Thomson's 'City of Dreadful Night' and other things at that time — they all seemed to my mind to come together, very much as you were saying in your book in fact, which I've just finished reading [*The Savage and the City in the Work of T. S. Eliot*, OUP, 1987]. Yes, that was strong. I liked Baudelaire especially, I think, because . . . In fact, I think, I got into him before I got into Eliot and it seemed to me that he was one of the few who had, at a very early date really, the sense in poetry of what was going to be a modern city and I liked that tremendously. I think subconsciously I had been looking for that and not finding it, but it seemed to be there in Baudelaire.

Have any particular anthologies made an impact on you?

Well, I can think of two. One especially was the *Faber Book of Modern Verse* when it first came out. It was much changed later on. The more recent editions have diluted it. Now it doesn't have any unity, but when it first came out it had unity and was a very striking anthology and I think, for the first time probably, gave me an idea of what was happening in both British and American poetry of modern times, though it went back to Gerard Manley Hopkins. I read that about 1937, I think. Maybe it was 1936 when I read it. I'm not quite sure . . . but that I found *very* striking. Introduced me to people like Hart Crane and Laura Riding as well as the more obvious names, and I learned an awful lot from that. So that's a kind of landmark I think. And the other one is an anthology of foreign poetry, *An Anthology of World Poetry* it was called, which came out about 1930, edited by Mark van Doren, and consisted of — it's a big book — translations from many many languages, very often by poets, and I remember being struck by some of these, from different periods. A lot of the Oriental material in that, which I'd never seen before, made a big impression, and probably chimed in later on when I went to the Middle East and I began to put these sort of things together. Among the more exotic contents of that book I remember being greatly struck by some of the Arabic and Persian and Indian poems, and I think a lot of the Arabian translations by a man called E. Powys Mathers seemed to me to be very good, and they opened up really a new kind of poetry. He, of course, was translating (and also writing about elsewhere) poems from different Oriental countries, but it wasn't just they were presenting a kind of exotic scene that was interesting because it was exotic. Often it was strange story-telling or very powerful erotic imagery that was just that little bit different from what you'd get in Western poetry and yet at the same time was obviously the real thing. It was just as much human experience — even bits he'd translate from the *Thousand and One Nights* have got this mixture of something — you seem to believe it could actually have happened — and yet it's all very highly imaginative at the same time. There was something about that. Hafiz, the Persian poet, also came into that anthology and there was something about that that I think must have struck me a lot, and later on perhaps when I began to write about it probably that was somewhere at the back of my mind: this early anthology which certainly I devoured at the time, just before the war.

When did you *start writing poetry?*

When I was about ten or eleven, I'm not quite sure exactly. I had poems written at school. Some were in the school magazine. Some I just wrote myself. And at the same time I was writing prose, stories, usually long rather strange adventure stories which I suppose — I haven't got any of them now so I can't check on this — but I think they were abutting on, verging on, science fiction; possibly they were science fiction. Not for any purpose. Just because I liked doing them. They were never published anywhere, and probably they were too long to publish. I remember once I finished one and it was about a hundred and odd pages long, and I think my grandfather thought there might be a possibility of getting it published, but it didn't come to anything at the time, and eventually it just disappeared. Round about that time, between ten and fourteen, I was writing a great deal, probably more in prose actually than in verse.

Your first book of poems, published when you were thirty-two, was called The Vision of Cathkin Braes. *Were you wanting to bring Langland to Glasgow?*

I think possibly that there's a bit of the alliterative style certainly in the poem. I'm not sure whether it was as literary a thing as all that. I was living in Rutherglen at the time when

I wrote that and very often was actually on Cathkin Braes. I suppose it was a kind of local poem in a way, looking back to ballads and poems of that kind where the dreamer, if you like, goes out into the landscape and has a strange dream and wakes up at the end. Things like that were perhaps there.

Did the 1960s give you a second life?

Yes, I think probably I would say they did for a number of different reasons. It's hard to say it was just one thing. The whole feeling of the decade seemed to me to be very stimulating and liberating and I liked it a lot and found I was able to write more and probably better than I'd been doing before. I didn't like the period before that. I didn't enjoy the 1950s very much at all. I was sort of casting around for different ways to write without really making it. But towards the end of the 1950s, things began to get better; in the 1960s especially. Just the climate of the time just seemed to suit me for some reason.

Did it matter to you to attempt a poetry that was both joyous and Scottish?

Well, I suppose so. I think it's maybe partly a temperament thing and partly a sense of Scottish poetry — I think there has been a good deal of recognition of the comic in the whole Scottish tradition, which I liked. If I was reading Dunbar or Burns or MacDiarmid, comedy was obviously important to all three of them, even though they were serious poets, and I liked that and I think something positive comes through that that attracted me and still attracts me. So possibly . . . well, when I say 'positive' of course a lot of satire's involved too, but satire can have something positive about it. Maybe the energy of language that you get from satire can be in a way positive although you're attacking something.

From The Whittrick *to 'Cinquevalli' and perhaps beyond, are you attracted to mercurial, slightly elusive personalities?*

E

Yes, yes, I think I am, yes. It's partly the great liking I have for energy as a quality. I think that's what attracted me to Dunbar. It wasn't just a 'back to Dunbar' thing. It was loving Dunbar because he's a kind of whittrick, and I find the same with MacDiarmid, and with Burns too. I think the three of them are whittricks. Yes, and Cinquevalli obviously in a physical sense, was a kind of whittrick. Yes, I like this. The risk in liking it is perhaps the risk that you might miss the opposite liking for something that is very solid. But I don't think that that rules out a liking for the mercurial. I think you can see the mercurial in a number of contexts which, like overlapping worlds perhaps, or different spheres of existence, do amount perhaps to something very, very solid really because life might be just like that. It might be something that is just as mercurial as it is solid.

Has painting been important to you?

Oh yes, very. From an early age in fact I always liked doing what I could myself in drawing and painting. Art was one of the subjects I did at school. I took my Higher Art at school. In fact, I was going to go to the School of Art, and almost did. University was just a second thought really in the last minute. Yes, I think starting from that, just from my own enjoyment of it and learning a bit about it because I took Higher Art, having to learn a bit about the history of painting for the final exam, got me into it quite strongly. Although I haven't continued to do very much in a practical sense I've always enjoyed painting.

How about film?

Yes, film too. Maybe because when I was growing up it was very much a kind of film-going generation. The cinema was very very popular at that time, in the 1930s particularly, and I did see a great many films. My parents took me at a quite early age to go and see various selected films, which they thought would be good for me I suppose! Maybe I got the bug then, but yes I always liked the film. And when the Cosmo (the G[lasgow] F[ilm] T[heatre] as it now is — what used to be the Cosmo before the war) was started, that was a great thing in

Glasgow because you were able to *see* things that you'd read about — classical film which you would never have hoped you would see before — but now they were able to be seen and I remember going there just before the war and catching up, as it were, with the history of film and being very excited by it. I was very much persuaded by the early theory of film — that this was going to be one of the most important arts, possibly the most important art of the twentieth century. I think I accepted that and was sorry in a way that I wasn't going to be going into film. Though I didn't do anything about it practically, I was *greatly* attracted by the way in which imagery was used in film, even if it was at the expense of words. I was never quite sure about how important language was in films. Although I've been saying before that language was what attracted me right from the earliest years, nevertheless that was qualified to some extent when I began looking at film seriously and learning how much could come through imagery and not through language. You might have a very good film in which hardly a word was spoken; and it forced me to rethink some of my ideas about how the arts worked. But I was greatly impressed by film.

How about music?

Yes, music too. I think I liked all the arts. When I was at school we were taken occasionally to classical concerts in the old St Andrew's Halls and I got a kind of inkling of classical music from that and got my own favourites coming out of it: Beethoven and Sibelius, mostly. And it was mostly classical music until the period we were talking about, the 1960s, or the late 1950s anyway, when what is now called Pop or Rock music seemed suddenly to me to become something that I enjoyed listening to very forcefully. Before that, I was brought up, if you like, at home on what you would call the popular music of the time — the 1920s, the 1930s. We had a gramophone. The most popular records were bought and played on that. Neither of my parents had any particular interest in classical music at all and all the majority was for the popular music of the time. But looking back on that, I think it was just the kind of background of the scene as it were and although I remembered the songs and they often have a kind of emotional resonance, I don't think probably as songs they were really as good as the songs that began to appear throughout the 1960s. That made a different impression on me, because it seemed to me this was a new kind of music where there was a sort of poetry in it as well as often very catchy tunes or even interesting orchestration as you got with the Beatles. The Beatles and Bob Dylan, and many of the other groups at that time gave me something from music that I hadn't been getting before and possibly that chimed in with the sense of getting involved myself in the whole creative scene. It added to the enjoyment of the 1960s as a kind of liberating period for me.

Your 1973 collection is called From Glasgow to Saturn. *Your selected translations carry the title* Rites of Passage. *The idea of constant translation — linguistic, cultural, and geographic — seems central to your work as a whole. Do you feel that that's the case?*

Translation in all senses! Well, maybe so. I like translation itself as an activity, the challenge of translation, of trying to do it as well as I can. Yes, also I like various kinds of confrontation, I suppose — like going back to these old encyclopaedias that I mentioned, the different kind of subjects being brought together. I like the idea, say, in *From Glasgow to Saturn*, of living in a place, like Glasgow, acknowledging that as your base, seeing the place where you have your being as it were, but at the same time feeling that you're not by any means bound to be only writing about that; you're quite entitled to think of Saturn or some other place outside our world and as far as you can to have ideas or feelings about it and to bring that into your writing too. And the whole business of communication — I suppose that comes into translation — always interested me a lot and it was partly the difficulties of communication (I suppose that's often a theme in what I write) or even imaginary communication, but again the idea of bringing things together and of giving things a voice through what I write, even if they don't have an actual voice — giving animals or inanimate objects a voice — that attracts me a lot, and I suppose that is a kind of translation in a way. If I write a poem called 'The Apple's Song', the apple is being translated if you like into *human* language. Who knows what an apple thinks! We don't really know — it doesn't give signs of thinking, but because we don't get signs of what an animal or a plant or a fruit really is thinking, I don't think we're entitled to just switch off and say it's not feeling or thinking. I like the idea particularly that in a sense we're surrounded by messages that we perhaps ought to be trying to interpret. I remember in 'The Starlings in George Square' I brought in the bit about 'Someday we'll decipher that sweet frenzied whistling', which in a sense I suppose I believed actually — although it seems just a fantastic idea.

Messages from the past and the future also?

I think probably also. Yes, yes, yes. The writer or the poet being in *receipt*, if you like, of messages, just like people listening for stars' messages, astronomers listening for that. I think the writer too does that kind of thing. He does his best. He tries to decode, if you like, the messages that he thinks he gets from everything that surrounds him. Nothing is not giving messages, I think.

'CHANGE RULES.' Does that sentence have a wide significance for your work?

Yes, I think so. Because, I suppose, so much of my work has been about something that is in the process of change, and I like, I think, even the idea of change more than I like the idea of tradition. Obviously tradition exists and you are a part of some kind of tradition, whether you want to be that or not, but it's not something that particularly interests me — I'm more interested in what does change than in what has been and what is constant.

Like the novels of Alasdair Gray, your own work blends ludic fantasy with the sometimes grim depiction of urban life, particularly in the West of Scotland. Again, like Alasdair Gray, you've chosen to live in Glasgow. Do you see many links between your work and his?

I suppose so in a way. I know I remember seeing parts of the work long before it was actually published, and liking it, and going out towards it and wanting to encourage him and so on. Yes, I felt there was something there that was similar. The difference is I suppose that what he's doing is a novel, a large novel [*Lanark*] which presents different problems and different ways of dealing with them from what we get in poetry. But, yes, it was something that I liked a lot. I felt that what he was doing there was what ought perhaps to have been done in fiction a long time ago, but had never been done. He was perhaps the first person to see that Glasgow could be, well 'mythologised' is perhaps the wrong word — but something like mythologised. It had to be a real presence, it was a real place, but at the same time it had to be given a resonating, a reverberating kind of existence that you would expect a big place to have, and he was able to do that.

Embedding parts of your own biography in the text at the same time as going way into the distance strikes me as something that, as a partly subterranean structural device, would again connect you with Alasdair Gray.

Yes, I think that's true. Yes, because his own life is very much embedded in *Lanark*, as my own life is embedded in 'The New Divan' and many of the other poems too. I think 'embedding' is the word, because it's not always immediately straight-forwardly clear that the life is there, but it is in fact there and various clues are dropped here and there just to make sure that the real person *is* in the poetry. Sometimes people say that it's not a very personal poetry, that it tends to be an impersonal poetry. I don't think it is. You can't talk about your own poetry, obviously, in an objective way in that sense, but I don't think that is really true. I think in fact that it's just as personal a poetry as anybody else's, but the clues are not perhaps as clearly spelt out as they would be in other people's poetry. But I'm quite sure that the personal life, the autobiography if you like, is there, and is there quite strongly in all the things that I do.

Do you think that your own prose — your early essay on Dunbar, for instance — is bound up with your own poetry?

Yes, I think that probably early things were bound up a bit with what I was doing and what interested me particularly and sometimes even the style of somebody; early essays would fit in with that idea. Yes, I think you're often drawn to subjects that you want to write about for reasons that are not just concerned with critical estimates of writing you're taking up. At the same time, of course, that has to be qualified by the fact that you're *asked* to write this or that. You're asked to review a book or to write an essay on somebody and so you're constantly — CHANGE RULES again — changing your views on certain things or you're extending your views on certain things because of accident. I think that quite often when you're reading an early essay on someone you can tell that it comes from an interest that's of primary creative concern to that person, as being different from what he's been asked to do for some particular occasion.

Looking back, it seems as if there's a strong line in modern Scottish poetry that passes through John Davidson, Hugh MacDiarmid, and Edwin Morgan. Are you happy about being seen as part of any particular position?

Well, with these names, yes, I would accept that that is so, and I like that kind of association. I suppose that (just going back to what I've said about tradition) I'm not myself particularly interested in that really; but yes, I do take this as being something that, looking back, I would certainly feel to be true. I know that when I did come across Davidson, and Thomson — Thomson even more in some ways than Davidson . . . I do feel there's something there that is a kind of link, but it would probably be complicated in other ways. We've already mentioned people like Dunbar, and I suppose they're in the background too. But in so far as it's recent time we're talking about, yes, I think so, and maybe it is a tradition that is not one that's always thought of. Perhaps it should be thought of more.

Like several Scottish poets, including Davidson and MacDiarmid, you're interested in using scientific materials in your work. Why does your science usually take the form of science fiction?

Well, I suppose I was always interested in science fiction. I was interested in the sciences as well, but in a very amateurish kind of way. I remember at school enjoying the American science fiction magazines and, although some of the stories had a good science basis, others were much nearer fantasy. I think probably it was a combination of two things. I liked the idea that, if possible, you should keep the arts and sciences going together; if you had any interest at all in the sciences you shouldn't let it drop if you happened to be an artist of some kind. But I think particularly as far as actual writing was concerned, it had something to do with what was happening in the sciences from about the late 1950s onwards, when especially perhaps in space exploration (but also in biology and biochemistry) the most extraordinary things were happening. With space exploration it was as if for the first time life was really catching up with science fiction, and somehow it seemed to be more of a subject for poetry because in poetry — you could write science fiction poetry before that time, there was some, not very good most of it — but it was really from that time, the time of the first Sputnik, and then the first man in space — the first dog, then the first man in space — it was really from that quite a lot of poets began to feel that you would write *genuine* poetry which would once perhaps have been called science fiction, and perhaps you would still call it that, but nevertheless it has a basis in what is happening in the sense that the area for human operations is moving out, it's extending itself to other places than the earth. And you have there something that is perfectly real and will someday perhaps be even ordinary, and yet at the same time highly appealing to the imagination and to the sense of the adventurous and the heroic.

Has organised religion meant much to you?

No, not really. It was a church-going environment. I don't think my parents would be called really 'religious' in the way people use that word, but, yes, there was church and Sunday school every Sunday, so that inevitably you got to know a good deal about it. You got to know the Bible very well, learning a lot of it by heart and so on. So that background is there and I know I often use Bible imagery in what I write — it is simply there — but organised religion as such did not, I think, really mean very much to me and I didn't go to church after about fifteen or sixteen. I think I felt it was something I really couldn't honestly go on doing. So it's maybe a difference between organised religion in that sense of church-going, and the sense of getting something from the Bible — which one shouldn't split off from that, but nevertheless one does in many cases. Obviously certain bits of the Bible, and partly the language, I suppose, of the Bible, did make a strong impression and that is no doubt still there somewhere.

Do you have a particular interest in the structural devices which can govern poems?

Yes, quite a lot. Though, obviously, beginning to write poetry when I did, there was a great deal of free verse around and one tended to use free verse a lot — though even free verse has its ways of structuring things. Yes, I've always felt that it's important to find or to have structure, and sometimes it can be a use of existing structures like the sonnet or rhyming couplets which are still available and can be done something with; they don't really disappear. At other times, I suppose in some kinds of concrete poetry, you are searching for new ways of structuring which are perhaps harder to combine with traditional ways of thinking about poetry, but, yes, I think structure has always been important — maybe a structure of ideas, maybe a structure of events, a narrative, or whatever, but yes, I have thought a lot about structure.

Are you interested in randomness?

Yes, yes. That is a kind of structure too I suppose [*laughter*]. But, yes, I think again this was to some extent a kind of 1960s thing. There was a lot of discussion of randomness and I was reading people like Jackson MacLow in America who made a great deal of this, and of course John Cage was interesting too. I think the question is just how do you do this, and how far you can do this. I suppose in a sense I made use of randomness if you like in the hundred poems of 'The New Divan' which are not . . . They have a *kind* of structure. It's not randomness obviously. It has a beginning, it has an end, and I think the one in the middle (the fiftieth one) is of some importance too, but apart from that (if you can say apart from that) it deliberately does use a kind of randomness in the sense that one is not following a story that really goes forward step by step. Characters appear and reappear. You're not certain whether the characters are autobiographical or not. That kind of randomness is something that did attract me. And, if you like, the idea of non-structure almost as a structural idea in itself — in a sense that a good deal of poetry of the Middle East (which I got to learn something about when I was in the Middle East) deliberately is almost anti-structural and almost in fact thinks that we in the West are too obsessed by structure, and we drive our readers too hard. In Arabic or Persian poetry they're rather fond of the idea that a 'divan' as they call it, a collection of poems, is something that you enter; you move around; you can cast your eye here and there, you look, you pick, you perhaps retrace your steps. But you're not as in, say, *Paradise Lost* being driven from point A to point B, to point C, or being driven perhaps back but then forward again but in a very clearly defined kind of way. That appealed to me. Whether you call it in a strict sense 'structure' or not I'm not quite sure, but it's one way of doing it. The idea that if you were writing a divan, a collection of poems, although it wouldn't be something that a critic could very easily analyse as having structure, nevertheless there would be something that in a more mysterious, subterranean sense would be structure, an emotional structure, a structure perhaps relating to the life of the person who had written it. But you'd have to know something about that life, if you like, to get the key to the structure. So the structure is underground, it's tantalising, but it may perhaps even — who knows? be there — in a more profound sense than the structure of a very highly organised poem.

Is the idea of a quest important in 'The New Divan' and your poetry generally?

I think it is, yes. That means saying, I suppose, that 'The New Divan' is not really a narrative structure in the ordinary sense of the term and very often of course a narrative structure — a story — does have some kind of search in it, but it is a kind of quest poem in many ways, I think. And very often I am attracted by the idea of a quest, partly I suppose because I tend not to start off from having a firm basis of ideas or of belief. There's a search for ideas or a search for belief which is often translated into a search in physical terms, and I like again the idea of coming to something that hadn't been quite foreseen or foretold; maybe that links back with the liking for change itself and the sense of something unknown as something that looms and is worth thinking about even though more immediate concerns are obviously going to be a large part of your life. That has always I think been there, as far back as I can think; and it's partly the feeling that poetry has got to reach out in that kind of way — whether it's science fiction or even a straightforward story, poetry has to look outwards towards something that hasn't happened yet. It feeds on that, if you like, and it's meant to help its readers to feed on that too. It draws things forward, it draws life forward, it draws people forward. The way in which I like Shelley, for example — of all the Romantic poets probably Shelley makes that appeal very strongly — and I always liked the ideas in Shelley of reaching out to something which you perhaps *cannot* define and the more you could define it the less value it would have. The danger of that of course is that you have the whole thing beginning to be something that disappears out of view altogether. But I would hope that, with the other kind of interest I have in the immediate and the real, in the documentary and so on, there would be a check on that, and it would be an attempt if possible to combine the idea of something very immediate in human terms with an extraordinary outreaching hand as it were, outreaching as far as you can think at all.

What do you feel you've taken from American writing?

Oh, I'm sure a lot. I think Whitman was probably the earliest American poet that I really enjoyed, and that goes right back to certainly early university days, maybe even at school I think I may have come across some of his poetry, and I liked him a lot. But also much later when the Beat writers came on the scene — Ginsberg, Corso, Ferlinghetti — I enjoyed them and could understand what they were doing. That, when I read them (again in the late 1950s and early 1960s) was again part of that sort of liberating process of the 1960s. In America they were deliberately doing this of course as part of a reaction against what they thought of as the over-academic poetry, and they didn't quite catch on in this country in that way. There was perhaps an English and even a Scottish Beat poetry movement, but it was a much weaker imitation of what they were doing across there. But I liked what they were doing, and it seemed to me in a way something that was important to me not in a very direct sense, but it seemed to unlock something in me that I could certainly use; and it also helped to get me into other kinds of American poetry which I hadn't liked before at all. William Carlos Williams had just seemed prosy and dull to me before the Beats, although they were very different from Williams (Ginsberg acknowledged Williams of course and liked him); I got into Williams from them. It seemed to me again that it was a sense that there was nothing you couldn't write about. The thing was just to feel for it and to allow yourself certain kinds of spontaneity that perhaps had been difficult to get before.

Have you learned from Russian and East European writers?

It's probably easier for other people to say what you've learned from. I've enjoyed and read and translated a lot. It must have been influential. The influence must show in some ways. When I took the Russian class at university I remember getting very interested in a lot of Russian poetry. Mayakovsky was probably the first one that made a really big impact, though Pushkin too about the same time in a different way. But Mayakovsky particularly. That was a kind of revelation. That was a bit like the kind of Baudelaire/Rimbaud thing, I think, because they were happening about the same time too, in my first two years as a student. With Mayakovsky what attracted me particularly there — again it was something I hadn't seen before but had perhaps subconsciously been looking for — it was the combination of a very strong, committed political content and a very adventurous style. He was a revolutionary poet as regards his style, but whereas in Anglo-American poetry the revolution had tended to go with a right-wing view of politics in Eliot and Pound and people like that, this, for the first time for me anyway, was a poet who was committed to the left but being revolutionary in language. I was fascinated by the struggle Mayakovsky had in trying to persuade people, not immediately after the revolution but as the 1920s went on, that his way of doing it was the only way to do it; that you couldn't in fact constantly dilute your poetry for the popular market just because you were left wing, or just because you were a socialist, that it must still be good powerful poetry; and the way in which he still kept doing this, trying in various ways to be a good communicative poet but not giving up the sense that an innovative use of language was still very important and must be kept up at all costs.

Someone once said that you represent Modernism at its most acceptable. Do you like that description?

[*Laughter*] Ah! Should I or should I not? Well, I like Modernism. I suppose I always was a Modernist in the sense that, for example, even in the 1920s I remember being greatly taken by, say, modern architecture. I suppose that's a kind of touchstone in many ways. You tend either to like or dislike what's called Modernist architecture. I always right from the start really liked it, and I remember seeing books which happened to be brought into the house from somebody, showing modern architecture in various countries, mostly the Le Corbusier type of architecture, and my eyes were lighting up at this and I was saying 'Why is Glasgow not more like that?' I did feel that. And I felt the same about the other arts too. When I was doing my art course at school it was quite a good course. They went really quite up to date — far more up to date than they did in the literature department — and I did know about Picasso and Matisse and the Cubists and the Fauves and so on when I was still at school. And there again I was attracted by the modern developments and didn't see them as something that had to be fought against. I felt it to be somehow part of my world and I continued to feel that.

Do you like the idea of a documentary poetry?

Yes and no. Yes, I do obviously — I must to some extent since I've done quite a bit of this. Yes, I like the idea of especially recording things that are not being recorded in other ways. A great deal that happens simply flashes past in the media — whether it's radio, television, or newspapers — often things that are of the greatest interest flash past, and nothing really fixes them. Artists no longer fix them; painters don't fix them any more. Sculptors don't fix them. So it's left, if you like, to the writer. Novelists can do it, of course, in their way, but I think poets also can do something about this and when I was doing the *Instamatic Poems* (which I suppose are an example of that kind of thing) I was, really, I suppose, saying 'Here are all these events being recorded very briefly in newspapers — not followed up, many of them — just there, perhaps even just one day — of great interest whether they're perhaps strange or comic or frightening or bizarre or whatever, but of great human interest. It was always the human story that attracted me. Why should the poet not try to do something with this? The question is 'What?' And there is a problem there, because the more you do use this immediate contemporary material, things that are going past very quickly, the more you may be finding yourself stuck in the position of the camera-artist as against the painter. People will say 'Well, why do it? Is this a poem at all?' Or 'Why are you not adding more to it?' And I was tempted by the idea of opening out all these little *Instamatic Poems* into longer pieces and working them up into various comments about the world that was of that particular year. But I didn't do this, and I felt in the end that perhaps it was best left as if the camera had been there and had taken a shot, just to see what would happen with this. Again, it's a bit like the divan idea. Taken one by one in isolation this wouldn't mean very much, but I hoped that a collection of them in a book would in fact add more and that you would see a context for the whole thing. It would be a context of those particular years when this thing happened. It would be a kind of unusual but nevertheless perfectly real picture of what human beings had been up to at that particular time. So it's partly recording things, it's partly documentary, but also it is exploring the whole idea of what a collection of poems can perhaps do which an individual poem can't do.

How did you come to write Sonnets from Scotland?

That didn't begin with the idea of the whole thing. It began with the idea of writing one or two, I think as a kind of reaction, probably, to the failure of the Referendum to give Scotland political devolution and any idea of a Scottish Assembly. I think at that time there was a sense of a kind of gap, a hiatus, a numbness in Scottish thinking. There had been such a build-up towards the possibility of not independence, obviously, but some kind of Assembly, and I think lots of people had felt that really it was going to happen. It didn't happen, of course, and there was this great deflation. But the deflation led to (not just in myself but in other people too) a great deal of thinking about it, not necessarily picking over what had gone wrong. I think there was a kind of 'Nevertheless' feeling. We hadn't got our Assembly, and everything seemed to have gone back to square one as it were, but. And it was the but that seemed to be important. I had very strong feelings about Scotland at that time and wanted perhaps to put something down that would make this 'Nevertheless' feeling quite palpable and tangible. Although there's only one of the sonnets about the Referendum itself and the sense of deflation, nevertheless the whole thing is meant to be related to that. It's a kind of comeback, an attempt to show that Scotland was there, was alive and kicking, that people were living there, were thinking and feeling about it and were going to go on writing about it even if political change was at that time certainly pretty unlikely. It was just a kind of desire to show that Scotland was there and that one mustn't write it off just because the Assembly had not come into being.

What's your attitude to Scottish Nationalism?

Well in general I approve of it [*laughter*]. That's a kind of very blunt answer. It's become quite a complex subject nowadays really. The family was not inclined that way. My parents were both Conservative — not Thatcherite Conservative — I suppose they were kind of natural Conservatives. It was their belief that anything that wasn't Conservative was 'political'. If they called anyone 'political' it meant that he was probably left wing. But when I began to think for myself about these things I tended to do the opposite. I tended to vote Labour, but when it came to the 1960s I began to feel more strongly about the possibility of some change in the constitutional arrangements and some sense of Scotland's difference from England being acknowledged politically. And I then tended to vote for the SNP without joining it. I never joined any political party, but I would tend to vote SNP, and have gone on doing it. I still do, with lots of doubts about the actual party itself which doesn't seem to me to be a charismatic party at all. But it seems to me to be the only party that is really committed to Scotland as an entity, so I tend to give it my support. I feel Scottish — I suppose it really comes down to something as simple as that on a kind of basic level. You have a passport which says you're UK or British, and you obviously have to acknowledge that in a purely official sense but I don't feel British. I don't feel, certainly, English. I don't feel anything but Scottish. I suppose in that sense, a bit like MacDiarmid, you want the political arrangement to reflect the way you feel about it. I think I go along with him in that sense. So, yes, I would like a Scottish Republic really. That's what it comes down to.

Your next collection will be published by Carcanet later this year. What attracted you to the title, Themes on a Variation?

Well, the phrase actually came from a reviewer who had been looking at some of my poems and feeling that what I was doing was not so much variations on a theme, as it might seem on the surface to be, but rather the opposite — that it was really themes on a variation. And when I read this, my ears seemed to prick up somehow, and although it was a strange sort of reversal I began to think about it and thought that there was probably some truth in it. It seemed to me that it did apply (although I didn't want to work it out) — I just liked the phrase. It seemed to me to apply to a lot of the things I had been doing recently, so I just used it as the title.

Are you interested in a sort of 'themes on a variation' in some modern composers — Philip Glass, for instance?

Yes, I am, though I see from the current number of *The List* that Philip Glass is on his way out already — that's pretty quick, isn't it! [*laughter*] But, anyway, yes, I do enjoy Philip

Glass. I suppose I came to it really rather late, but, yes, I liked it and I like the way in which he's been able to move. I suppose he had originally a pretty small audience and he thought of himself as a sort of avant-garde composer, to whom it was suggested that he might broaden his scope and write operas. He tried it out and in fact they were successful and probably among his best things. I like the idea — maybe again this is the acceptable face of Modernism — he seemed to me to be able to devise a style that at first seemed to be almost perversely repetitive, and in that sense not having broad appeal, into something that, although it is still repetitive, does somehow unfold very good stories and ideas as well in his operas.

You spoke earlier of autobiographical 'clues' embedded in your work. In what direction do you want these clues to be followed up? I mean, would you be happy, say, with a biographical reading of your poetry?

I wouldn't object to it. I think this kind of thing can be done and can be useful, can be helpful. I suppose if that had been meant to be the *whole* thing, then the poetry would have been itself more obviously autobiographical. It isn't that. But, yes, I don't see why every aspect of a poem couldn't be investigated and, as, eventually, when you pop off and people begin to wonder about you, perhaps to think about your life, and ask questions, and trace you up and so on, they *will* go back to the poetry and they will see things that weren't immediately clear perhaps at the beginning. And I think that this can be useful. It probably is one approach, because the other things that you've been asking questions about — the structure, and interest in various subjects and so on, influences from other poets and poetry — that obviously is part of it. So it's only a part of it, but I think that the person in the poem is still an important idea. I don't think critics will ever really get away from it. I know some have tried very hard [*laughter*] and are still trying very hard to get away from it, but I don't think you ever will. I think that the poetry *is* a man's life as well as being whatever else that it clearly would be to an analytical critic.

*interview with Robert Crawford (Glasgow,
7 January 1988) in* Verse *5:1, February 1988, pp. 27-42*

Power from things not declared

When I first read your poems, I remember noticing that there were signs you might be gay, there was more room in the love lyrics than I would normally expect. But it was your poem about the soldier back from Aden on the bus which struck me as something of a declaration.

Yes, that one makes it very clear. Tom McGrath interviewed me some years ago for a piece he never actually got round to writing, as far as I know, and made the point that a lot of the love poems, to him at any rate, were quite obviously about men and not about women. He asked me to confirm something that was merely a fact for him, and I did confirm it. I wouldn't have minded if it had got into print at that time. All the same, very few of them were actually explicit. The ambiguity was something I just had to come to terms with. It was partly the sheer difficulty, particularly at the time when I grew up, of even thinking, far less writing openly about these things. I think I must have, maybe half-consciously, put in all these clues, even in the early books. When I wrote 'Glasgow Green' back in 1963, to me that was a clear declaration. There was something nightmarish about the whole scene, and the sex of the people involved wasn't entirely clear to readers, though it was clear to me. As I saw it, the thing was becoming gradually more explicit, for example in some of the 'New Divan' poems. Writing 'Glasgow Green' was a bold thing to do in the early 1960s, and it was a long time before I actually submitted it to a magazine. I suppose I was afraid of the reaction, and yet it's done in schools now! [*laughter*] Possibly a younger poet in a similar situation today wouldn't feel so inhibited as I certainly did, not just when I was very young, but even later, even after the war, about making it clear, but in fact all the love poems which I have published are gay.

I think it's really only people who have been brought up since the early 1970s who are beginning to have a more direct attitude.

The question is just how you do bring these subjects into poetry at all, whether you're hoping to keep a general audience by writing in such a way that you're not offending the majority sensibilities, or whether you have a duty to address a minority sensibility. That was something I found difficult when I began writing. I hoped the love poems would reach a general audience and could be taken in different ways sexually and that did work out all right. But I have written about half a dozen other poems which I haven't published which are very clearly gay, even erotic, and I don't know whether I ever will publish them. I still, even today, you see, have that apprehension about doing that kind of thing.

But you haven't destroyed them.

No, and I haven't given any instructions to my literary executor to destroy them either. So they probably will be published some day.

In terms of being gay in Scotland, living and writing, yours is something of a success story.

I suppose in a way that is true. It wasn't something you could easily ever work out and work towards. You just had to hope that what you were doing would work out.

There was really no equivalent of a gay identity available when you were growing up. How did you define yourself then?

Oh, it was a difficult and painful time, and I remember it very vividly. Most of my schooling was at an ordinary mixed school, Rutherglen Academy, what would be called nowadays a comprehensive school. I was there till I was fourteen and my parents thought I wasn't doing terribly well there. The teachers probably weren't all that great at that time. They made me sit a scholarship for Glasgow High School which I did, and I won the scholarship, and the last three years, from fourteen to seventeen, I was at Glasgow High School, a boys' school. But even in this mixed school, I was aware of the fact that I was being attracted to boys more than to girls. When I was twelve or thirteen, before I left that school, the girls were obviously showing their sexuality. We were all aware of it and made jokes about the girls with their jumpers showing that they were not just the same as what they were a year ago. There were some boys too who, even at that age, twelve or thirteen, were clearly very sexual. One boy in particular who was very well developed, wearing shorts, we all wore shorts until we were fourteen or fifteen, and he always wore a very tight, old pair of shorts, he was just bursting out from all over [*laughter*], and he used to take his cock out in the class and show it to his companions. The teacher would perhaps be at the blackboard and he would quickly poke it out and we would all admire this enormous object [*laughter*] and a lot of people did come and have a stroke. The girls would do it too, it was a joint boy-girl thing at that time, but I remember being fascinated by this boy with his large member more than by the breasts of the girls on the other side of the room. So I knew at that age, twelve or thirteen, certainly fourteen, that there was something, although I couldn't really define it, you could hardly read about it at that time, there was very little one could learn about it. But at the High School, the boys' school, a great deal of activity went on, and I soon learned a great deal more about it there. We went on a school trip to Germany, to the Rhine. This was 1937, not long before the war, but there were good relations with Germany even up till that time. We were all told to wear the kilt, must wear the kilt, there was an order that you must wear nothing under the kilt, an order which we duly obeyed with great pleasure. That trip was [*laughter*] quite amazing. It would take a chapter to write about that [*more laughter*].

I hope you will write about it . . .

Oh, I don't think so! Although I can laugh and joke about it, looking back at it, and that was enjoyable enough, I was also worried. I was aware that this is what very often goes on in a boys' school, and we joked about it and it wasn't taken all that seriously. At the same time, when I got to the end of the school years — I didn't stay on for the sixth year, but left at seventeen — I was aware that my interest was very strongly focused on boys, not on girls, and it *did* begin to worry me. At that time — sixteen, seventeen, eighteen, seventeen especially, I did have very strong guilt feelings about it. It wasn't so much fourteen to sixteen, when I was just enjoying the new world that was opening out. I had a puritanical period with myself — 'I'm going to travel on the bus and not look out to see who's nice down there. I'll read a book or do nothing about it. It'll go away, I'll meet a nice girl and get married, and that'll be it.'

So you thought it would change?

Yes, I thought it was a phase. I think someone had said that. And I made myself very miserable by this self-repression, which was quite strong and went on for more than a year. It fitted in with the fact that I was attracted by this boy Frank, who was straight, and by a girl, Jean. That was also a purely platonic thing, apart from a few cuddles. I knew there was something wrong somewhere, and that I would have to deal with this as well as I could, but I tried to deal with it by getting rid of it, at that age. I suppose things would have developed more regularly or steadily if it hadn't been for the war, but then I had this sudden, very great change going into the army, when I was twenty. And it's surprising how much activity goes on in the forces even during a war. It's a very odd thing and it doesn't get into the history books, but it's amazing how much sexual activity does go on.

So your time in the forces was a very liberating time?

Yes. That's partly what went into 'The New Divan'. At the time I couldn't write anything, during the war. I tried but couldn't write a thing, maybe because I couldn't be alone. You were always in a tent or a barrack room with other people. That confirmed the feeling that if I was going to write I would have to be by myself. The various figures appear in the 'Divan'. It must be a difficult poem to interpret because it's partly imaginary, with invented characters, and partly has real characters, including myself. Two people in particular — Cosgrove, who's mentioned, I don't know whether you remember, about number 80 something, there are two poems [86, 87] about Cosgrove, whom I was very fond of indeed. Like Frank, the earlier boy, he was not sexually inclined that way at all, but we went about together a great deal. He goes in the poem by name, but there was also a strong sexual thing with someone else, which didn't involve an emotional relationship at all, who appears towards the end, in number 98, Arthur. His name's not in the book, a chap in the Dental Corps, actually. Number 98 is completely autobiographical, with the reference to going up Mount Carmel, and him getting this turd on his shirt front because he was lying on the ground, and I was on top of him [*laughter*]. That was what he wanted, and I gave it to him all over Haifa [*more laughter*]. It was strange. It went on for quite a long time. We were stationed in Haifa for about a year. We got on very well just simply sexually. We talked to each other all right, but we weren't really attracted to each other temperamentally or emotionally. We would wander away in the evening, saying to the others we were going out for a walk. Maybe someone did wonder what we were up to. We would go in a deserted building — there were lots of them in Haifa — down by the harbour somewhere or up Mount Carmel. It was intensely pleasurable in a bodily sense, but that's all there was to it. That's why I say at the end that this 'unwashable laundry . . . had to be thrown away' [*laughter*].

So that sequence is really largely about the war, and you were writing it more than thirty years after it all happened?

It's really largely about the war, though it goes back in time, into prehistory, in fact. It's not just one thing, but to me, it's my war poem.

And why did it take so long to get written?

I really don't know. As I said, at the time I wasn't able to write at all, but I must have been storing up very strong impressions of actual places that I was in. When it came to be written, I think it was probably because the Middle East was again so much in the news. It brought it all back to me. The places that were in the news I had been in and had very strong feelings about.

The references to violence can read like references to the 1970s . . .

It's mixed that way, it's got such a long time span, it's quite hard to work out, I'm sure.

So you were feeling very guilty, and repressing yourself, and then the war came.

And the war removed the guilt to a large extent. I don't know why, maybe because I had these two experiences, one just a love experience, the other a very physical experience. The sexual expression came in a way that involved considerable risks, and yet I was clearly quite willing to do it. Although I use the phrase 'unwashable laundry', I don't mean by that that I felt guilty about it. It was just something that wasn't going to lead to anything. He was posted away from the unit, I think because somebody had either observed or suspected very strongly what we had been doing, and it was serious, sodomy, that would have been a court martial offence. What would make it likely that it would become known was that — it's all to do with mosquito nets [*laughter*]. I think I mentioned mosquito nets in one of the poems in 'The New Divan', one of the poems towards the end where Arthur in fact comes into it. It was a barrack room we were in, probably about twenty men I imagine, and we used to wait at night, both stay awake till maybe about one o'clock or so, and hope that all the rest would be asleep, and he would go up out of his bed, all the beds were covered with these mosquito nets, he would go up to the toilet, go outside to the toilet, and spend quite a while there and come back in. But instead of going back to his bed he would come to my bed and I'd be waiting for him, and he'd just slide underneath me and I would fuck him, that's what he wanted, he liked to have it done to him and I liked to do it so

I just did it, always as quietly and unobtrusively as possible. This couldn't have been done, obviously, unless there were mosquito nets there.

Because you couldn't see through the mosquito nets?

You could up to a point, but it offered a kind of concealment. If anybody had been awake and watching, then clearly they would have known who it was. Looking back on it, it was an appalling risk to take, with all these other men sleeping round about you [*laughter*]. It shows the strength of these sexual feelings, that you should take risks like that. We were both just privates, we had no rank at all. One of the officers must have said 'We'll just break it up, without making a great thing out of it'.

We're very much taught that unrequited love, somebody you desired very much and who rejected you, is somehow much more noble than the sheer physical enjoyment of fulfilling sex, yet in retrospect the latter is very important indeed . . .

Both seem to be important in different ways, the Arthur thing and the other chap Cosgrove, although one was physical and the other was totally unphysical. You could easily feel you ought to be ashamed of the one and proud of the other. Moralists would probably tell you that, though it's not quite so easy as that, not quite so straightforward. It was probably, just for sheer physical pleasure, the height, the most intense. We were both very young of course, the youth heightens it enormously. I recognised the feeling for Cosgrove, and didn't try at all to repress it. I knew right away that it wasn't going to be reciprocated, but somehow I was able to accept it on the level of just intense friendship and go about with him a good deal and I seemed to feel that that was perhaps enough. No doubt I still hoped there would be some way of bringing the two things together. It was perhaps more a breaking down of inhibitions than anything else, during the war.

Did you feel the need to come up with some kind of an explanation of your sexuality, to fit it into a wider context?

I don't think I consciously tried to. When I was a boy, if it ever came up in conversation with parents or friends, there was probably a certain element of joking about stereotypes. When I was about fifteen or sixteen, my parents thought I ought to learn the piano, though they didn't play themselves, and they got a tutor for me, who was in fact a student at Glasgow University, not many years older than myself. I remember before he came to give me my first lesson my father saying to my mother, 'He's an awful jessie, you know'. That was the way he talked about it. They accepted the fact that he was effeminate looking and possibly inclined that way. He was a very interesting man, very intelligent and widely read. We got on very well and he talked often about literature and music and it was fine.

How did the discussion on modern literature fit into the piano lessons?

His name was Lex Allan. He was generally interested in all the arts, as I was, and that was what made it easy to get on with him and have these conversations with him. He also taught me Latin.

So he would be just twenty, twenty-one?

Yes. I had been meaning to go in for art, that was my main aim in later years at school . . .

Painting . . .?

Yes, I took Higher Art, but I changed my mind just in the last year at school and decided to go to university instead and take English. To do that you had to have Latin, and I had dropped Latin at school, I'd had very little of it, so I had suddenly to get my Lower Latin, and my parents thought the best way to do it would be to get a tutor. He knew his Latin just as well as he knew his piano so he gave me Latin lessons and I got through the exam all right. It was music and Latin and all the arts, he was very interested in all the arts, especially literature, so we just talked about what was happening at that time, the general writing scene in the 1930s, which he was very well up in.

If he talked about gay authors, you must have been quite out with each other . . .

He was, in a sense, yes. I wasn't. Whether he knew or guessed that I was already somewhat knowledgeable about it, I just don't know. It didn't come up in personal terms. He was quite open about it. Though I remember the first time he talked about all these gay authors, he said at the end of it, 'I don't know how we got onto this subject!', joking about it.

A disclaimer . . .

A disclaimer, if you like, yes [*laughter*].

Can you tell me your feelings about Lorca?

Lorca came up really in a more political connection, in the sense that I remember quite vividly the conversation we had at that time, it must have been 1936. It was during the Spanish Civil War, anyway. I must have been sixteen, yes. It was in the context of Auden and the other political poets of the 1930s and going to Spain and writing about Spain, and so on. Auden's poem hadn't come out by that time, but there was a good deal of talk about British writers going to Spain to fight on the anti-Fascist side. I remember Lex saying just quite suddenly to me 'If you were a couple of years older, would you not be going to Spain?' I'd never thought of this kind of thing before, probably growing up in a very conservative kind of household. To my parents, to be political meant to be left wing. To be right wing was the natural scheme of things!

And yet your parents chose someone who had very specific and very valuable things to give you . . .

Yes, that was fascinating. He didn't go himself, he was already committed to his studies at university and didn't want to break that, but he was aware of the fact that very important political things were happening, and Lorca came up in the context of that conversation. I remember getting hold of some of Lorca's work after that and having a look at it and being quite surprised, I suppose, that there seemed to be so little about it that one would identify with writing about being gay or writing on gay subjects. Because there isn't really all that much that is directly so, except when you get his poems about America, about New York, and even then they're not apparently all that sympathetic, certainly towards effeminate gays. So I was left wondering a great deal about Lorca, but being very much impressed by him, liking his work a lot.

Were you reading him in translation at this time?

Yes, these were all translations. Later I did manage to get up a good deal of Spanish and looked at the original.

I recently saw Communicado's production of Blood Wedding, and tried, as maybe you did then, to see where the gay theme was behind it. By about the second act I had twigged that it was about a woman being forced to marry when in fact she's in love with someone else whom she cannot marry for social reasons, and when she acknowledges this love the result is catastrophe for both of them. There I could see a quite clear gay theme. But it all struck me as rather hopeless and, in a curious kind of way, rather prim . . .

That's probably very Spanish, something to do with certain conventions of what you say and what you don't say in Spain. I didn't see that production but I know what you mean. I had that problem with Lorca too. I remember Lex saying (he did bring up the point of the dramatic writing) that very often you had to decode these. Although it would be written apparently very much from a woman's angle, the central character might very well be a woman, you had to get underneath that and see that it was about something else.

Did the piano teacher tell you he was gay himself?

No, nothing was actually said. He talked a lot about it, and I just twigged [*laughter*].

And who was the next important gay writer you came across?

Hart Crane, probably. I had seen his poems without knowing very much about the man, before the war, because in the *Faber Book of Modern Verse* there were poems by Hart Crane there, and I liked them a lot, and meant to find out more about him. But I didn't know very much about him until the later 1940s, probably after the war. Then I did read his biography. I was very much attracted to his work and just the kind of pathos of his life, and when his letters were published, I thought they were wonderful letters, remarkably vivid and also very touching, very moving letters. Both the family situation with his mother and father and later on the fascination with sea and sailors and so on, it all meant a lot to me. I suppose probably I've a kind of romantic temperament myself, and there was something very romantic about Crane which made it appeal to me.

'Floating off to Timor' . . .

Probably so, that probably fits in, yes. In fact, the long sequence, the long poem 'Cape of Good Hope' was originally dedicated to Hart Crane, though I don't think I included that when I reprinted it.

Did you realise at quite an early stage that Crane was a gay poet?

No, I didn't know that. It was only after the war that I found out a little bit more about him. I took French when I was a student, and obviously Proust came into the picture. I read quite a bit of him, and liked it a lot. But of course, I found him a difficult writer, and didn't get properly into him. And it was the same problem as with Lorca, it wasn't obvious, except in some parts of the novel, that this is what he was writing about. The man's life didn't attract me at all, the very opposite from Hart Crane's. I don't think I really understood him. I was reading the book more just as what was regarded as a very good and very famous novel that everyone must read. And I was more interested in the way it was written, in the style (I was doing it painfully in French). It was more an aesthetic thing than anything else, getting into Proust. He didn't make any tremendous impact on me from the point of view of his being a gay writer.

The kind of decoding which we are talking about suggests that you were looking for other writers who treated gay themes ...

Yes, I think so, that is the case I'm sure.

What books would you want to put into a young gay writer's hands today?

I don't know really. I think it would depend very much on the exact situation of the person and the place, as it were. I don't know if it would be easy to give a general recommendation. In recent years there have been some very good, very well-written gay novels which have in fact reached quite a wide public, like Alan Hollinghurst's *The Swimming-Pool Library*, and books of that kind, obviously extremely well written, yet they also sell very well. They must be getting across to heterosexual readers as well as to gay readers. Books like that or possibly Joe Orton, all his writings, whether it's biographical or his plays. Or Edmund White, again, well worth reading from a literary point of view. I think it would have been hard to find books like that which you could claim to be literature, worth reading, and yet which also said something about the gay condition. Post-AIDS problems arise as to who you recommend, what you recommend, with Larry Kramer's *Faggots* for example. Books like that already belong to a historical period, I suppose.

Can you talk about what it was like to be gay in Glasgow in the 1950s and 1960s?

Although it was a subject that wasn't very much talked about, by the middle of the 1950s it was being more talked about than it was before the war. The Wolfenden Report came out in the 1950s and there were a number of very famous cases in the courts, Montagu and Wildeblood and Gielgud and all these people. It was being discussed slightly more openly but still with very great disapproval.

And what did you feel when you read about these things?

Great interest, a painful interest, and also various worries and apprehensions whether the fact that people like that were getting into the papers and having their lives disrupted would apply to me too. You couldn't help but apply it to yourself. There was a lot of gay activity in Scotland, in Glasgow at that time, especially perhaps after the war, places where people met, cafés and bars and so on, which have all gone now.

Can you remember some of them?

Oh yes [*laughter*], a big café called the Oak Café which was somewhat louche, even very louche, but very interesting, you never knew what was going to happen there! It was the kind of place that people would say was not recommended, but everyone went nevertheless. There weren't any clubs in the proper sense of the term, as you would define it perhaps nowadays. But one, the Good Companions, was a much more select place. They looked at you very carefully before they let you in, you had to be gay to get in. And there was the Royal Bar on West Nile Street which was one of the main places, gone now. So you did go round and you did meet people in these places. In that sense it was not tremendously different from what it is today, except just that always at the back of your mind was the knowledge of what you were doing, in relation to the law. It wasn't exactly inhibiting to behaviour, but it was at the back of your mind all the time. All these places were in the centre of town. The Oak was probably in St Vincent Street or perhaps West George Street, fairly near the city centre. The Good Companions was further up towards Bath Street or possibly Blythswood Square kind of area. I'm sorry I can't remember exactly, but these were roughly where they were. There were little groups in Glasgow, before the SMG or SHRG, as it later became, were established. There was one which called itself the Bachelor Clan [*laughter*], this was a disguised name. It didn't last very long, I think very often these groups don't last very long. I dare say there were similar things in Edinburgh though I didn't know about them. In Glasgow there were one or two. This one simply consisted of possibly never more than about fifteen or twenty people. We met in each other's houses and talked about the situation and occasionally there were outings arranged. But it was so difficult because Glasgow is such a big place and everyone was so scattered. Not so many people had cars and it was difficult getting people together for meetings. It just gradually split apart because of these purely practical difficulties. But that was the way in which things were beginning to be very slightly organised in a cautious kind of way before the big organisation was set up later.

Can you describe what a meeting was like, what people talked about, who was there? What did you see as the objectives of it?

I think the objectives were just to break out of the awful kind of isolation that most people felt at that time, after the war. Either there were those cafés you could go to or bars, there were some bars too of course, I mentioned the Royal in West Nile Street. There were places like that certainly where you could meet people. But I think there was also beginning to be this feeling that there should be some kind of grouping and it was just a very general discussion about the whole matter, there were no minutes kept as far as I know, or anything like that. It was a pretty informal kind of thing altogether. If books came out which were on a gay theme they would perhaps be discussed. Somebody would say 'I was reading so and so', and there would be a discussion of that, I don't know if you know or remember that there was in fact quite a succession of gay novels in the 1950s. I suppose Gore Vidal's *The City and The Pillar* would be the first one. That was the end of the 1940s in fact. And through the 1950s there were quite a surprising number.

Giovanni's Room *by Baldwin* . . .

That was another one, yes. I just scribbled down some names here because I remembered them. Not famous people at all — or some of them may be extremely famous in fact — Fritz Peters *Finistère*, Rodney Garland *The Heart in Exile*, Charles Jackson *The Fall of Valour*, and of course *The City and the Pillar*. One came across these books, not that they were widely talked about or widely advertised, but there were beginning to be things like — there was a book club, which was in fact really a gay book club, although it didn't call itself that, which had an exchange scheme. Once you joined and got your first novel they would exchange it for another gay novel, all through the 1950s. This was one method of getting all the books of that kind. I remember joining and getting these books. So there was a gradual emergence of awareness at that time, but still very tentative throughout the 1950s.

How did you find out about the book club, and how did you go about joining?

Oh, it was something I saw in a magazine being advertised, I'm not quite sure where it was now. I don't think there were any British gay magazines as such at that time. I'm sorry, I've just forgotten. It certainly wasn't an American publication, this was purely British. Many of the books were by American authors.

Was the book club British rather than Scottish?

Oh yes, I think it all came up through London, probably. It came by post. I don't think there was anything quite like that in Scotland.

Tell me about a meeting. When did they take place?

In the evenings usually, in somebody's house. We just had coffee or tea, it wasn't a drinking thing. It was in rotation.

Was it not quite an emotional moment when you first went?

It was a bit, yes. It was the first time I had come across this kind of thing. A kind of awkwardness too, not knowing what to do, what to say, how to behave. It might be much easier nowadays, or perhaps these things are always awkward, when you're meeting a lot of people for the first time and you don't really know how to relate to them, what they'll be like and so on. Maybe the awkwardness never was entirely broken down. You might meet someone that you would like and possibly not go back to the group, though that wasn't a primary objective. In that case, it didn't work tremendously well as a group, because it wasn't really ever designed to exert any great pressure on changing a more general situation. It was much more a kind of ad hoc thing which people hoped would help a little bit without taking it too far. That's probably why its name doesn't give very much away! [*laughter*] But it was a beginning, it was something.

And who was the moving spirit behind all this? Did someone in particular lend their house for meetings?

I never wrote anything down about this, I've no record at all. It's such a long time ago that I really don't exactly remember who the people were.

What sort of feelings did people express? Did they want to have the law changed, or was it fairly lighthearted and camp?

Fairly lighthearted, I suppose, sometimes camp. There were one or two camp people there. There wasn't any great, serious discussion about getting the law changed, as far as I can remember. That didn't really come into it. I don't think it was really a campaigning kind of thing at that date, that only came in later on.

Did any particular friendships come out of it for you?

Yes, for a while, yes . . .

F

Were you aware of what was happening when the Scottish Minorities Group got moving in the 1960s? How did you react to what was happening?

When the SMG started, I knew about it, and they were in contact. I didn't in fact join, I felt probably that I should have done, but I gave some money. They wanted either subscriptions or members. It wasn't that I didn't want to help them, it was just that I'm not really fond of joining things. I'm really quite a solitary person and I just don't like that kind of thing very much.

How have you responded to gay liberation, as someone who was actively and consciously gay both before and after? A lot of older gay men have very ambivalent attitudes to the liberation movement. They feel that things were better when they were worse, that when no one said anything about it much more could be done, whereas now, when things have to be named, everything has become much more complicated.

I think in some ways I would go along with that, that is quite true. I look at it partly from a creative, from a writer's point of view, from any artist's point of view. It's the old idea of where your power as a writer comes from. Very often your power comes from things that are not in fact declared and open, and if that's one of them, then it doesn't necessarily mean you're going to write any more easily because it is more generally written about. This maybe clashes with what I said earlier about the good novels that have been appearing in the last ten years but, still, in poetry anyway, I'm not so sure about prose, very often you have some kind of sense that if you're of my generation your power is in some way linked with the fact that there are these undeclared feelings and, if they were fully declared, you might lose some of your power. There's a curious kind of ancient feeling you have, like the old idea of having a mystery in two senses, there's a mystery about writing, it's also your profession, your 'mystère' is your profession, but at the same time there's something mysterious about it, you don't want to lose your mystery. We mentioned Proust or Lorca or Hart Crane too, for that matter, he's not a very openly gay poet at all, and their power probably comes from the huge amount of repression of emotion you feel there is, in an undeclared kind of way. So yes, one does have, I think, divided feelings about that. In the abstract you agree that it's better, in general, for honesty in these matters, and for people in the general public to be aware of what writers and other artists are really like, to be sure of the whole situation. But from the writer's point of view, probably, there is some ambiguity still about that.

So it's good to be repressed?

No, I don't think I really believe that [*laughter*], but it is probably a generation thing. I'm quite sure that in my generation it's obviously still hard to write openly about these things, whether you believe it ought to be done or not. For a younger writer now, in his twenties say, this wouldn't be the same. I'm sure they would feel it much more possible, much more natural to write openly and yet not to lose anything in doing so. I think there has been a change there. Writing openly — well, of course, as I mentioned to you, I have written openly on some occasions, unpublished poems, erotic poems if you like to call them that. The fact that I haven't published them, and still don't publish them, must indicate something. It's probably my age that makes it pretty well impossible for me to publish these things. I'm not saying they should never be published, I suppose they will be some day. I won't destroy them or whatever. A younger writer would probably just go ahead and publish these poems, I imagine, today.

When I think of Lorca or Hart Crane, I can't help thinking of the enormous amount of psychological damage, of psychological suffering the repression has caused . . .

This may just all be part of the necessary plan. Don't you think in a sense that the suffering there may be is probably just a part of the man's whole situation and also the man as a writer, and it probably just adds something, adds the particular flavour to what he's doing, it may be just a part of the whole thing that you cannot really get rid of?

Would that not imply then that heterosexual writers are at a disadvantage because they're so much less repressed?

I'm not sure about this whole business of repression. You want on the one hand to say that people shouldn't be repressed and yet you sense in your bones that it's not necessarily a bad thing to be repressed . . . [*laughter*]

Why is it not a bad thing? [*laughter*]

Just because it leads to pressures. Creative activity of any kind is not hindered by pressures and difficulties and tensions, in fact it's often helped by these things, so I don't think one should rush to get rid of all one's problems in the hope that this will lead to better art. I don't think that this would necessarily be true. It's very hard to imagine a thoroughly joyful art that comes out of no tension, don't you think? There must be something that sets the artist going, and there must be something about this that is emotionally unusual and pressing on him, something he feels he must express in some kind of way. It might be a very great joy, I suppose there are examples of very joyful love poetry, but on the whole most things seem to come out of some kind of difficulty.

Though a lot of your finest poetry is very joyful poetry indeed . . .

Yes, I'm condemned out of my own mouth! [*laughter*] It's quite a difficult thing to decide that, quite a complex thing. There are probably arguments on both sides. I know it's true that a lot of the love poems come out of a positive and happy love affair, and other ones don't. It's probably hard to sum it up actually.

The tension in the Glasgow sonnets is a tension of unhappiness and deprivation in the environment.

Yes, it's much harder to write about central Glasgow today, which has had its face lifted; this doesn't give rise to feelings from which poems come. It may be more pleasant to walk about it and so on, very nice, very agreeable to look at, but it doesn't give rise to the kind of poems that people were writing, or that I was writing anyway, in the 1960s and 1970s. Possibly with human relations you can have joyful or sad and difficult and frustrated poems equally. Perhaps if you're writing about a place and a city, writing about its problems, it's more productive than just writing a kind of PR job for the new Glasgow.

How specifically Scottish were the groups that met in the 1950s? Was there something about them that would make them different from groups in England or elsewhere?

They were Scottish obviously, in the sense that they had no links with anything outside the locality. The only one I knew really, was a member of, was this one I mentioned in Glasgow, the Bachelor Clan. That was purely a Glasgow thing, and it was very conscious, I suppose, of being a Glasgow thing. Everybody at it belonged to Glasgow or thereabouts. It's maybe mixed a little bit in my mind with the war years just before that. I was with a Scottish unit of course, when I joined up first of all. We did our training near Peebles at a camp called Glentress near Peebles, and it was 42nd General Hospital, which was a Scottish unit then. But as time went on and as we went overseas and changes took place, people were posted away or died or whatever, it became more English, towards the end of the war, much more mixed, and many of the people that I knew well, including the chap called Arthur that I had the very sort of sexual thing with, were English.

Was Cosgrove English?

No, Cosgrove was from Glasgow. It was mixed in that sense. I wasn't thinking specifically, I suppose, at the end of the war, just in terms of any kind of sort of Scottish sexuality or anything of that kind. But as time went on, into the 1960s, obviously there was going to be something that meant there were going to be Scottish organisations, as distinct from English ones, although they would probably always have links with them. We always had a feeling, I think, even at that time, that there was more of a fight in Scotland than in England, things were much more difficult, as turned out to be, of course, the case.

What were the reasons for that?

Well, we thought it was simply the Calvinist inheritance. It's too simple a phrase, obviously, because there's a similar thing among Catholics, probably, but we felt that it had something to do with religious conservatism and also I suppose political conservatism. Even Labour in Scotland was thought to be very conservative in many ways. We felt that it would be harder to do very much about things and maybe to some extent we envied the Americans and English, who were apparently being more active, although it might have been easier for them to be more active. There was a general feeling that it was easier to discuss things in London or New York, rather than in Glasgow or Edinburgh, which was probably literally true, except in a private way.

Were you in a sense leading a double life in the 1950s?

Oh, very much so, entirely. When I came back after the war in 1947 I got my degree and got on the English staff [of Glasgow University], I was very much aware of the fact that I was going to these places and having activity, in public sometimes, and yet at the same time I had to keep up this respectability thing. I suppose at that date it would have been the end of your career if this kind of thing had come out. I was aware of the double life element, but felt this was something one had to do, and just watch out, be careful . . .

What sort of atmosphere was there? Which age group was involved?

Very mixed because, although a lot of the people were young, late teens early twenties kind of age, there were also lots of people like myself coming back from the forces, in their late twenties or in their thirties. It was older people too, really there was a very wide age range. And of course people met in houses as well, there were a good deal of parties going on. I was never much of a party person, so I don't know very much about that scene. I must be by nature, quite apart from this subject, somewhat solitary, so I didn't enjoy the great gettings together, except very occasionally. Certainly it did go on.

Where were the various boundaries? Who knew and who didn't know? Were there people at the university you could be open with?

No, I don't think there were. There were some that I might have been, but I wasn't. It was so much not a matter for discussion that it was very hard to find out about that. There were certainly others, some of whom I did know about, but I didn't always necessarily make up to such people. You tended to be a series of solitary people who were in fact gay, but there wasn't much of a sense of solidarity, hardly any solidarity at all at that stage.

Was it partly a class thing? Was it more difficult to talk about this to middle-class friends?

It was partly a middle-class thing, though as regards actually meeting people, talking to people and activity, it was a cross-class thing and in fact, the working-class involvement in it in Glasgow was considerable. Quite often working-class people themselves don't realise how much of it goes on among the working class. There was plenty of going across between classes. Glasgow has really no upper class, so it's either middle or lower class.

There's an idea that working-class people are more uninhibited about these things . . .

They very often are, but they're also much more conventional on the surface, often very prudish. But in fact [*laughter*], a great deal of it goes on.

Is that a form of bisexuality?

It's more bisexual. Glasgow's said to be the bisexual capital of the universe . . .

Who says that?

I read that somewhere or heard it somewhere, but there's some truth in it. The number of married men in Glasgow who are not at all averse from something else is large. A great many married men who are really quite happily married, they're not in a state of tension, do have homosexual as well as heterosexual experiences.

Do you think their wives are often aware of this?

I've been involved in several relationships of this kind. Some are, some are not, I don't know if one could generalise. In one case, a chap I knew, he was obviously perfectly happy with his wife, he had two young children, the whole family unit was perfectly well integrated and happy, he was out of work at the time, hoping to get another job, a perfectly ordinary kind of situation. He would never have dreamed of either telling his wife or wanting his wife to know about it. It was a completely separate thing from this point of view. It was almost like a Graham Greene novel, we had a trip to Amsterdam once and had to involve each other in the most extraordinary machinations to get this trip. The fact that we did it, we did get to Amsterdam and had our week, it was a kind of long weekend, shows on the one hand the power of the extramarital thing, the power of the homosexual thing with this character, and yet the fact that it was always done secretly shows that he wasn't going to want to break the family up, he was still a man who going back to his wife and was perfectly happy with his wife. It was not doing something because you're not satisfied with the other thing, it was doing something and doing something else, this curious double thing that I've come across several times in Glasgow. At other times — one of my closest friends, I don't see him all that much, we meet occasionally, he's lived down south for quite a while, he doesn't live in Glasgow at the moment, but I've known him for many years, and he's married and his wife knows all about it. But that was more, I think, a marriage of convenience, in the sense that she accepted the situation, they have children, she accepted this and they live together, get on with each other very well, are perfectly happy but in fact he is primarily gay. That's a different kind of case. There are these two different cases. But in both cases the man and the woman get on perfectly well together and would not see anything strange in their heterosexual relationship in that sense. And yet on the other hand, this other thing comes in very strongly sometimes. I don't know that it's ever been investigated by sociologists and so on. It is real, and it's a very interesting situation. It seems to me to be a very Glasgow thing. I don't know if it happens in Edinburgh or London or other places in the same way. Tom Leonard has some poems which seem to me to link in with this kind of situation.

I like the one that goes 'The popularity in Scotland of the line "A man's a man for a' that", is enhanced by the fact that so many Scottish men are uncertain of their sexuality.' [laughter]

Traditionally, the Scottish male has always hated being accused of being effeminate to any extent. I remember when I was a boy that any man who wore scent of any kind was thought to be terribly suspect. It was as bad as having suede shoes to have any kind of scent on you. Nowadays, of course, it's almost universal. Young people go into the shops and choose which scent they want to have. It's called aftershave, but it's still scent. That's a real change, in the sense that younger people now don't have this fear of being thought to be effeminate because they know that society in general doesn't regard it as being effeminate to have a pleasant smell about you.

Did you find it painful to be involved with somebody who was married?

I think at the time I just accepted it as being something we both wanted to do and that was very exciting on a physical level. It was probably the excitement of it more than anything else that [weighed] in my mind. I wrote a poem about it, published in an obscure magazine [*laughter*], it's not in a book! Perhaps the collected poems will have it! It was a bit like with Arthur during the war, a very exciting physical thing and possibly not really very much more. Feelings of guilt maybe, to some extent, but they didn't get very far because obviously I wasn't trying to drag him away from his wife or break up a marriage, it wasn't that at all, he was very anxious to do this and to make it something that wasn't going to be found out. It's something that obviously you're not proud of, but at the same time it was physically very strong.

Did you have friends who were gay, but not sexual partners?

Going back before the war, when I was a student, my closest friend was not gay, and I was absolutely in love with him, completely infatuated.

What age was this?

Seventeen — eighteen — nineteen. Mainly eighteen. In fact, that was the only reason I took Russian [*laughter*], because he took Russian.

So Scottish poetry has a lot to thank him for!

Yes, yes . . . He was very political, he was communist in fact. We had great political discussions. He took Russian as part of his political thing, and I just went along to the class but got very interested right away, because of its literary and linguistic qualities. That friendship didn't come to anything. We both went into the army. He was in the Artillery, I was in the Medical Corps and we were scattered in different places but there was a time, I think it was 1941 or 2, I'm not sure exactly, when I was stationed in Egypt and his unit was going to be in Egypt, and there was some chance of a leave for both of us. We might actually meet in Cairo or Alexandria. We'd kept a correspondence going, and I wrote to him. It was partly being separated, and this possibility of meeting a couple of years later made me, probably very foolishly, confess my feelings, and that was the end of that! He just said that while he could understand my feelings, he could not sympathise with

168

them. Actually it wasn't a total break, we did meet after the war on an ordinary level, and it was okay, though I haven't seen very much of him since. But that was a real infatuation, very very strong at the time.

Did you make a conscious effort in your earlier poetry to avoid the subject of love and everything connected with it, as something you couldn't really deal with safely?

I did also write autobiographical poems, mostly unpublished. One, for example, about this chap Frank. I didn't write it during the war, but just after, in 1946 probably. It's got his name inserted into it in a punning way. I used the word 'frank' and the word 'mason', that was his second name, in their ordinary meanings, so that the name is embedded there in a hidden kind of way. [*laughter*] The poem is about the letter I wrote to him in Egypt and his cold reaction to it, which haunted me, terrible to get, at that time. But I didn't attempt to publish it or to write more poems like it, so I must have felt it wasn't possible then. At that early time in the 1940s, before I wrote the poems that are included in the big book, I did write quite a lot of verse letters to various people. In some of them I would talk quite openly about these things, to W. S. Graham, Sydney Graham, he knew that I was gay. He was one of the first people I was quite open with. Not that he was gay hmself, but he understood these things pretty well.

What made you feel that you could be open with him?

In the first place I was attracted by him physically. We met first of all in our teens, and he was a very dashing, good-looking person then. We went about quite a bit together and got on very well together actually. He probably did suspect my feelings though I didn't say very much about it. Then he went down south to London and to Cornwall. We did meet occasionally, here, in London or elsewhere and we somehow did talk about the thing and he said 'Yes, I always thought so' [*laughter*]. And so in some letters I would talk about that to him but these were just letters passed between two people, they weren't really meant for publication. They might be published some day. I don't know whether his widow has kept the letters or not. They do exist. So I was able to write about these things but in that kind of 'sub' way, not in a way that was intended for general publication. But possibly the fact that I did write about them, on paper, typed out, letters actually sent to people, indicates I must have felt they could be written about, should be written about. I was feeling my way towards something that didn't really happen until after 1960.

Did it happen to you more than once to fall in love with someone who defined himself as straight?

I suppose it's something you recognise will happen and you can't do very much about it, can't force the thing to any happy conclusion. But you realise too that anything that happens to you is going to be used somehow in the art you practise, to get into the poetry somehow. You perhaps fall back on art when life fails in that sense. I'm not sure about that. Maybe I should have persisted and written more poems about this chap Frank, just to get these feelings sorted out more in my mind. That happened more than once, it continued to happen in fact, feeling very strongly for someone who didn't return the feeling, and on the other hand having affairs with people I wasn't perhaps particularly attracted to on an emotional level.

So the two tended to remain fairly separate ...

Until I met John Scott. That's the man I dedicated the big book to. That was really the first time it had worked both ways, a very strong sexual thing, and yet emotional too, a love thing at the same time. My love poems really came out of meeting him.

What age were you when you met him?

That was in 1963, I was old [*laughter*], think of that! A long wait, I've always believed in waiting. If you wait, things sometimes do happen [*more laughter*]. That was just luck, it had never happened before that.

But it sounds as if you quite enjoyed yourself while you were waiting . . .

Yes, yes, that's true. Looking back, I suppose the curious business of public activity, semi-orgies, no doubt very much disapproved of, but it's surprising how much of that there was going on, even at that time just after the war. I never seemed to have any hesitation in joining in that kind of activity. There was a café, near the Buchanan Street bus station, gone now, where this kind of thing — I shouldn't be saying this, should I? [*laughter*]

I think everything's been knocked down . . .

Everything's completely gone, so one can say that. That was a place where, an upstairs place with a toilet, and really pretty well anything went on, it was obviously very very risky, but people did go there and enjoy this, and you could see a dozen or more people there at any one time . . .

Did this give you, from an early age, an ironical angle on the Glasgow hard men?

Yes, I think that's true. You know Tom Leonard's little poem . . .

'wotchyir bawz' . . .

That's bang on, absolutely true. He's a very strange character, the Glasgow hard man. I remember going once with somebody who was a real kind of hard man, young, very good looking, but no expression, that strange, blank, good-looking expression you often get in Glasgow. It was a frightening little experience. It's reflected in the 'Glasgow Green' poem, though that's not exactly it. Although I was frightened, it worked out in a kind of way and afterwards, after *he* was satisfied, he changed, and became quite sort of affable and said — we were up at the canal bank, which is a horrible place — 'You know the way back doon?' So we parted quite amicably.

Why was it frightening?

Because he threatened me, he said if I didn't do exactly what he wanted he would get the boys to me. I used this in the poem, 'get the boys t'ye'. And he meant it too. The poem was meant to be a plea for some kind of recognition or liberation or acceptance, though it's not expressed as clearly as it could be, a sort of gay lib poem before there was such a thing. It was only because such a strong and frightening experience lay behind it — actually, it was a condensation of more than one experience — and yet there was something quite positive in it, too, the poem gained meaning from this.

Did the syndrome of the hard man, which used to be so prevalent in Glasgow, raise questions of masculinity for you, of what it means to be a man?

I don't think so. I was always attracted by the masculine without feeling that I was effeminate myself.

Can you tell me some more about John Scott?

He was almost two years older than myself, working class, mostly working as a storeman in different places. He came from the Carluke area, a big Catholic family, sisters and so on, a general sense of a large family circle. Because it was so close-knit, he regarded himself as more Lanarkshire than Glasgow. He tended more to come to Glasgow, but I did sometimes go down to his place to meet his family.

Was he married?

No, he wasn't. We met every weekend and went on holidays together, we didn't live together. That just wouldn't have worked out.

Was that for personal reasons or social reasons?

A mixture of both. I felt that I probably couldn't do the work I wanted to do, that is, write, and live with anyone. I've done it for very short periods, but it's never really worked out, and I seem to need to be on my own in order to write.

And you're happy that way?

I don't know about happy, yes, I suppose so [*laughter*], intermittently. I know it's necessary, I found that out, I just have to be by myself.

For long periods, for a day or two days . . .?

To be able to when I need to, that's the point. Living with someone else, unless there's a very free and understanding relationship, you can't just suddenly say 'You must give me a week to be by myself'. It might work out with someone, but even just the presence of somebody, not just in the same room but in the same house, puts me off my stride.

There's a stereotype in the West of Scotland that sees Catholic families as more sensual, more relaxed and accepting than Protestant ones.

I suppose I didn't see John's family often enough to make very much of it. He broke his leg once, and I had to go and see him at home. It wasn't even Carluke, it was Law, which is a very difficult place to get to. I don't have a car, so it took hours to get there [*laughter*]. But in a way the stereotype possibly was true. They were always meeting each other, a very affectionate family. I was an only child, very different in that sense. He had brothers and sisters and all sorts of cousins and nieces and so on, whereas I had only my mother and father and a few aunts and uncles. So I was conscious of it being different. I don't know how much they . . . It was obviously a very close relationship, and they accepted me very readily, and I thought that was very good. When he died and they phoned me, and I went to the funeral, I was quite surprised that at the burial they gave me a cord to hold, which normally would only be the family

173

circle, so they must have reckoned that this was something they accepted.

But nothing was ever said . . .

Nothing was ever said.

How long were you close to one another?

For sixteen years.

Until John died . . .

Yes, though unfortunately, I never regretted anything more, we had a quarrel just about a year before that and didn't properly make it up. About nothing, the way people who are very close to each other do quarrel sometimes. I hadn't seen him for quite a while before he died, and I very bitterly regret that. But that's just the way these things happen sometimes.

Would you like to say something about the poems you wrote to him?

Meeting him in 1963 was probably the thing that unleashed most of the poems in the 1960s, quite apart from what they were about. It was something that had a big effect on me. All the love poems from the 1960s were started off by meeting him and were about him in various ways. For me, it was a new kind of poetry. I had written kinds of love poems, in fact, when I was eighteen or nineteen I had a few unpublished love poems to a girl called Jean whom I was very close to then, the same time as I was in love with Frank, the man I mentioned. The two of them were together [*laughter*] in my mind, and I wrote some poems to her but that didn't come to anything at all. The only love poems that I've had published were the ones that started off when I met John.

174

It was really quite a new time in your life.

Yes it was, and just about the same time I came to live here, so the change of environment, and meeting him, and added to that, the general feeling of liberation in the 1960s, it was that kind of decade, also would come together.

So the fact of homosexuality still being illegal didn't matter that much.

I was aware of it, but it didn't matter all that much. I didn't think of this as being homosexuality, it was just that I was in love and it happened to be a man. That was really all there was to it. I just wrote about it because I felt so strongly about it.

I did a lecture and two tutorials on your poetry just a couple of weeks ago, and I spoke about the problems of decoding your love poetry. I asked the students if they had realised that these weren't just ordinary heterosexual love poems, and most of them were flabbergasted! Mind you, one of them did point out that all your poetry needs to be decoded in one way or another, the 'Emergent Poems', or the experimental poems. But it does suggest that you have trodden a middle path, between explicitness and concealment, very successfully. A reader who is not fairly aware would not be forced to look at the underlying implications.

I can understand that reaction. Though I would have thought there were some, two or three, that it would be hard to interpret except from a gay point of view. 'In Glasgow', for example. If a woman was speaking, it would make the last bit unlikely. I'm not sure, but 'pal', 'old pal', I don't think a woman would say 'pal', would she? That one always seemed to me to be more definite than some of the others. I suppose it's a bit mysterious in the sense that you might wonder why on earth there's all this bit about washing the feet. It was a long distance lorry driver, and of course, if you drive lorries for long distances, your feet get very hot and sweaty and swollen, so the washing of the feet did actually take place [*laughter*].

It's quite a biblical note too, isn't it?

Oh yes, it has that too, I know, and the throwing on of the shirt. That seemed to me, when I was writing it, to be much more open. Do you think even that they would . . .?

They were using the Carcanet selection, where some of the more explicit poems aren't included.

And there's a kind of sequence too, about another person, in *The New Divan*, the ones from 'The Divide' to 'Resurrection'. I would have thought that those, 'Smoke', for example, with the reference to Iago and Cassio, would have made it fairly obvious. Again, that's not in the *Selected Poems*. Maybe if you saw them all, it probably would be different.

I get the impression from the way you are reacting that it's important to you that people should understand what the poems are really about.

Yes, that's right, although I know that many of them are just quite simply ambiguous. I knew that when I was writing them, that they must be ambiguous and that comes in many cases, I suppose, from a kind of apprehension, more than anything else.

Apprehension about the consequences of speaking very directly?

Yes.

I noticed in 'Strawberries' that the only word which might be gender specific turns out to be child, which is neither male nor female, and one of my students pointed out that there were two forks on the empty plates, not a knife and a fork . . . [*laughter*]

Yes, this did once strike me too, when I was thinking about the poem, but after I'd written it. I thought a psychologist would probably seize on that.

Do you want to say anything about the genesis of this and the other love poems in the same book?

Most of them, not every one exactly, but most of them did come out of things that actually happened. 'Strawberries' came out of eating strawberries on that French window there in fact [*points*], from which you can see the Kilpatrick Hills, so that just comes from life if you like. It just happened really pretty well exactly as it is there. Most of them are rather like that, though in some cases a bit of imagination comes into it. These are all about John Scott.

I was quite struck when you told me that 'After the Party' was totally invented. If anything, 'Strawberries' seems the more idealised of the two.

It's odd that, isn't it, because the party one is so specific you think it must have happened, but no, not at all. I dare say something like 'After the Party' must have occurred. Mainly just the idea that there might be the beginning of a contact which comes to nothing. This might take place very well at a party rather than in any other kind of situation. Somebody might just touch somebody else in a way that would seem to be significant, and then that's the end of it, you might spend your life searching for that other person and never find them again. I think it was that sort of thing and, I can't remember this actually happening, but I'm quite sure something like that probably did happen. It must have stuck in my mind, and I just invented the circumstances to make it hopefully seem probable.

There's a marvellous Cavafy poem, 'He asked about the quality', that your poem reminds me of. Although both men there know what's going on, it can never come out as language, one man can't say 'I rather like you, what are you doing this evening?', what he says is 'Do you sell coloured handkerchiefs?'

Yes, I remember that very well, their hands actually touch as they're looking over the handkerchiefs, yes . . .

In your poem there's a similar situation, because nothing can actually be said, there's only the touch, the physical thing, crossing the boundary into talking about what's happened is very difficult. 'Strawberries' and 'Glasgow Green' give two very different sides of gay experience. 'Strawberries' is very idealised, very sugary . . .

Apart from the last line. That suggests the storm is going to come, the storm is always there, somewhere. You're quite right, both are really required. Both are true, both aspects do exist, so possibly it's good to have both the romantic and the realistic.

I feel that often, by focusing on the objects around the lovers, you can avoid having to be explicit about their sex. In 'One Cigarette', for example, you had to wait until the other had gone before writing the poem, otherwise you'd have had to be more direct.

Didn't they get that one? 'I am drunk on your tobacco lips'?

Yes, although they pointed out that women smoke, too . . .

Yes, all that was done in a very unconscious way, in the sense that this again actually happened, it was just looking at the cigarette that somehow gave rise to the whole poem. People have said 'There's an awful lot of cigarettes in your poems, Morgan' [*laughter*], and I don't know about the phallic symbolism. This is the 1960s, you see. Perhaps nowadays that we're more anti-smoking it's a different kind of thing, it's a bad image. At that time there was really nothing bad about it, most people did in fact smoke. It was more unusual if you didn't smoke. I had smoked in the army myself, but I didn't carry it on when I came back. To me the act of smoking, and the smell of a cigarette, perhaps just because of the fact that this person smoked and I didn't, became very erotic, became very loaded with all sorts of feelings and emotions which were quite strong, and positive, not anti [*laughter*]. So I still rather like people who smoke. It's an odd thing, for a non-smoker. I rather like the smell of cigarettes, and tobacco, and cigars.

I think it's defined as quite a masculine thing . . .

It probably is, yes. John smoked a lot, he was quite a heavy smoker.

Looking at 'The Second Life' again, I saw it as to some extent a coming-out poem. 'Many things are unspoken in the life of a man . . . there is an unspoken love . . . men will still be warm . . . Slip out of darkness, it is time'. Like somebody saying 'It's time to throw off concealments or half statements, to begin to speak much more directly'.

I think you're right, I did in fact feel that, although as you know from the dates it didn't lead to very much at that time, apart from perhaps 'Glasgow Green', which takes things a bit further forward.

Did a long time pass between writing 'The Second Life' and meeting John?

No, that all happened about the same time, early 1960s. Most of the Glasgow poems and the love poems came just at that time, when I met John. It must have been itself something that unlocked a few gates, and I found I was writing a great deal, different kinds of poems in fact, all through the 1960s, just after I met him, so these things all sort of came together at the same time.

There's a tremendous elation in the poem.

Yes, that's what I felt at the time, having met him. It just seemed to fit in neatly with what was happening to Glasgow. I know people have different views about what was happening to Glasgow's architecture, but at the time I felt very optimistic about it.

To come back to the students, one of the brightest of them, a chap from Fife, had a reaction I found very honest, and very amusing. When we spoke about the love poems, he was taken aback. 'Edwin Morgan's a great poet, a great Scottish poet,' he said, 'how can he be a homosexual?' It said a lot about his ideas of what being Scottish meant.

But then you might say, there are no precedents here, starting something up . . . [*laughter*] Was he upset?

I think it just meant that some of his ideas had to be broken down and reconstructed, because someone who for him was very central . . .

Could also be, from another point of view, not central . . . In that case it's probably quite useful. I can understand that reaction.

The students were also very resistant to the idea of there being in a real sense a Glasgow school of writing, drawing together yourself and Tom Leonard, Jim Kelman, Liz Lochhead, Alasdair Gray and others . . .

You can't put it into manifesto terms, I don't think it's a school of writers in that sense. I can see why you might think that. We are I suppose really pretty different in many ways. On the other hand, we see each other quite a lot and get on alright together, discuss things. I suppose we do feel a kind of common purpose, maybe just because we have a kind of commitment to the place, not much more than that. On the whole, we still live there and write there and quite often write about it. Maybe that's not enough to define what you might call a movement or school or group, but there certainly is something. The Glasgow spirit is so hard to define, it's got so many incongruous opposites and bizarre elements about it that it's probably quite hard for people outside to see it as being one thing. If you live in the place you do see it as being one thing, but you still find it, because of its amorphousness, very hard to put into words. But I would feel there was some linking . . .

How much of the Glasgow spirit do you think you can put into words?

Possibly very little. It is probably elusive.

For me the very fact of giving each other support and encouragement and solidarity is the best aspect of a group . . .

That's partly it. Maybe that is partly the Glasgow spirit, that this should take place, instead of the kind of backbiting you got often in the past in the Scottish Renaissance period, MacDiarmid and Muir, MacDiarmid and Gunn. There was so much of that going on that wasn't really terribly helpful. I think the Glasgow friendliness — I'm sentimental about it, obviously, because we have very sharply differing ideas in many ways — there is something that seems to keep people together in Glasgow. Maybe it is specifically the place, I'm not sure. That was always part of the image of Glasgow in the past, that it was both dangerous and friendly. You were likely to meet a friend for life or get your throat cut, it was one or the other, or perhaps both together! [*laughter*]

Something else that brings you and Liz Lochhead and Tom Leonard together is an interest in what it means to be male or female.

That is a theme, yes. In Tom Leonard there's a lot about that, and in Liz. She's a feminist, not an abrasive type of feminist, but she's very conscious of the fact that she's writing as a woman. For me, there's the fact that I have poems about female characters quite a lot, whether it's Marilyn Monroe, or the one where Eve speaks as she looks down on Adam ['Eve and Adam']. I wonder if people would decode that one. It's in Paradise, Adam's asleep, and Eve is not asleep, she's looking down on him and I tried to get into Eve's mind, to speak as she would speak, but also I know that in looking down and describing Adam there's something that comes from me as much as her, the 'black hair lying tangled in a helpless mass' and so on, all this actual description of the sleeping man, looking down on a sleeping man, is something that could be taken in a way quite differently from just Eve looking at him. There's a gay element in that, although it is a poem about Adam and Eve. But I always loved Milton, and I loved the Paradise scenes in *Paradise Lost*, so those things are probably there as well.

When at the beginning of 'The Second Life' you bring in Thomas Wolfe, it's almost not clear whether you're talking about New York or Glasgow. So something else you have in common with Liz Lochhead and Tom Leonard is the enabling influence of American writing, using it as a lever to open up new spaces. Does this apply to writing about gay experience? Whitman, for example?

Yes, I came across him even at school, when I was a student I read a lot of him and felt this enormous attraction to what he was doing and to the way he did it too. He must have had quite an influence on me. The Thomas Wolfe thing was slightly different, I'd read all his novels and liked them, though I could see their faults. It was more just the image he has of the young man in a city that appealed to me. I'd always felt that, though it's on a smaller scale, Glasgow is quite like some of the big American cities, and a young man in Glasgow would have something of the same sort of feelings that he had. I linked Wolfe up with Hart Crane as having this special feeling for New York, and got something from both of them that did feed into what I was doing myself in Glasgow.

What makes you feel that Glasgow is like some of the big American cities?

I think it's got something of that American feeling of doing what you want to do, just going ahead and making your mistakes, put up a big building and if it's not liked in twenty years' time, well we'll take it down and put up another one.

It's so different from Edinburgh. Edinburgh is stuck with its history, its past, it's awfully hard to renew Edinburgh physically, the Cockburn Society will say no, and that's it! [*laughter*] Whereas in Glasgow I suppose people are brasher, and they have something of this thrusting sense urban Americans have, and they've also got something of the American boastfulness. New Yorkers or people from Chicago are always boasting about the height of their buildings, each one claiming that it's higher than the other. It's perhaps an unamiable characteristic, but I think it is true of the place. And just the modernity, I like the modernity in Glasgow. There are some old buildings [*laughter*], Mungo's church, which goes back quite a time. The city is more nineteenth century than earlier really. It would please me if somebody discovered the original Mungo's church, the real sixth-century church, a few lintels or doorposts, I wouldn't object to that at all. I like to think of Glasgow as being a place that is quite willing to renew itself in a fairly devastating sort of way. The drawing in of horns that's been going on in the 1980s, against the changes of the 1960s and 1970s and the fact that refurbishment is taking the place of putting up new buildings, in general anyway, is not something that pleases me tremendously because I like to think of the new buildings going up, even the Red Road flats. I think these are feelings that are more West of Scotland than East of Scotland, more Glasgow than Edinburgh, and it may just be that Edinburgh faces Europe and Glasgow faces America, and Glasgow people, if they get the chance, do like to go across there, if they can afford it they really would like to get to New York.

I'm often struck by the way sexuality and creativity are so closely linked. Would that be true for you?

Yes, I think probably so, yes. That would certainly fit in with the 1960s thing, the fact that that was the first really satisfactory relationship I'd had, both emotional and sexual, and at the same time I found that I was able to write much more and, I'm quite sure, better than I ever did before. Though I think it can also come from a frustrated sense, it can still be very sexual even though it's frustrated, and that can also give rise to quite strong poetry.

Can you think of examples of that in your own work?

I suppose the little sequence I mentioned, there in *The New Divan*, where in fact it doesn't really come to anything, but is very intense, even two people sleeping together but nothing happening, 'Smoke', that's probably the main one. There's a lot of feeling in these ones that it was something that was only tentative and incomplete. It's all true to life, meeting this person, all just as it actually happened. We met quite a bit, and played a lot of music, and so on, and it was just one of those things where in actual fact, in one sense you get quite close to another person, in another sense you probably realise it's not going to amount to anything, and it just does come to an end.

'Instructions to an Actor' struck me as very clearly a gay love poem, although it's motivated by the setting.

I was conscious of this, obviously, in writing the poem . . .

Things like 'you're a dead queen' . . .

I knew that was all sort of there, though at the same time it's still meant to be a poem about what it says it's about, about this particular play and this particular part.

How far have you been able to assess people's reaction to it?

It's a poem that people enjoy, and I often get asked to read it. It's used quite a lot in educational contexts, drama colleges use it, and schools use it too. And of course the Shakespeare side of it is also felt to be interesting by people. As regards the other possible meanings, I don't know, I haven't had any token reactions about it until you mentioned it yourself. I imagine there must be something that people would possibly think about. I don't know how much they really think about how Shakespeare's plays were acted and how good the boys were in women's parts. We know that from various accounts of quite remarkable performances, truly professional and often very convincing. So it's doing different things, it's about Shakespeare and about the theatre and about love, it is about all these things, and forgiveness, that obviously comes into it, that links it up with other things. It was objected to by the Puritans at the time that there were relations between the older actors and the boys, which was thought to be a great scandal, this was so common, obviously inevitably it would happen. When Shakespeare was young, or in his early period, it would be taken probably just for granted, but very quickly it was commented on in Puritan pamphlets.

Do you believe that a specifically gay sensibility exists, that the experience of gay men is specific in some way?

I'm not tremendously attracted by that kind of idea. It may well be there is such a thing, but I've always tended to feel that in writing poetry you're just writing for human beings, you're writing for everybody, although there maybe are some poems which you know are going to be read differently by people who are in a minority. On the whole I've felt that I'm writing just for people to read. From that point of view I'm a bit reluctant to say there is a specifically gay sensibility. In any case, a gay sensibility, if it does exist, must change continually, as society changes, and from country to country. I don't think there could be one gay sensibility. There was certainly a very marked American gay sensibility before AIDS, which resulted in very outspoken works of literature and the other arts too. There was never anything exactly like that in Britain. There are things which have been written for direct appeal to a gay audience. That's alright, but I think in my own case, the way I've been working, the way I see it, I don't take it from that angle. I'd probably just say I'm a writer, I write poetry, it's meant for anybody who takes it up to get what he or she can out of it. I'm not trying to say I'm writing for a gay audience, although I know that in so far as it's realised then that audience will be there, will react differently. I know there's bound to be a different reaction to works of art, that is true. Whether that means it's been written from a gay sensibility I'm not sure. You may have a gay subject matter, and that will appeal to people who are inclined in that direction, and it may cause offence or problems with a different kind of audience. But a great many things seems to me to have a general appeal, even though they have a special appeal as well. I think that would be the kind of thing that I would probably prefer.

So you wouldn't mind people failing to perceive the actual situation behind the poems?

The more specific reading is an extra, a bonus, something that is there. I'm not saying they must be taken in that kind of way, though obviously the other meaning will come out more and more as time goes on, as the readership changes, and as more is known about it, I think that's part of it too. It's an eternal problem, isn't it, it's like Shakespeare's sonnets. They still divide people, even today, hundreds of years after the event. I remember many, many years ago, it must have been during the 1940s, I was involved in a radio programme in Scotland with George Bruce, something to do with Shakespeare's sonnets. They were being quoted, and we were having a discussion before the programme. 'Shall I compare thee to a summer's day' was one of the sonnets mentioned and I just dropped into the conversation 'Of course, you realise it's to a man, not to a woman', and this gave rise to cries of disbelief [*laughter*]. It was extraordinary, but they couldn't believe that anybody would call a man a summer's day. This was impossible, and yet it really is pretty clear from the way the sonnets are arranged that this belongs to the group that was about the young man, not the woman. There is still obviously great resistance to accepting the truth of the matter with things like that, where there is an apparent either ambiguity or an apparent non-gay content.

Obviously when two men are in a relationship they are just two human beings in love, but I think there is a particular quality to that experience that makes it a very new kind of subject matter.

That does make sense, and I think it should be written about, and it should be known. Do you think it should have been spelt out more in my work, just to make the point, or is it in fact done adequately the way I have done it? That there is something new, something that is not just quite like other love poems?

I think that what you have done is very powerful, because it's not couched in a way that is going to provoke a suppressive reaction, and yet when younger and younger generations come to this, they can find the gay elements in a very central, a very accessible place in Scottish literature. It seems to me a very successful tactic.

Perhaps it was, not so cowardly. I really did wonder if I should be more open about these things.

What kind of attitudes do you think prevail among other members of the Scottish literary pantheon — it's an ugly phrase — as regards homosexuality?

It's more a question of wondering what, wondering what if. I'm not at all sure what the reaction would be, it might very well be inimical, in many cases. I've never tested it so I don't know. Where there was not much awareness of even the fact of gayness then you could expect perhaps a very inimical sort of reation. It's hard to know how much some of the established writers in Scotland would know about it or be willing to consider the fact. We sometimes say things are changing, but I think with some of the writers possibly not. They would never consider the question at all, and would be upset by the revelation. That remains to be seen. It raises the old apprehension that I've mentioned more than once already.

I think you can afford not to be apprehensive now ...

You think so?

conflation of two interviews with Christopher
Whyte (Glasgow, 21 October and 18 November
1988); this is their first publication

II

II

A poetry before poetry

There is a poetry before poetry — that is what I seem to see if
I look back to my boyhood. Ours was not a particularly
bookish house, and neither of my parents was interested in
poetry or the other arts, though my father had been a great
theatregoer in his youth, and kept the cast-lists from old
programmes pasted in an album. Nor did any poetry I learned
at school leave a very strong impression until my last two
years, when Keats and Tennyson suddenly took hold of me.
(Modern poetry was not taught at all. I got as far as Bridges
and Brooke.) But the imagination of someone who is going to
write poetry can be stirred in all sorts of preparatory ways —
through popular songs, through nature, through prose,
through visual images, through knowledge. In this context
there are things I remember most vividly: my uncle Frank, who
had a good tenor voice, sitting at the piano to sing 'Pale hands
I loved beside the Shalimar' or 'Ramona' or 'Charmaine', the
strange longing filtering out over playing-cards, bobbed heads
and cigarette-smoke; my father (who worked for a firm of iron
and steel scrap merchants) describing on a long Sunday walk
how steel was made, the whole process — lurid, fearsome, yet
controlled, an image of power and danger — coming alive in
my mind simply through the evocative force of words; looking
again and again through a Victorian volume of my grand-
mother's filled with engravings of storms, wrecks and exotic
atolls and icebergs, and stories of maritime adventure and
endurance; poring with a torch under the bedclothes over sets
of cigarette-cards like 'Romance of the Heavens' and being
equally fascinated by the 'romance' and the scientific facts;
discovering, on a family holiday at North Berwick, that the
newly intense feelings I was having about the sea and sun, and
fields of poppies, and the passing of time and the seasons were
going to give me no rest or satisfaction until I had put them

into my own words, sometimes in essays, sometimes in letters, sometimes in verse. At that time, while I was still at school, I was writing more prose than poetry, and took great pleasure in creating huge fantastic narratives which probably reflected my liking for Verne, Wells and Edgar Rice Burroughs. It may be that more of my 'poetry' was channelled into prose tales and imaginative essays (on both of which I spent much time and energy) than into verse, though I was also beginning to explore verse expression; and this may be linked with the fact that I knew almost nothing of modern poetry till I went to university at the age of seventeen. Then I read Eliot in English, Rimbaud in French, and Mayakovsky in Russian, and a whole world, or series of worlds, of which I had not had the remotest inkling, began to explode in my mind as the novas on the cigarette-cards had done, in their own way, years before.

I think of poetry as partly an instrument of exploration, like a spaceship, into new fields of feeling or experience (or old fields which become new in new contexts and environments), and partly a special way of recording moments and events (taking the 'prose' of them, the grit of the facts of the case, as being in our age extremely important). I don't find myself relating what I do to other poetry to any great extent. I have had a long and hard search, through my own writing rather than through any conscious apprenticeships to other poets, to find a voice that I could call mine.

It would be wrong not to acknowledge the liberating effect of the American non-academic poets I read in the late 1950s (the Beats led me on to Black Mountain, Williams, Creeley), and then of the Brazilian concrete poets I discovered in 1962. I am also aware of a deep, almost spooky underground debt to some poetry in the Scotch tradition (certain aspects of Dunbar and Burns). And I have learned much from translating foreign poets (Montale and Mayakovsky in particular). But I like poetry that comes not out of 'poetry' but out of a story in today's newspaper, or a chance personal encounter in a city street, or the death of a famous person: I am very strongly moved by the absolute force of what actually happens, because after all, that is it, there is really nothing else that has its poignance, its razor edge. It is not an easy poetry to write, and I think it requires a peculiar kind of imagination that is willing to bend itself to meet a world which is lying there in the rain like an old shoe.

Maybe it is for the same reason that my concrete poems have titles and are 'about' something. If the element of wit is to succeed in such poems, reality must be around and must be able to be appealed to. In the concrete poems, it is the strange mixture of a strict structural idea and verbal play that I find exhilarating — not so strange perhaps in the end, since 'play' is only within limits 'free' and usually implies a 'game' which of necessity has its own rules. Only in poetry the game cannot be played twice, and the element of exploration is always there, whether of form or of experience.

Geoffrey Summerfield, putting together his anthology Worlds *for Penguin Education (1974; reissued 1986), asked the contributors (Charles Causley, Thom Gunn, Seamus Heaney, Ted Hughes, Norman MacCaig, Adrian Mitchell and Edwin Morgan) for 'an account of their own ways into the making of poetry, of what fed their minds and imaginations, of what provoked and sustained them'.*

The don as poet or the poet as don

In this country the poet in the university is an untypical figure, and on the whole I think he should remain so. This is not to say that for some poets it will not be the best solution of the problem every writer has to face — the problem, how to live. Many writers pare down this problem to vanishing-point, and are ruthless, or successfully naive, in the demands they make on society; but there are others who feel that devotion to art ought not to be incompatible with leading a fairly useful life on society's terms. If they have brains, and can apply themselves, they may well drift into quadrangles and laboratories in search of an attractive compromise. But this attraction, though not illusory, must be interpreted. It is the spaces inside a glove that make it useful. The university writer discovers that he must guard a certain modicum of unassimilability; even if he is a good teacher, he must now allow himself merely to 'become' a university teacher — he has to keep, and fiercely keep, the kind of independence that every writer has by nature. In so far as a university is an absorbing and protecting world of its own, he must gently fight it. In so far as it has links with the worlds of business or the arts, he must warily scrutinise the links. Above all he must diligently preserve his own non-university interests, contacts, and friends. The difficulty of meeting these requirements is my reason for believing that the university writer will continue to be a genuine but uncommon species.

I am opposed to the American experiment of complete rationalisation of the creative writer's position and function within the universities, because it has produced (at least in the United States) a generation of technically advanced and professionally cultivated poets (and their professionalism we might envy) whose response to life itself has atrophied and whose poetry is impotent to move and inspire the human heart. The much-execrated *Howl* which arose a few years ago in California was the inevitable counter-attack, and when I read about Ginsberg's angelheaded hipsters who 'passed through universities with radiant cool eyes' and who were 'expelled from the academies for crazy', I felt that perhaps it was high time they did and were.

For myself, I don't regard my university post as either an ideal solution or (at the other extreme) simply a bread-and-butter device. It is somewhere between the two. Although when I was at school I had no thought of entering a university, I always had a vast curiosity, took prizes, and read indiscriminately and with speed and passion, and looking back now I sometimes wonder how that intellectual curiosity would have been satisfied had I left school at fifteen and taken a job in the designing department of a carpet factory as I very nearly did. No writer has no problems, but the would-be poet or painter who cannot shake off a seemingly irrelevant hunger for learning is faced with particularly hard decisions in our specialised civilisation. Those like myself who take the risk of keeping up both the poetry and the learning may still be useful to their community (in teaching or research) and to their university department (where they can add a quirky leaven to the discipline); but their main anxiety is that they will be left sufficiently at liberty to forget the learning from time to time, or to combine the learning and the poetry in their own peculiar way.

EM's contribution to a symposium in
Universities Quarterly XIII:4 *(August-*
October 1959) pp. 359-60

Notes on the poet's working day

I'm a Reader in English at Glasgow University. Glasgow is a big university, and the English classes are large — 450 in the first-year class at the moment (which has to be split into two and the lectures given twice). The Scottish MA Honours is a four-year course, so we have these four classes plus a fifth, called the Advanced, which is an alternative third year course for those who are taking an Ordinary not an Honours degree. So we've these five classes, which involve a mixture of lectures, seminars, and tutorials. This year I'm teaching four out of the five classes. I have five courses of lectures to give, on Medieval Scots poetry, Victorian poetry, Emily Bronte's *Wuthering Heights*, Robert Burns, and James Hogg's *Confessions of a Justified Sinner*. I also have a regular series of seminars on Scottish literature for those who are taking a special optional paper in the final on that subject, and of course I have also some postgraduate students to supervise.

That's the bare bones of the job. It's difficult to describe a typical day because every day is different. Some days are relatively free, with only an hour or two of seminars or tutorials, others are really packed on a ten-till-five basis. But here's a sample day from earlier this week: Alarm goes off at eight o'clock. While I'm having my tea and toast and rice krispies I'm listening to the radio and when I get to the last cup of tea I look through the papers — never quite relaxed because I'm always thinking about what's going to come up during the day and I'm by nature an anxious sort of character. I don't usually have to leave the house till about half-past nine. There's generally a good deal of mail and I like to go through this before I leave. This day there's a couple of invoices which I add to a large clip marked DAMNED BILLS; there's an invitation to read my poetry at a school in Dumfriesshire and I spend some time looking up timetables to see how possible it would be to get there; and there is also Part 26 of the *Dictionary of the Older Scottish Tongue*, from Naturall to Nyxttocum, which I know it would be fatal to start dipping into.

I get to the university, partly by bus partly by walking, shortly before ten, collect my mail there, go to my room, and hold an individual tutorial from ten to eleven, discussing with a man in his final year two essays he'd written on Dickens and Tennyson. I have a lecture at twelve, on Tennyson — on *Maud,* which I haven't done before, so I look over my notes and make some last-minute changes and additions and make sure I can quickly find the passages I want to read. Also, in this hour before twelve, I answer one or two letters, answer the telephone once or twice, and for quarter of an hour go to the staff club for a coffee.

Conversation in club: Did you know our new colleague has arrived? No, what's her name? Heather Glen. You're joking. No, it really is Heather Glen; she comes from Australia, via Cambridge. And is she medieval? No no, she's Blake and Wordsworth. But I thought we were short of early Renascence characters? Maybe so, but she's not one. Is she Miss, Mrs, Dr, or what? The answer to this question never emerged — in comes someone waving an old briefcase. Is this what you're looking for Hannah? I don't know, it's so long since I mislaid it, has it got a lock? Yes it's got a lock, and there's a tiny wee key tied on with a bit of string, should we open it? I'm not sure. I'm just not sure, let me feel it, it should have my Pope notes in it. Go on, give it a squeeze Hannah, it won't do it any harm. All right, let's open it. Sorry, the string's not long enough to get the key in, we'll have to cut it. Anybody got a knife or something? Morgan supplies pocket scissors. Oh man, that's a dangerous weapon. It's all right, it's for self-defence. Snap. Lock's open. Hannah rummages. Yes, here's old Pope, it's mine. At that moment the university clock chimes out twelve and I scurry off to my lecture.

After the lecture at one o'clock I go to staff club, have lunch, back to my room at two. For a minute or two I stand looking down into the quadrangle. It's a dark showery day, with gusts of wind, and I watch one of the gardeners trying to sweep up fallen leaves into a sack, letting the wind blow them in as much as he can. Three girls run past, hurrying for a class. Miniskirts under maxicoats, which is always rather eyecatching. The gardener stops and looks up and grins as they fly past. Everything about them is streaming in the wind — their hair, scarves, coats, shoulder-bags — they are like figures in a Japanese print. I wonder if anyone else at some other window is watching me watching the gardener watching the girls. It is all gone in a minute, but is beginning to compose itself into a sort of poetic experience, or the first hint or essence of a poetic experience. I recognise the feeling. But it isn't demanding enough for me to do anything about it there and then. I store the observation away in my mind. If it had been stronger I probably would have tried to write something down, though this is always difficult within the university's surroundings and I seldom in fact do it.

Anyway I have other things to do: I have to look over a poem which is to be analysed at a seminar at four o'clock (Donne's 'Air and Angels'), and I have to work out a programme for a couple of postgraduate students — I know these things will take me till about four. So — the seminar on Donne, ending at five. I have a long wait for a bus, get back home about a quarter to six. A friend comes in at six and we have tea; he had been out of work (he's a factory storeman) for more than six months and he has just got a new job; we decide to go out and see a film, *The Godfather,* which at least makes a nice contrast to 'Air and Angels'. I get back to the flat at eleven o'clock, make tea, read an essay for a tutorial the following morning (this takes about an hour, as it's a long essay: but it has to be done). Then I take a paperknife and cut the pages of Part 26 of the DOST, stopping at some of the fascinating words on the way, over a sip of whisky and a nibble of shortbread. Bed about 1 am.

In this sort of job, poems usually have to be written either in the evenings or at the weekend or during vacations. You can accommodate to this, you can accommodate to the specific rhythm of the work, though not without tensions and frustrations. The worst part of the job, in a big university like Glasgow, is the marking of essays and exam-papers — even with a substantial staff this is a heavy and soul-battering operation, and it normally has to be done at home. There's often a real clash between the desire to write poetry and the necessity to get so many papers marked by a certain deadline. And there's no way out of this except by burning the midnight oil. This may not happen frequently, as far as the really large batches of papers are concerned, but it is bad enough, and it is at these moments that you feel like giving up the job. But the moments pass, and I have found — and I can only speak for myself — that with its various disadvantages the job seems to suit me. I seem to need some tension, some anxiety, some clash of responsibilities, and if I am too free I may be less creative. I don't find the academic life deadening (though I'm sure some people do), partly because I enjoy teaching and partly because I keep a lot of other interests going which are non-academic and even anti-academic. I like to keep a separation between my academic working life and my life outside the university hours. For this reason, being an ordinary member of the English Department suits me better, I think, than having a special position as a campus poet, which I have never sought. This is obviously not an argument against having campus writers. But speaking for myself, I would only make the point that it's not impossible to combine an academic job with creative work.

EM took part in a symposium, 'The Poet's Life — 1972 style', organised by the magazine Ambit *(54, 1973, pp. 29-31) for the London Borough of Camden in 1972. EM and Jim Burns were the opening speakers of a session entitled 'The Poet's Working Day'. The day chosen by EM as illustration was 11 November 1972. The interrupted poem which follows on the next page was published in* College Courant *[Glasgow University] 75 (September 1985) p. 25*

Cantus Interruptus

(A poem which would have been written in
November 1972 if the writer had not had to take a
seminar.)

The little I can see of sky is grey,
dark grey massed clouds ragged in the wind.
Below me the quadrangle trees shake, thinned
by the gusts, and papery leaves cartwheel away:
the gardener takes them as he can, his sack
a waving hell-mouth for russet souls; he lacks
more than he takes. Three girls in maxi-macs
and mini-skirts rush past, their hair flares back,
their coats and shoulder-bags are streaming as
he pauses to grin up at them as I gaze down
at him and as who knows what face is pressed
to what far window to watch me. It has
already stopped, become the linenfold gown,
crouched satyr, painted leaves wildly at rest.

What if feels like to be a Scottish poet

I prefer being called a Scottish poet, do not mind being called a Glasgow poet, find being called a British poet faintly absurd but acceptable, and become highly irritated if called an English poet. Normally it ought to be enough to be called a poet, *tout court*, but I feel the present moment of Scottish history very strongly and want to acknowledge it, despite the fact that my interests extend to languages, genres, and disciplines outwith Scotland or its traditions. Much modern Scottish poetry differs from poetry in the rest of the British Isles by being written in Gaelic or in some form of Scots, but my point would be that even if it is written in English it may be part of a hardly definable intention in the author to help to build up the image of poetry which his country presents to the world. If Scotland became independent tomorrow, there is no guarantee that it would enter a golden age of literary expression. Yet I am sure I am not mistaken in sensing, even among those who are less than sympathetic to devolutionary or wider political change, an awareness of such change which in subtle ways affects creative endeavour, suggests a gathering of forces, a desire to 'show' what can be done. The 'Scottishness' may be no more than a writer deciding to remain and work in Scotland, though wooed elsewhere; and despite my phrase 'no more than', I regard this as being important. More and more writers now take this decision. The result will be, I hope, that dedication to the art of writing will not be unaccompanied, by the other dedication — to a society, to a place, to a nation — which can and will run the whole gamut from the rabid to the near-invisible. Scottish poetry is less easy to define than Irish or Northern Irish or Welsh poetry, but this is possibly in its favour, taking the long-term view that it is gestatorily the poetry of a nation-state, and therefore no more necessarily definable than French poetry or Hungarian poetry. Perhaps

Scottish poets should not — though I dare say they do — feel envious of the greater attention paid at present by English reviewers and critics to the poets of Ireland. Irish poetry is good, but I suspect the English praise of it is not unlinked to some subconscious guilt about the Irish situation, coupled with the fact that the Irish poetry is very accessible and manageable. Poetry in Scotland seems more various and adventurous, more willing to take risks, as witness Hugh MacDiarmid's work, classically 'unplaceable', or more recent exploratory work from Ian Hamilton Finlay or Tom Leonard or myself which must complicate the impression of what 'Scottish poetry' is really like to the outside eye (or ear). The hope is that as the 'idea of Scotland' begins again to emerge, the parts and pieces of its literary production will be seen to belong to the same animal, and that this animal will be worth a bit of describing and investigating.

contribution to a symposium in Aquarius 11
(1979) pp. 72—73

Pageant of Worthies

The Lanark teachers' magazine, Lantern 3:1 *(Winter 1985) p. 6, asked a number of 'celebrities' which worthies in Shakespeare, or literature in general, reminded them of themselves in some way, and printed the replies under the above heading. Rikki Fulton and Eileen McCallum were the other contributors.*

My immediate reaction was to recall that in my schooldays our class acted out some scenes from *Julius Caesar*, which was a set text, and as I was already known to be a writer of verse I was given the part of Cinna the Poet. The plebeians fell on me with a fine relish, crying 'Tear him for his bad verses!' as soon as I tried to explain that I was Cinna the Poet and not Cinna the Conspirator. Obviously I cannot claim this was traumatic or put me off writing poetry, but I remember thinking Shakespeare was a bit unfair in using the figure of the poet merely in order to establish a point about the mad logic of the mob. But he made amends elsewhere, and I always strongly identify with the 'enchanted' poetry of *A Midsummer Night's Dream*, the transformations and illusions, the shifts from comic to grave, the dreaming and the waking, the different levels of reality. Perhaps a cross between Bottom and Theseus would fit me: I sometimes wear the magic ass's head like Bottom, and have dreams that 'the eye of man hath not heard, the ear of man hath not seen', but then I am also the Duke and can place all these things in a context, and know about imagination and its shaping power, and how even 'the best in this kind are but shadows'. In fact, though, I must suppose like everyone else that I am unique, and therefore 'not in Shakespeare'.

Poets in schools

The idea of inviting a writer, whether poet, novelist, or playwright, to a school to read and talk about his work and to initiate discussion both about his own writing and about the art of writing in general, seems now to be well established in Scotland. I have always supported this idea, and taken an active part in the process, so perhaps a few thoughts on how I see the meaning and value of these visits might be of interest.

I have been to schools in most parts of Scotland, from Oban to Aberdeen and from Thurso to Duns (and also, I should add, to some schools in England, comprehensive, grammar, and public, and to a fair number of high schools in the United States). I have been caught in snowdrifts and held up in railway tunnels by rockfalls; I have found myself walking a golf course at 7 am, and listening to oilmen's talk during hours of waiting at Aberdeen airport; I have had every kind of school hospitality from the statutory coffee to a mammoth and scrumptious afternoon tea home-baked by the domestic science department; like Matthew Arnold, I have had to become a great student of train timetables and a great connoisseur of railway buns. Many schools have taken advantage of the Scottish Arts Council's 'Writers in Schools' scheme since it was started in 1972, and the general feeling seems to be that this scheme has been very useful. In a sense, the Scottish Arts Council was recognising and facilitating the expansion of a situation which already existed. I know that in my own case — and probably other writers had the same experience — I had visited schools before the Scottish Arts Council proposals emerged, usually without payment and on the invitation of some teacher who knew me and who was using my work in school. After the publication of my book *The Second Life* in 1968, which included poems about Glasgow and Scotland as well as 'concrete' poems involving verbal play, teachers seem to have been using these poems increasingly in the classroom, and it was natural that they might want to hear the author read some of the poems or give his comments on how they came to be written. This is itself not unconnected with the new popularity of public poetry-readings by poets during the 1960s and especially in the latter parts of that decade. Much 1960s poetry had a considerable communicative quality, and bonds were forged between poet and public around that time which have at other periods often proved elusive and recalcitrant. A sense of this was certainly not lacking among teachers, who began to see that much could be done in classroom terms to capitalise on these communicative possibilities. If recent poetry had this character of 'availableness' to young people, who after all are searching for aesthetic as well as other sorts of experience, even if they are not always aware of the fact, then why not extend this 'availableness' to the author, if he could be persuaded to talk about his own work? School pupils could see, and feel, that literature was something that was still being made, that it was not merely 'historical', and that writers who were names in a book actually existed and had to cope with the same problems and general affairs of life as those who read them. Even where the problems differed, they could see that the writer's job was nevertheless to sympathise or empathise with people whose experiences varied from his own. Through the question-and-answer of a personal contact, even the limited contact of a reading session in classroom or library or assembly hall, many things about the place and function of a writer, many things about what art can and cannot do, even things about the nature of art itself (it is curious how often the ancient and no doubt unanswerable question 'What is poetry?' — though one tries to answer it — turns up in these sessions), can be aired in an undogmatic, non-destructive atmosphere. (Not that there are no smart-alecs or needlers, of course: 'What do they pay you if you get a poem published?' 'Oh, maybe about £5.' 'I don't understand some of your poems; I think that's taking money under false pretences.')

Whether there is any 'best way' of conducting a reading, I am not sure, since schools, audiences, and writers themselves differ so widely. I have spoken to audiences ranging in size from twenty or thirty to several hundred. With a small group it is possible to develop a more intimate kind of reading;

gentler, lyrical poems may have a better chance; and it may be easier to get a lively, uninhibited discussion going. On the other hand, a very large audience can generate its own kind of excitement, and through feedback (if the reader is on form) a much more electric atmosphere can be created; the situation becomes a sort of 'theatre', and the drama within a poem, together with the ongoing drama of the juxtaposition of poems of varying types, can help to keep the audience interested, surprised, and entertained. The disadvantage may be — though this is not always true — that questions and comments are less forthcoming (or are so far away that they are inaudible!) and that unless the questions have some fairly general implications the reader's answer may cause some of the audience to fidget. In fact the reader has to play every occasion by ear, be flexible, be ready to make lightning decisions about which poems to include, be able to gauge a decent length of reply to queries.

Schools have different preferences about whether pupils should have cyclostyled texts of poems to be read. I think it often helps if they have texts of *some* of the poems, but I believe there is value also in exposing them to work they may not have seen. It obviously facilitates discussion if they have studied, or at least read, a few of the poems in class beforehand. They may come primed with questions about things which have puzzled them, or which they disagree with, or which they would simply like to have more (and as they think, more authoritative) information about, but quite often the questions will relate to something that the live reading has brought out or suggested to them for the first time, and although this *can* complicate the issues (which is the *real* poem, the one on the printed page or the spoken one?), I think it also shows the value of being able to call attention to minute but important features of style as the author's voice indicates them — matters of rhythm, pause, emphasis, tone, all of them difficult to talk about in the abstract from the poem on the page. No doubt there are dangers here of over-dramatisation. Is a poem a script for performance, or not? My own view is that unless a reader is carried away by the Severn bore of his own impetuous virtuosity, he can have the valuable function of making the essential double point: that a poem, at least in post-Gutenberg society, should be able to stand up to silent mental scrutiny, and yet at the same time it should, by being read aloud, be tested for its music, its rhythmical coherence, its tone, its 'voice'. By agreeing to 'perform' his poems, and also later in the same session to talk fairly rationally about them, the poet can help to remind people of the enormously powerful oral component poetry has, while not denying that printing and the book have introduced other qualities and possibilities, including purely visual effects that cannot be indicated at all in reading aloud. Perhaps no one can succeed in being both inspiring and sensible, but that should be the aim.

The questions asked do fall into a pattern, but there are always surprises, and some questions are remarkably acute and searching. The expected ones are: When did you start writing poetry? How long does it take you to write a poem? How many poems have you written? What poets have influenced you? What's your favourite poem among those you've written? How d'you feel about your poems being 'done' in schools? Don't you think it spoils a poem to study it in detail? Where do you get your poems from — are they based on things that have really happened? D'you think it's right to use Glasgow speech? Do you use Scots? Do you really call that poetry (ie concrete poems or sound poems)? Do you go over your poems and change them? Do you just write poetry or do you write other things? What is poetry? But also questions like these: Are you Aquarius? ('No, I'm Taurus.' 'Oh, I thought you'd be Aquarius.' 'No, really Taurus.' 'Oh well, yes, I see you could be Taurus.') Some of your poems make me think of the Pink Floyd: were you influenced by them? (Questions like that are a little uncanny, because I *do* like Pink Floyd, and yet I can't imagine how this could possibly show in the poetry, unless through some passage of surreal imagery or maybe through some special use of science-fictionish sound-effects.) Many of your poems have religious themes: are you religious? (The directness of the question, though perfectly natural and proper, makes it hard to answer. A yes or no seems impossible, yet one doesn't want to seem evasive. The answer can only be something like: 'I don't *think* of myself as being particularly religious, but it's true that I do find myself recurring to religious subjects or religious implications . . .' and then put it in the context of (a) Scotland, and especially Glasgow, where religion still crops up frequently in everyday talk and argument, in football, in entertainment, and (b) my interest in man's place and destiny within an ill-explored cosmos of space

and time, where questions of religion will always tend to lurk.
. . . But in the end it's only other people who can say if you're
religious.)

Many of the questions, even if they are addressed to the
work and experience of a particular writer, will quite naturally
open up general thoughts and speculations in the answer. The
poet is there not only to present his own ideas but to represent
poetry, first as an art or craft or profession with its own
characteristics and also as a curious and persistent human
activity which can be defended against the wider social,
political, and scientific background. It is my own belief that a
case can be made — during an hour, anyway! — for the
relevance of a creative art like poetry, even to a large undiffer-
entiated audience many of whom may have little interest in
literature and may be sceptical of cultural impositions. The
audience will at the same time contain a minority of people
who are already interested in literature and are perhaps doing
some writing. They are not being directly helped by the writer
on his flying visit, though they may come up at the end of a
session to ask some special questions or occasionally to show
him some of their work. The only way of dealing with this
problem is perhaps to have a 'writer-in-residence', either at a
chosen school or peripatetic round a circuit, who would hold
workshop sessions with small groups and get to know
individual pupils and how to help and encourage their writing.
Such schemes may have difficulties of the integration (or non-
integration) of the writer into the normally tight teaching
schedule, but when they can be worked out they clearly offer
a useful complement to the one-off visit. I would still think that
there is a great value in the single visit, if only because everyone
can be brought in, to consider for a moment what the art of
writing can do within, for, and to a community.

Community! Dread word! A writer is of, and yet not of, a
community. In part he is voyaging to Arcturus, or is 20,000
leagues under the sea, or is searching not for her but for She. In
some ways one must regret that an accessible, down-to-earth
poetry, with strong roots in recognisable experience, offers so
much tempting aid to teachers who can use it to catch the
attention of those suspicious of the airy-fairy or the high-
flown. A poet is, as Wordsworth said, a man speaking to men.
But the means by which he does so may range very far from
realism. A poem by a Renascence sonneteer, knee-deep in

conventions, or a poem by Shelley, pinnacled dim in the intense inane, may be a very fine poem, and it would be a pity if we reached a stage where it became impossible to persuade young people that this was so. (My Pink Floyd questioner would perhaps accept Shelley.) I often, at school readings, try to make the point that although many poems are based more or less directly on experience, many are not, and there is no need for them to be so based; that the art of writing is an art of the imagination, and that the imagination is an important faculty which asks to be fed and nourished — in everyone, not just poets.

from Bookmark *(Moray House, Edinburgh)*
3 (Winter 1979) pp. 2, 4-11

Poet in person

We had a visit at our school last term by the poet Edwin Morgan, and I found this visit very helpful in elucidating his work. We had studied some of his poems in class, and although I liked the poems I was also at times forced to admit to myself that I found aspects of them puzzling or difficult, and I was looking forward to hearing what the writer himself had to say. Mr Morgan read about a dozen poems, talked about them, and answered questions from the audience. My teacher told us that he was born as long ago as 1920, but he seemed very fit, and read the poems very fluently and in a great variety of tones and voices. I think there must be something of the actor in anyone who reads his work in public in such a way as to get it across — and Mr Morgan's work really did come across — but perhaps the difference is that the poet is concerned to bring out the meaning of the poem and not only its emotional impact.

The visit was helpful in different ways. In the first place, the writer is able to introduce each poem and give something of its background, perhaps saying where or when it was written, what set it off, or what problems there may have been in writing it. Mr Morgan said that it was not always possible to say very much about a poem, especially if it was written some years ago, because writing it was a very emotional and even partly subconscious experience, and you could never quite get back into the frame of mind you were in when you were writing it. This was a new idea to me, but it gave me an insight into what makes a poem different from some other kinds of writing. But Mr Morgan did tell us interesting and helpful things about a number of his poems; he talked about the bad social conditions that lay behind the gang-fights in 'King Billy', and told us that the poem was written not from having been at the funeral but after reading newspaper accounts and then working it all up within the imagination, and he emphasised that imagination was important in poetry as well as working direct from life. He also talked about 'Trio', and said that he knew some people took the poem in a very symbolic way, with the infant Christ, the wise men bringing their gifts, etc, but that he had written it more out of an actual incident and would not want to insist on a religious interpretation, although he knew the suggestions were there. I found this helpful, not in 'elucidating' the poem, but in reminding me that you can never completely pin down a poem, with one single meaning — otherwise it would not be a poem.

The poet also read a few of what he called his 'science fiction' poems, including 'From the Domain of Arnheim' and 'The First Men on Mercury'. Science fiction is not in fact a great favourite with me, but I must say that Mr Morgan made me look at it in a new way, by explaining what he was doing in these two poems. He said it was very easy to be too indulgent in that kind of poetry, because you could write about the most fantastic happenings as freely as you liked, but he always tried to give science fiction poems some kind of point, and so that they would reflect real human life and its fears and hopes and possibilities. I could see what he meant by this in 'The First Men on Mercury', which is about man's supposed conquest of space and whether he has the right to take his arrogance and imperialism out to other planets. The poem is entertaining, but there is more to it than the fun of inventing an imaginary language.

It was very helpful to hear 'The First Men on Mercury' read aloud, because I had really had no idea how it should sound, and I thought this was even more true of the group of poems which he called his 'sound-poems' or experimental poems. He read 'The Loch Ness Monster's Song', 'Canedolia', and 'The Computer's First Christmas Card'. I had seen the first of these, but the other two were new to me. I was amazed to hear how convincing the Loch Ness Monster sounded, and how much more there was to the poem than it seemed to have on the printed page. The poet told us something about how he chose the right kinds of gurgling, plopping, and throaty sounds to try to convey the speech of a large aquatic creature. The other two poems showed me what one could do with place-names, and what relation the computer might have to the human mind in creating works of art. Talking about these poems, the author gave us some useful background information about recent movements in poetry, and also raised in my mind some fascinating questions about where exactly poetry might go in future.

Mr Morgan answered many questions, both about his own work and on poetry and writing in general, and I thought his answers were very fair and helpful, though sometimes surprising (he was asked how long it took to write a poem, and revealed that he once wrote twenty-six poems in one week, even if that was unusual). I asked him whether he ever exaggerated things in his poems, for greater effect, and he said, 'That's a good question. I try to be truthful as a general rule, especially where a poem is about something that actually happened, but yes, I think sometimes you do have to heighten some effect, because you want the poem to communicate, to get across to other people — but I still don't like to think of it as "exaggeration" in a bad sense!'

I found Mr Morgan's visit to the school stimulating and enjoyable. It made me go back to his poetry, and to see it more clearly, but I also felt that his enthusiasm would help many of us to realise that poetry was very much a living art and not something lying fixed in dusty books.

EM's answer to question 18, SCE Higher Grade English, Section 3 — Poetry, 1985: 'Demonstrate how your engagement with a poet in person, perhaps on a school visit or at a poetry reading, has been instrumental in elucidating his work.' EM, Cliff Hanley and Hector MacMillan were asked to submit anonymously answers on their own work; they were then assessed by English Adviser Jim Duffin who discussed the results with the authors on the Jimmy Mack Show, Radio Scotland, 17 May 1985: they all passed!

The poet's voice and craft

My first reaction on reading through the questionnaire which the poets were sent, and asked to investigate and comment on, was that to many of the questions my answer was 'I don't know', with the even stronger rider 'And I don't want to know'! It seemed to me that the whole exercise was misguided, and was a job for critics, not for the writers themselves. If I may quote Barnett Newman: 'Aesthetics is for the Artists like Ornithology is for the Birds.' As I see it, it is not healthy for poets to become so acutely self-conscious about their own work. I cannot imagine anything more likely to inhibit them from writing their next poem, and that, after all, is their function. Our labour and devotion are to create, to produce, to deliver the goods, not to analyse how the goods came to be made.

My first basic objection, then, is that it is not any part of the duty of a writer of poetry to make a detailed examination of his own work. Perhaps that should be rephrased as 'to *try* to make a detailed examination of his own work', since the question arises immediately, how far it is *possible* to make such an examination of the creative process as we were asked to do. Supposing I believed it was worth while (which I don't), could I do it? The possibilities of rationalisation after the event are endless. Either out of a desire to please the enquirers, or carried along on a wave of enthusiasm for one's own past ingenuity in having solved creative problems as they arose, the poet could well present an apparently persuasive account, but how much trust would you place in it? Edgar Allan Poe's essay on 'The Philosophy of Composition' stands as a warning. This bouncy, step-by-step putative recollection of how he came to write his poem 'The Raven' is really a sort of charming imaginative fiction of how a mad rationalist might go about the task, rather than a true memory of the creative process.

Poe gives seven steps of deliberate creative choice: (1) the length of the poem (short); (2) main impression to be conveyed (beauty); (3) the tone (sadness); (4) the constructional keynote (a refrain); (5) the word in the refrain which would best convey the sadness of the tone ('Nevermore'); (6) speaker of the refrain, human or animal? (raven); (7) topic or theme (death of a beautiful woman — bringing together sadness, beauty, and universal poetic feeling). Well, poems are not written like that, and Poe knew it. He very interestingly, in the same essay, gives the game away in a passage quite apart from his description of the evolving of 'The Raven'. He is talking about other poets than himself, those who do not share his claimed ability of total recall of the creative process. He mocks them, but in doing so, despite himself, he gives what is in fact a strong and true evocation of the real creative state of affairs: it emerges gradually out of the mockery until the mockery disappears, and it is clear that in this paragraph he is genuinely recalling, in terms that any poet would recognise, the messy and imperfect, but intense and devoted business of creation:

> Most writers — poets in especial — prefer having it understood that they compose by a species of fine frenzy — an ecstatic intuition — and would positively shudder at letting the public take a peep behind the scenes, at the elaborate and vacillating crudities of thought — at the true purposes seized only at the last moment — at the innumerable glimpses of idea that arrived not at the maturity of full view — at the fully matured fancies discarded in despair as unmanageable — at the cautious selections and rejections — at the painful erasures and interpolations — in a word, at the wheels and pinions — the tackle for scene-shifting — the step-ladders and demon-traps, the cock's feathers, the red paint and the black patches, which, in ninety-nine cases out of the hundred, constitute the properties of the literary *histrio*.

What is remarkable about that passage — and Poe, for all his persiflage about 'The Raven', was a real poet and had things to say — is the honesty of its generalisations: the 'elaborate and vacillating crudities of thought', the 'true purposes seized only at the last moment', the 'glimpses of idea' that never came into full view, the apparently mature and ready imaginative touches 'discarded in despair as unmanageable'. I would underwrite all these ideas, and I'm interested too in the imagery that underlies them: (1) suggestion of large complex bulky oscillating machines, (2) sense of a hunt or chase, (3) a vision which keeps tantalisingly appearing in parts but not as a whole, and (4) kinetic sense of something fully made but unwieldy being thrown away. . . . These visual, tactile, and kinetic images seem to me to be very much to the point, and their understatement is in nice contrast to the full-blown dramatic images of the last part of the quotation, where the previous struggle of the poet to manage the growth of the poem is now identified with the theatrical preparations to stage a play — the wheels and tackle, the ladders and trapdoors, the paint and feathers — and the poet himself becomes the *histrio*, the actor in his own drama, and by 'his own drama' I do not mean the interior drama of his own soul but the exteriorising, projective drama of the poem he is gradually, painfully, yet also joyfully dissociating himself from as he completes it. When the poem is finished, *finita la commedia*, he stands back, his part is over; and the general public and the critic can then step in.

In citing Edgar Allan Poe, I wanted to suggest that a mighty struggle with intangibles, a drama of conflicting moods, is what goes on in the composition of a poem, rather than a series of conscious choices to produce certain effects as is suggested by the questionnaire. If this idea of a struggle or drama has any truth in it, it would mean that it would in fact be difficult for any poet to work himself back into the frame of mind he was in when he was writing the poem, since that frame of mind would have had a very active subconscious element, virtually irretrievable. As Shelley wrote in his *A Defence of Poetry:*

> Poetry is not like reasoning, a power to be exerted according to the determination of the will. A man cannot say, 'I will compose poetry'. The greatest poet even cannot say it; for the mind in creation is as a fading coal, which some invisible influence, like an inconstant wind, awakens to transitory brightness. . . . This instinct and intuition of the poetical faculty is still more observable in the plastic and pictorial arts . . . and the very mind which directs the hands in formation is incapable of accounting to itself for the origin, the gradations, or the media of the process.

Shelley's phrase about the mind being 'incapable of accounting to itself' for the creative process might be questioned by someone who had read Henry James's prefaces to his own novels, which don't show any apparent 'incapability'. Yet even there, what you discover is that the preface is not necessarily very helpful or relevant; the account he gives of how a story began may or may not be truthful, and is never the whole truth; he often fudges, playfully and tantalisingly, some crucial point of character or action; and in fact what he is doing is giving you a little ancillary work of art which you may or may not find easy to attach to the story — like the blindfolded man with the donkey's tail.

This would suggest that readers ought to be suspicious of authorial claims or attempts to lay bare the bones of their own creations. Either in the case of apparently (but not really) highly cooperative authors like Henry James, or in the case of highly reluctant authors like myself, there may well be some underlying protective mechanism at work, in the sense that literary creation is a 'mystery' in both senses of the word, ie it is a skilled craft or trade or profession as the word implied in medieval and Renascence times, and it is also the delivery of a mysterious object, not reducible to full analysis whether by the producer or by anyone else, the link between the two meanings being the fact that every trade has its secrets, from the magic ingredient in Coca-Cola to the sound of a Stradivarius. It's a question of where the creative power resides. When Delilah found out that Samson's hair was not just an ordinary head-covering, she cut it off. Is there a lesson there? Perhaps not! The creative spirit is fairly strong, and indeed is made to overcome obstacles (witness Hopkins and Milton). But I have a strong feeling — and I don't know what the previous speakers in this series of lectures have said, but I imagine it must be quite a general feeling — that the persistence of the mysteriousness of poetry, which even critics cannot dissolve, though it is part of their duty to try to, ought to be important to poets themselves, if they want to go on writing it. Pasternak has a poem called 'Definition of Poetry' which begins:

> It is a sharply discharged whistle,
> It is a cracking of squeezed ice-blocks,
> It is night frosting leaves,
> It is a duel of two nightingales.

A critic, especially a Formalist critic, would be overjoyed to be asked to analyse what that stanza told him about how a poem begins to emerge, and he would have no shortage of topics, from anaphora to onomatopoeia, to discuss. Yet the stanza seems almost designed to ensure that the poet himself would say 'pass' if he was asked the same question. Unlike Pope in 'An Essay on Criticism', who tells you exactly how to produce the effects you want, Pasternak makes an immediate imaginative leap into regions beyond technique. Only a high-powered technique could have produced the stanza, but the poet's real concern is to push himself, and us, into startling and unexplored contrasts of sound and silence ('whistle' and 'night'), isolated and seasonal happenings ('whistle' and 'ice-blocks'), and single and double or dialectical voice ('whistle' and 'duel'). He himself, I'm sure, would not want to say even as much as I have said in that last sentence. Mandelshtam has an interesting comment on that poem and others like it from Pasternak's early period. In his essay 'Notes on Poetry' (1923) he does first of all make a gesture of relating the force of this poetry to something specific — Pasternak's fresh use of what he calls the secular Russian vernacular — but very soon he falls back on metaphor — 'falls back' is the wrong phrase, he 'mounts up' on metaphor — in his attempt to convey how Pasternak's power emerges:

When a ship stops coasting along the shallows and moves out into the open sea, those who cannot stand the rolling return to shore. After Khlebnikov and Pasternak, Russian poetry is again moving out to the open sea, and to many of the customary passengers the time has come to say goodbye to the ship. I can see them already, standing with their suitcases at the gangway leading down to dry land. And yet how welcome is each new passenger stepping onto the deck at this very moment! . . . This 'burning salt' of certain kinds of speech, this whistling, crackling, rustling, glittering, splashing, this fullness of sound, fullness of life, flood of images and feelings, leaps out at us with unprecedented force from the poetry of Pasternak. . . . To read Pasternak's poetry is to clear your throat, to strengthen your breathing, to restore your lungs: poetry like this must surely cure tuberculosis. We have no poetry that is more healthy at the present time. It is *kumys* after tinned milk.

That passage of prose could itself afford a nice prospect of analysis to a critic! The point I want to make is that Mandelshtam was himself a poet, and figurative language seems to him the best or perhaps the only means of re-presenting the creative process.

What I have tried to put forward so far is the grounds of doubt or objection regarding the lecture project. Obviously this does not mean that I think the 'craft' of poetry is a misnomer. Poetry may succeed in spite of faults or weaknesses of craft (as with Spenser's *The Faerie Queene*), and even in spite of apparent overindulgence in craft (Hopkins's 'The Wreck of the *Deutschland*'), but it is certainly true that poets have to have an apprenticeship in the craft side of their writing. What is important to remember, however, is that the other side of writing, the inspirational or imaginative, is equally necessary and may loom large. To meet, to woo, to tempt, to attract the inspirational and imaginative spirits, no amount of craft will help, and the mind of the would-be poet must at all costs be prepared to be open and tentative and exploratory, open above all, even at times to the edge of passiveness:

> He will watch from dawn to gloom
> The lake-reflected sun illume
> The yellow bees in the ivy-bloom,
> Nor heed nor see, what things they be;
> But from these create he can
> Forms more real than living man,
> Nurslings of immortality!
> (Shelley, *Prometheus Unbound*, Act 1 — 4th Spirit)

Because there is this *given* element in poetry, the concept of craft becomes a variable. I'd like to discuss the balance between craft and givenness from some examples of my own poetry. This is outside the terms of reference of the series of lectures, which concern the structural components within the poems, but it relates to it by bringing to bear elements which the terms of reference omit.

At one end of the scale are some poems which are largely or almost entirely given. These in the nature of things will tend to be short; they are always surprising because they are totally unpremeditated; and they almost write themselves, with very little working on, very little applied craft. The first one I'd like to read was written on a train, a long-distance train, after I'd been looking through the window in a desultory sort of way at a rather dreary greyish landscape going past, not thinking of anything in particular, when suddenly the lines of this poem began to come into my head one after the other, and I wrote them down on a scrap of paper, feeling immediately excited and involved with the words, jolted out of my lackadaisical mood. Without any intention whatsoever of writing a poem, I was writing a poem. I called it 'The Sheaf':

> My life, as a slant of rain
> on the grey earth fields
> is gathered in thirsty silence, disappears.
> I cannot even guess
> the roots, but feel them sighing
> in the stir of the soil I die to.   Let this rain
> be on the children of my heart,
> I have no other ones.
> > On the generations,
> on the packed cells and dreaming shoots,
> the untried hopes, the waiting good
> I send this drop to melt.

The grey fields and the rain came from the landscape I had been looking at, but why at that particular moment I should have had that sharp emotion, mixing a sense of mortality with the hope that the act of writing — in this case a mere 'drop', a short poem — might reach and stimulate future readers as the rain stimulates the growth of plants, I have no idea. Nor do I want to know. To me, the event is all that matters, and I pass it on to you as a thing in itself which you may find interesting, and might even want to think about further, and which you could not guess from the poem as it is printed.

Another rather similar example of the given element is one that struck me even more forcibly. I was lying in bed, with the light out, getting ready to go to sleep, but with the mind very active, as often happens in that situation (it's the opposite of the experience in the train, when my mind was lying fallow), and again very suddenly, with no warning and no preparation, and with no follow-on as far as I am aware from anything I had been thinking about during the evening or seeing on television or reading, the first four rhyming lines of a sonnet came strongly into my head with a sense of great urgency, and I put on the bed-light and wrote them down on the telephone pad;

at once the further development of the sonnet became clear, and again this unforeseen poem took shape, in this instance almost against my will, because of its terrifying subject — I felt that if poets were prophets, as they are sometimes thought to be, this was a fearful poem to be writing. The area just north and west of Glasgow contains the largest concentration of nuclear weapons and installations in these islands, so that in the event of a major conflict the Glasgow conurbation, with about two and a half million people, would be a prime target. I called the poem 'The Target':

> Then they were running with fire in their hair,
> men and women were running anywhere,
> women and children burning everywhere,
> ovens of death were falling from the air.
> Lucky seemed those at the heart of the blast
> who left no flesh or ash or blood or bone,
> only a shadow on dead Glasgow's stone,
> when the black angel had gestured and passed.
> Rhu was a demons' pit, Faslane a grave;
> the shattered basking sharks that thrashed Loch Fyne
> were their killer's tocsin: 'Where I am, watch;
> when I raise one arm to destroy, I save
> none; increase, multiply; vengeance is mine;
> in no universe will man find his match.'

What was perhaps surprising in that poem, as compared with 'The Sheaf', is that the structure of metre and rhyme was itself a given, whereas 'The Sheaf' was in free verse. There was something almost frightening, though also thrilling, in this revelation of the power of the subconscious mind to erupt, not formlessly but with order, into full consciousness. I remember I was shaking, and wondering if these midnight creative excitements which I had scribbled down would really survive the cold light of morning. But they did; they still seemed good and the poem did not need much working over. The thing that made my hair stand on end was the fact that these first four lines had roused me wide awake from near-sleep and forced me to write them down.

Perhaps the other extreme from these two poems would be a poem where the exercise of craft was so continuous and so demanding that the danger would be that not enough space, not enough interstices, might be left for the spirit of inspiration to slip in. Some concrete poems, if they depend on a largely mechanical or rigorous rearrangement of their component words or letters or sounds, run this risk unless the poet allows an element of strangeness, like the deliberate asymmetries of the best oriental carpet design, to break the expectations — or alternatively, unless he allows his chosen basic pattern to be only the impetus for some freewheeling, so that the poem can develop in a partly open way. An example of this latter point would be my poem 'Opening the Cage', where the overall conception is very strict, a fourteenfold variation of the fourteen words in John Cage's definition of poetry, 'I have nothing to say and I am saying it and that is poetry', but I allowed the rearrangements of the words to come as they suggested themselves to me line by line and not within a prearranged grid — so that the accidents, inspired accidents one would like to call them, of connections from line to line, and even a certain narrative quality, could emerge and make the poem more interesting:

> I have to say poetry and is that nothing and am I saying it
> I am and I have poetry to say and is that nothing saying it
> I am nothing and I have poetry to say and that is saying it
> I that am saying poetry have nothing and it is I and to say
> And I say that I am to have poetry and saying it is nothing
> I am poetry and nothing and saying it is to say that I have
> To have nothing is poetry and I am saying that and I say it
> Poetry is saying I have nothing and I am to say that and it
> Saying nothing I am poetry and I have to say that and it is
> It is and I am and I have poetry saying say that to nothing
> It is saying poetry to nothing and I say I have and am that
> Poetry is saying I have it and I am nothing and to say that
> And that nothing is poetry I am saying and I have to say it
> Saying poetry is nothing and to that I say I am and have it

In another poem, not concrete, I had a different mixture of the deliberate and the open. This poem is in Scots, and is called 'The Birkie and the Howdie'; it's a dialogue or flyting between a young man and an old woman. It is one of a group of imaginary computer poems, in this case one of the computer's first attempts at dialect, Lowland Scots. The mechanical part of its composition comes from the fact that I culled from the glossary of Robert Burns's complete poems (in Kinsley's big three-volume edition) the most Scottish, the most ethnic words, like a computer programmed to spot and spit out everything non-English. Out of this bizarre list of words I then made up the little story of the poem, allowing both meaning and sound to suggest what they could, within their limited provenance, the result being somewhat like what the Scottish language might be if it had had a complete development away from English:

> A dorty, vogie, chanler-chaftit birkie
> brattled the aizles o the clachan chimlie,
> glunched at his jaupin quaich o usquebae,
> scunnered red-wud at the clarty lyart howdie
> snirtlin by the ingle-neuk sae laithron and tozie,
> and gied the thowless quine a blaud wi his gully
> till she skreighed like a cut-luggit houlet and dang her tassie
> aff-loof at his unco doup, the glaikit tawpie.
> The skellum callan goaved at her fell drumlie:
> 'Ye tocherless wanchancie staumrel hizzie,
> ye groazlin, driddlin grumphie, ye awnie ferlie,
> deil gie your kyte curmurrings o scroggy crowdie,
> and bogles graizle ilka ramfeezl't hurdie
> till aa your snash is steekit, ye duddie hoodie!'

> —'Ach, I hae warlock-briefs, stegh the collieshangie!
> Aa your ier-oes sall gang sae muckle agley
> they'se turn to blitters and bauckie-birds, and in a brulzie
> they'se mak their joes o taeds, aa thrang and sonsie,
> snowkin in aidle whaur asks and clegs are grushie:
> yon is an ourie pliskie!'
>   Wha wan the tulzie?

The majority of my poems come somewhere between these four examples of the extremes of givenness and craft, and I would only add that in any ordinary poem, craft must lead to givenness at some point, and often the best parts of a poem are those lightning discoveries that fly into the mind, unplanned, from sources that may seem to be remote from the ongoing discourse of the poem. Doubtless everything in the universe has a cause, but in the heat of composition the causes, the concatenations, are like a chain that melts *into* being instead of out of it. And there are few things stranger than that. If we lose sight of the strangeness, we lose sight of poetry.

What I have been saying may apply with less force to poetic translation, of which I've done a good deal, since by its nature translation is a more conscious and deliberate art, and many initial or early decisions may have to be made on purely technical matters — whether the general structure or metre of the original poem is to be retained or imitated, whether rhyme is important, whether imperfections are to be improved or smoothed out, whether difficulties are to be left as difficulties, whether faithfulness or paraphrase seems the best approach, and so on, a series of reconnoitrings on the intellectual level before translation properly begins.

Yet even here it is important to let the poem float into or through your mind on a much more emotional and imaginative level, as a series and also a cluster of impressions which you must store up and eventually combine with the more consciously worked-out ideas you have about the status and nature of the language-transfer. I try to sum up the general appearance of the poem, its symmetry or ruggedness, length of line, close or open texture, curious or common vocabulary, even such basic things as shape and length. In the end one has to be faithful to these first shocks and splashes of impact, representing as they do one's first sudden glimpse of the foreign poet's world, the poet's foreign world, which one is about to enter. For example, when I began translating the Italian poet Montale, long before I really understood his often quite difficult poems, I watched his poetic 'world' stirring and revealing itself: a shimmer, a play of light on water and on crumbling buildings, a face glancing in a mirror, an accordion being played in the twilight. . . . Absorbing this atmosphere is a step in comprehension, and one grasps at this point not only the tone of the particular poem but the signature of the author's style, if he has an identifiable style. Of course the semantic plod, phrase by phrase and line by line, has to be undertaken too. But in so far as translation aspires to the state of poetry, as it ought to do, it must not keep its nose continuously to the grindstone, as the books on translation always assume; it should be able to look up suddenly and see the whole poem, like a cloud or a constellation or a lighted city, twinkling within its form, even slightly changing its form, somehow active rather than passive, pulsing, something alive, something beyond grammar and lexis though obviously containing these. I again, you will notice, refer to indefinable things and use simile and metaphor to indicate the power I believe these indefinables have. Perhaps the best test of this is when you have to translate into a sister language, say from

Scots into English or English into Scots. The temptation would be simply to find the nearest dictionary equivalent for individual words, keep the syntax and figures of speech just as they are, and produce as a result a version which looked something like the original out of focus. An example would be William Kean Seymour's translation of Burns into English. 'To a Haggis' begins:

> Good luck to your plump honest face . . .
> (Fair fa' your honest sonsie face . . .)

Something more thoroughgoing is required. The whole passage or poem has to be re-felt, re-seen, re-created, bringing out, if possible, the differences between the two languages as idiomatically used. I made this attempt in a Scottish version of a scene from Shakespeare's *Macbeth*, Act 1 Scene 5, when Lady Macbeth has received her husband's letter about the witches' prophecy that he will be king hereafter. Since her soliloquy (broken only by some words from the Messenger telling her Duncan is coming to the castle) is a fairly well-known passage, I thought I might read the Scottish version, to give some idea of this attempt at whole re-experiencing the speech in terms of a Scottish Lady Macbeth. I hope you will find it, therefore, both familiar and very unfamiliar.

> LM
> Aye, ye are Glamis, ye are Cawdor, and ae thing mair
> ye sall be, ae thing mair. But och, I traistna
> sic herts as yours: sic fouth o mense and cherity:
> ower-guid for that undeemous breenge! Ye'd hae
> the gloir, the gree, the tap-rung, but ye want
> the malefice the tap-rung taks. Ye'd hae
> the pooer, gin pooer cam by prayin; ye carena
> for fause pley, but ye'd win whit's no won fair.
> Yon thing ye'd hae, gret Glamis, that caas 'Dae this
> to hae me, or hae nane' — and then yon thing
> that ye mair fear nor hate to dae. Come ye,
> come ye, I maun unfauld, maun speak, maun whup
> wi this tongue's dauntonin aa thing that hinners
> your progress to thon perfit circumgowdie
> aa thae wanearthly warnishments and weird
> shaw as your croon to be.

> [*Enter a castle carle.*]
>
> Ye bring me news?

224

CC
This nicht ye hae a guest — the king.

LM
                                              Are ye wud?
Your maister's wi the king. I'm shair he kens
we maun mak preparations for the king?

CC
My leddy, it is true. Ye'll see erelang
oor laird hissel. The message cam fae him:
wan o his men run on aheid, tellt me it
aa pechin and forfochten.

LM
                                              Tak tent o'm,
his news is guid. [*Exit castle carle.*] —Pechin? The gorbie itsel
micht hauch and rauch to tell me Duncan's come
like a deid man in-through my castle-waas.
Cwa sichtless cailleachs o the warks o daith,
transtreind my sex, drive into ilka sinnow
carl-cruelty allutterly, mak thrang my bluid,
sneck up aa yetts whaur peety micht walk furth,
that nae saft chappin o wemen's nature shak
my fey and fiendly thocht, nor slaw my steps
fae thocht to fack! Cwa to thir breists o mine
you murder-fidgin spreits, and turn their milk
to venim and to verjuice, fae your sheddows
waukrife ower erd's evil! Cwa starnless nicht,
rowed i the smeek and reek o daurkest hell,
that my ain eident knife gang blinly in,
and heaven keekna through the skuggy thack
to cry 'Haud back!'

                                    (*Macbeth* 1:5, 16-55)

That translation is obviously not word for word, but it is
accurate in the sense that what is in Shakespeare is there,
including the difficulties, which have not been shirked or
fudged. But it has been done along the lines of what I have been
saying throughout this paper — the craft, in this case the
accuracy, is not the be-all and end-all but must keep itself open
to the lyrical oestrus of unexpected, 'given' solutions. 'As
kingfishers catch fire, dragonflies draw flame.' I hope that in
not answering the questions proposed in these lectures, I have
nevertheless set a perspective on them which you will find

suggestive and (in its *lucus a non lucendo* way) useful. I am very willing to investigate the poetry of other people, but as far as my own work is concerned, my slogan is: Poetry to the Poet — Criticism to the Critic!

One of a series of lectures by twelve poets at Manchester University. Each lecture was to be based on a questionnaire sent to each poet. They were asked to 'engage with the structural questions which your work in either contemporary English or in verse-translation necessarily involves' and to consider particularly the following areas of interest: 1. Sound-structure and metrics; 2. Syntax; 3. Lexis. EM's anti-lecture was given in the Poetry Centre, Manchester, 16 February 1989.

Poetry and translation

I see the translation of poetry as a gradually developing art which still has a long way to go. I see it as a study which requires a great deal of patience, and the avoidance of too easily reached or ready-made conclusions. It is a study which has special interest today, for various reasons. The twentieth century has seen an enormous amount of translation being done, and some well-known poets have been involved in this, as for example T. S. Eliot, Ezra Pound, W. H. Auden, Salvatore Quasimodo and Boris Pasternak. It is an age that has known more international contact than ever before, there has been a great deal of cultural cross-fertilisation, and there is a much quicker demand for information about poets in other countries than there used to be. There is therefore a constant and growing demand for translations of poetry, even from those who have a low opinion of the translator's art. But stimulus for translation, and for the theory of translation, has come from other sources too: from the scientific study of language, from comparative studies in literature and stylistics, anthropology and sociology. And most recently, in the last ten years or so, a stimulus has come from an unexpected quarter — from the theory and practice of machine translation, still of course in its earliest and most elementary stages. In this, there may well be grounds for thinking of translation as a science rather than an art, since the mathematical possibilities of what one can do in a given language, within its grammatical structure, idioms, sound-patterns and vocabulary, are very very large but not infinite. Every human translator knows, indeed, from going through lists of synonyms, or lists of rhymes, in his head, just how mechanical a part of his activity has to be. The question no one can answer yet is how much of the total translating activity is mechanical in this sense. Even if it does nothing else, machine translation has the great value of making us think very hard, for the first time, about what happens when material is translated.

The whole study of translation has therefore had a shake-up, and views on the translation of poetry are changing; they are not static, they are not so dogmatic as they used to be. It would be generally agreed that poetry is the most difficult kind of utterance to translate, but not everyone would go as far as the American poet Robert Frost who said that poetry is 'what gets lost in translation'. This rather cynical view is one that we may all have felt at some time, after reading some desperately bad version of a poet whom we have no other way of judging, and we may be tempted to say that if the translator gives us a good poem it can't be a close translation, and if it's a close translation it can't be a good poem. The man who knows the foreign text best is quite likely to be a scholar and no poet, and the poet who takes up translation is not likely to make use of the foreign poet for his own purposes and not be much concerned with fidelity. A famous example of such a poet in the English-speaking world is Ezra Pound, who has translated Latin, Chinese and Old English poetry from a very slender knowledge of these languages, making some absurd and elementary errors, but producing in the result what most people regard as good poetry. In a controversy some years ago over one of his translations, a version of the Old English poem 'The Seafarer', one writer called his version a piece of 'nonsense ... based on careless ignorance and misunderstanding', and another said it had 'deplorable marks of the literary fake'; and yet one of his defenders called it 'a magnificently effective modern English poem'. In the end no agreement was reached, and perhaps none could be reached, since the premisses of the arguments were never examined. To ask only for accuracy on the one hand, or only for liveliness on the other hand, is not going to take us very far in understanding what translation is. Ezra Pound is lively but inaccurate, and those who think this is how the thing should be done will argue that somehow the translator must produce the emotional 'lift' of poetry, and to get this he has to throw out ballast of various kinds, and the first thing to go, the least indispensable thing, will be literal accuracy. This view, or something like it, has been the main historical attitude among translators themselves (eg, Dryden and Pope, or the great Elizabethan translators) and it is quite clear that the main fault (and fatal fault) of close

228

translation especially by non-poets is always its flatness, its deadness, its uninterestingness: it fails to meet the very first demand, that it should make us want to go on reading it. What Ezra Pound does has at least the breath of life in it, and that for many readers is enough.

But although some poets are still using this method, writing what one might call adaptations rather than translations (eg, Robert Lowell's 'Imitations' as he calls them of Villon, Baudelaire, Rimbaud, Rilke, Montale, and Pasternak, or Donald Davie's adaption of Mickiewicz), the trend now is towards a greater accuracy, and towards a belief that the scholarly and creative powers can be combined. This might be exemplified by the translations of modern German poetry by Michael Hamburger and Christopher Middleton; also by the recent founding in London of a magazine called *Modern Poetry in Translation*. My own work in translation is sympathetic to this trend, and to a belief that a fairly high degree of fidelity is not incompatible with poetic effectiveness. I was interested to read some time ago (in *The Listener*, 1950) the remarks of a scholar of the Persian language, A. J. Arberry, on one of the best-known poems in English, the 'Rubaiyát of Omar Khayyám' which Edward FitzGerald freely translated from the Persian about a century ago. Arberry brought up the question of FitzGerald's infidelity to the original — a question which people had always said was irrelevant to the quality of the poem. 'Take for instance,' he said, 'the very famous lines:

> A book of verses underneath the bough,
> A jug of wine, a loaf of bread — and thou
> Beside me singing in the wilderness —
> O wilderness were paradise enow.

And [he said] the strictly literal version of that is:

> If there be available a loaf of the heart of wheat,
> And a two-pint flagon of wine, and a thigh of lamb,
> With little sweetheart seated in a desolation—
> That is a pleasure which is not the attainment of any sultan.

FitzGerald invented the book of verse, the bough, the singing, and the comparison of the wilderness with paradise; he rejected (no doubt as unpoetical) the thigh of lamb, which gives a very homely and amusing touch in the original, and jettisoned Omar's subtle contrast between the lovers' spot of desolation and the sultan's crowded splendour . . . Infidelity to the letter and the spirit could hardly be more complete.' And later he adds: 'I too love my FitzGerald. But what of the true Omar? He also has the right to be accurately understood and appreciated.'

This question, What of the true Omar? What of the true Mickiewicz, or Rimbaud, or József? is one that we increasingly want to ask, especially as the study of translation becomes more developed and intense. We do have a better idea now of what the difficulties and complexities are. The easiest things to reproduce are the intellectual part of the meaning, the arguments or statements, the action or story if any, but even in this we have to decide *how* clear we want the translation to be, since the process of trying to understand the foreign poem always tempts us to make the translation a little clearer or simpler than the original, and this may have a weakening effect. Then there are the associations of words to take care of, the connotative fringe or fuzz that so often surrounds words in poetry, the colour that words receive from their neighbours, the slightly new meaning in fact that accrues to a word in a strange and original placing; or a word may refer to a thing or an idea that doesn't exist, or doesn't quite exist, in our own language, in which case we have to decide whether to have an approximation, or a periphrasis, or the original word plus a footnote. There are no general rules, each case has to be decided on its merits within its context. Also, there's the whole range of sound-effects, the so-called music of poetry, both in individual words and phrases and in the overall structure of rhythm and rhyme. We have to decide how important the sound-effects are, how far it is worth straining other elements of the translation in order to reproduce them; and we have to remember that the less well we know a language the more we tend to read into its sound-effects. There may even be a visual or pictorial effect, as in 'concrete' poetry, or e. e. cummings, or perhaps in Chinese poetry. There is too the poet's characteristic grammar or syntax, which affects the movement of the poem (important in Milton, or Rilke), and behind that the grammar and syntax of his own language; we have to decide whether it is important that an attempt should be made to reproduce any alien effects, or at least to suggest them. And lastly, there is a tone or feeling in the poem which is almost indefinable but which has to be recreated somehow, and which is perhaps the most important thing of all.

I would say that to translate poetry well, you need not only great concentration, but a peculiar mixture of knowledge and feeling. It is a hard art, but it has its rewards.

New Hungarian Quarterly *VII:25 (Spring 1967)*
pp. 27-30

The translation of poetry

It is very difficult to describe what happens in translating poetry, which is perhaps why the theory of poetic translation has taken so long to develop, though much has been written about it. Judging from my own experience, I would say the process goes through several phases. First of all the aim is to sum up the general appearance of the poem: its symmetry or ruggedness, length of line, use of rhyme, close or open texture, curious or common vocabulary; to store this impressionistic information at the back of the mind, and then get down to reading the poem 'properly'. But again this early reading ought perhaps to be fairly impressionistic, since it is important to remain faithful to these shocks and splashes of impact, representing as they do one's first sudden glimpses of the foreign poet's world, the poet's foreign world, which one is about to enter. For example, long before one fully understands a difficult poem by Eugenio Montale, his world stirs and reveals itself: there is a shimmer, a play of light on water and on crumbling buildings, a face glancing in a mirror, an accordion being played in the twilight. . . . Absorbing this atmosphere is a step in comprehension, and one grasps at this point not only the tone of the particular poem but the signature of the author's style; one begins to sense his 'hand', his way of putting things. At this stage, too, most poems yield more unmistakable pleasure than they do at any later moment of understanding, and it is perhaps with great reluctance that the translator looks at them more closely. This, of course, is in line with Coleridge's remark that 'when no criticism is pretended to . . . the poetry gives most pleasure when only generally and not perfectly understood'. But then criticism must be pretended to; the poem must be treated as an object, degraded (if you like) to an intellectual puzzle or code, until the hard core of its meaning is laid bare with all external aids of dictionary and grammar, and the matter is gone through word by word and phrase by phrase from beginning to end. Once the poem has survived this ordeal, the translator should have at the front of his mind a grid or sequence (I might call it a pattern) of meanings, and somewhere at the back there is a flickering web (though again this might be called a pattern) of pictorial, acoustic, and generally atmospheric or sensuous impressions. The job is now to focus the grid of meaning onto the web of impressions; when they coincide, the translator feels he can really see the poem. This last process is a combination of rangefinding, piano-tuning, and sight-testing, it involves speaking the poem over many times, looking at it both quickly and long, and brooding over it in different moods. The point has been reached where translation can begin, and it is probably better to put off translating till this process has been completed, although possible words and phrases often suggest themselves right from the start. And something very curious happens here. Translating is searching for the English (or Scots) equivalent, but an equivalent of what? Not, apparently (and in this I can only appeal to what other translators may have experienced), the words of the foreign language so much as the words of *the poem itself*, which has attained some sort of non-verbal interlinguistic existence in the mind. When I used the metaphors of the hard grid and the moving web I tried to indicate something of this existence, but it is not easy to be at all precise about it. I can only assume that the brain has recorded a pattern of impulses which by their nature were only partly verbal in origin, and that in the process of organising the discrete impulses of the poem into an intelligible unit the brain transforms them into its own language, a language of nervous or electrical energy; and that the poem the brain stores, the deverbalised foreign poem, is in some way made accessible to the translator who proceeds to reverbalise it into his own tongue. Without desiring to be mystical, I believe there does seem to be some sense (and it is a sense unlocked not even by the devoted critic — only by the translator, who is committed to an *action* in a way that the critic is not) in which the poem exists independently of the language of its composition.

These remarks come from my own experience of translation, but perhaps further light could be thrown on them from Walter Benjamin's difficult but percipient essay 'The Task of the Translator' (1923), where he says:

> If there is such a thing as a language of truth, the
> tensionless and even silent depository of the ultimate
> truth which all thought strives for, then this language of
> truth is — the true language. And this very language . . .
> is concealed in concentrated fashion in translations. . . .
> It is the task of the translator to release in his own
> language that pure language which is under the spell of
> another, to liberate the language imprisoned in a work in
> his recreation of that work.
>
> (translated by Harry Zohn, in
> Illuminations, Collins/Fontana, 1973)

If there is any truth in this, as I believe there is, it means that the translator is involved in an almost paradoxical activity. Since he wishes to release the 'pure' or 'true' language that is hidden or imprisoned in the foreign poem, he has to bind himself like a slave to the obligations and restrictions and pains of this discovery. Yet on the other hand, he will not convey this released language into other people's minds unless he uses all the resources of his own tongue to give the impression of freedom and creative joy. A good translation, like a good original poem, has the effect of slightly altering the language it is written in, and I do not mean within the immediate context of the poem alone, but as regards the available potential of that language. This indeed is what languages do for one another, like strangers moved to embrace across a fence. Mencius say: 'Words near but signification far good words; the keeping simple but application extensive good principle.' A poem is written in a language, that is to say, in the idiosyncratic and cohesive shibboleth-system of a group of people, but a poem is also a poem, written in that third 'pure' language which Benjamin spoke of, and it may be that the most important part of translation in the end is to shake the shibboleths, not to intensify them. Here is another paradox; at times when states are anxious to establish their national identity and to prove the virtues of their language, they have very often in history indulged in widespread translation from other cultures; yet in the process of doing this they subtly alter their own language, joining it in many unforeseen ways to a greater continent of almost undefined and non-specific human expression. Whether one would take this as far as George Steiner does in *After Babel* when he calls translation 'a teleological imperative' in the search for an eventual linguistic unity (using the metaphor of Fall and Redemption, debabelisation being a long-term redemptive process), it is probably true that the translator must come to a very peculiar awareness of the way in which the quest for the most native will turn out to draw him into the most universal. He pauses in an astounding landscape, almost afraid to move. When he moves, he is no longer himself. And that is it.

from Scottish Review 2:5 *(Winter 1976) pp. 18-23*

Creator and critic: jekyll and hyde?

I put a question-mark after the title, because I didn't want to suggest quite so bluntly that the relationship between writer and critic is a monstrous one — that the critic is a monster, whereas the writer is a fairly reasonable fellow. But it is perhaps a good point to start from, that the popular idea of the critic and of the critic's function is far from complimentary, and even educated readers often express great scepticism about the usefulness of the critic. Last month there was a little conference in Glasgow on critics and criticism (in the Third Eye Centre); the *Glasgow Herald* published an article for the occasion, by Christopher Small, their literary editor and a noted drama critic. Christopher Small gave this picture of the critic as people see him (and it's a good deal more Hyde than Jekyll): 'Nobody likes a critic; nobody really has any use for such a person. The popular notion of him . . . is of a creature with a long, sharp nose, for sniffing out faults, a barbed and usually double tongue, hands without palms (never used for clapping) but long and bloodstained talons; a cold and slug-gish bloodstream, and a permanent expression of sour distaste.' Nor is Christopher Small alone in this opinion. In Beckett's play *Waiting for Godot*, when the two tramps are indulging in a bout of exchanging insults, they reach their crescendo as follows: 'Moron! Vermin! Abortion! Crablouse! Sewer-rat! Curate! Cretin! Crritic!'

So who would want to be a critic? Well, as we shall see, there are perhaps special reasons for the dislike of critics in the late twentieth century, but it is worth remembering that literary criticism as we use the term is a relatively recent development, from (shall we say) the late seventeenth century at the earliest. This means that Chaucer, Spenser, Shakespeare and Milton produced their works, major works by any reckoning, without the benefit or without the incubus of literary criticism breath-

236

ing down their necks. And I've seen this put forward as a great argument against critics. If Shakespeare and Milton didn't need critics, why should Joe Bloggs need a critic in 1979, if he's trying to write poetry or a novel or whatever? But this argument forgets the fact that writers in the later Middle Ages and the Renascence were educated in grammar and rhetoric and had studied the devices of style and eloquence and usually knew something about how the classical authors (at least) had attained their effects. So that even if Shakespeare wrote with great freedom in an unclassical way, he shows again and again an awareness of rhetoric and uses rhetoric as far as he needs it — often ironically, as if he was acting as his own literary critic. From *Love's Labour's Lost* and *A Midsummer Night's Dream* to *Hamlet* and *The Tempest*, you get a real sense of Shakespeare's *critical* intelligence, playing over matters of style and presentation, the relation of art to life, the nature of the poet and his inspiration. But if we say that criticism proper doesn't begin till you come to Dryden and Pope, it is a notable fact that most of our best critics have also been creative writers: Dryden, Johnson, Coleridge, Arnold, Eliot, Pound. And even below that rank of critic, Pope, Wordsworth, Shelley, Keats and Yeats have all contributed a great deal to both criticism and creative writing. None of these writers evidently felt it was beneath him, or somehow going really against the grain, to write critical prose (or critical verse as in the case of Pope). Well, perhaps the best critic is a minor poet, someone who is a good enough poet to know something about creative matters from the inside but not so committed to poetry as to make that his main work — eg, Dr Johnson, Coleridge, Arnold could be regarded as minor poets but major critics. T. S. Eliot, however, doesn't fit this pattern, since his creative and his critical work are of about equal importance, and both have been very influential. But in this he is possibly the exception that proves the rule. It's what has happened *since* Eliot's time that has changed the whole picture.

This is where Beckett's crrritic! begins to rear his ugly head. What has happened is that there has emerged a whole new race of professional literary critics and theorists, men like F. R. Leavis and Northrop Frye who are not themselves creative writers but whose entire job is to stimulate critical discussion or to formulate a theory of literature. It may be that in doing this, in carrying out these critical functions, they do themselves evince some kind of creative gift (the opposite of Shakespeare). F. R. Leavis has a nice line in critical invective. He had such an irritable personality, and stored up in himself so much bile and venom, that when the right target came along he was able to attack the target with some eloquence and style. Here is how he attacks the novelist C. P. Snow (lecture *Two Cultures?*, 1962): 'Snow is, of course, a — no, I can't say that; he isn't; Snow thinks of himself as a novelist. I don't want to discuss that aspect of him, but I can't avoid saying something. The widespread belief that he is a distinguished novelist (and that it should be widespread is significant of the conditions that produced him) has certainly its part in the success with which he has got himself accepted as a mind. The seriousness with which he takes himself as a novelist is complete — if seriousness can be so ineffably blank, so unaware. Explaining why he should have cut short a brilliant career (we are to understand) as a scientist, he tells us that it had always been his vocation to be a writer. . . . Confidence so astonishingly enjoyed might politely be called memorable — if one could imagine the memory of Snow the novelist long persisting; but it won't, it can't, in spite of the British Council's brochure on him (he is a British Council classic). I say "astonishingly enjoyed", for as a novelist he doesn't exist; he doesn't begin to exist. He can't be said to know what a novel is. . . . I am trying to remember where I heard (can I have dreamed it?) that they are composed for him by an electronic brain called Charlie, into which the instructions are fed in the form of the chapter-headings.'

In a very different way, Northrop Frye shows something creative in his habit of playing with the reader, teasing and provoking him, putting forward apparently absurd, entertaining, yet really very pointed suggestions in order to shake up the reader's sluggish mind and make him think along new lines. Eg, in his famous book *Anatomy of Criticism* (1957) he tries to stop us from thinking in terms of value-judgements, he's very very sceptical about value-judgements because he argues they are always based on the purely transitory values of the reader's class or society or beliefs. But he makes this point interesting, makes you think about it, by inviting you to try out an exercise: pick three big names at random, he says, work out the eight possible combinations of promotion and demotion, and defend each class in turn. Eg if the names are Shakespeare, Milton and Shelley, it might go like this:

'1. Demoting Shelley, on the ground that he is immature in technique and profundity of thought compared to the others.

2. Demoting Milton, on the ground that his religious obscurantism and heavy doctrinal content impair the spontaneity of his utterance.

3. Demoting Shakespeare, on the ground that his detachment from ideas makes his dramas a reflection of life rather than a creative attempt to improve it.

4. Promoting Shakespeare, on the ground that he preserves an integrity of poetic vision which in the others is obfuscated by didacticism.

5. Promoting Milton, on the ground that his penetration of the highest mysteries of faith raises him above Shakespeare's unvarying worldliness and Shelley's callousness.

6. Promoting Shelley, on the ground that his love of freedom speaks to the heart of modern man more immediately than poets who accepted outworn social or religious values.

7. Promoting all three (for this a special style, which we may call the peroration style, should be used).

8. Demoting all three, on the ground of the untidiness of the English genius when examined by French or Classical or Chinese standards.'

If you want to push this line of thought even further (links between critical and creative), there is the curious fact that the opening poem in *The Oxford Book of Modern Verse*, 'Mona Lisa', by Walter Pater, is not a poem at all but an extract from a critical essay on Leonardo da Vinci published by Pater seventy years before and rearranged in lines of verse by the editor of the anthology, W. B. Yeats:

> She is older than the rocks among which she sits;
> Like the Vampire,
> She has been dead many times,
> And learned the secrets of the grave;
> And has been a diver in deep seas,
> And keeps their fallen day about her;
> And trafficked for strange webs with Eastern merchants;
> And, as Leda,
> Was the mother of Helen of Troy,
> And, as St Anne,

Was the mother of Mary;
And all this has been to her but as the sound of lyres and flutes,
And lives
Only in the delicacy
With which it has moulded the changing lineaments,
And tinged the eyelids and the hands.

Is that poetry, or criticism? Pater was a critic, not a poet —
or was he? Yeats, as both poet and critic, wanted to suggest
that Pater foreshadowed something of the modern poetic
philosophy of flux as demonstrated by Pound and Eliot, and
made Pater 'modern' by reprinting his prose as *vers libre*. But
he was also calling attention to the formal or structural
elements which were actually there and which might seem to
be nearer poetry than prose, eg the repeated 'And'-phrases
which Yeats rightly used to begin most of the lines with. It's
worth mentioning, too, that Yeats made one alteration to the
original, for the sake of rhythmic and syntactic parallelism,
when he added 'Was' before 'the mother of Mary'.

So far, we seem to be saying that there isn't such a
diametrical opposition between the creative and the critical as
is commonly supposed. It would still be possible to argue, on
the Jekyll and Hyde analogy, that in the case of Coleridge and
Matthew Arnold, the poet (Jekyll) was gradually destroyed by
the critic (Hyde), simply because criticism came to exert so
much fascination for these two writers. We don't want to lose
Coleridge and Arnold as critics, but we wish they could have
written more poetry. If they could write as well as they did in
'The Ancient Mariner' and 'Sohrab and Rustum', what would
they not have gone on to do in poetry if they hadn't followed
the fatal will-o-the-wisp of criticism? Well, the truth is of
course that we don't know; perhaps they had written all the
poetry they ever could have written; perhaps we should be
glad that they were able to turn to a different kind of writing,
in prose, writing about ideas, and writing about them in ways
that are still interesting today.

And sometimes in fact when a writer is both creative and
critical you can get the sense that this is not from a rather
meagre choice between the two alternatives but that it comes
from superabundant energy, eg the prefaces Bernard Shaw
wrote for his plays and the prefaces Henry James wrote for his
novels. These prefaces are so important to both writers that

they virtually become an art form in themselves, they're equally critical and creative.

The opposite of this is also found: some writers who have a high reputation for their creative work would lose a lot of that reputation if you judged them by their critical work. Two major names in modern American poetry are Wallace Stevens and William Carlos Williams. They both wrote literary criticism as well as poetry, but in both cases it's disappointing. Stevens as a critic, to put it bluntly, is a pompous windbag, with all the ideas at second hand; and Williams, though not quite so bad, is certainly disappointingly thin and unpersuasive. In both men, it's a sort of second-rate quality of mind that seems to show itself. In a critic like T. S. Eliot — well, Eliot can at times be silly, but even when he's silly he's silly in an interesting way. With Stevens and Williams, you begin to wonder if you were right about the *poetry*, in judging it as of major quality. This would be unfair, since there's no *necessary* correlation between being a convincing critic and being a convincing poet. But there is a rather nice problem here, about what sort of mind a creative writer has or should have.

Duke Theseus, in a famous passage in *A Midsummer Night's Dream*, gives one answer:

> The lunatic, the lover, and the poet,
> Are of imagination all compact:
> One sees more devils than vast hell can hold,
> That is, the madman; the lover, all as frantic,
> Sees Helen's beauty in a brow of Egypt;
> The poet's eye, in a fine frenzy rolling,
> Doth glance from heaven to earth, from earth to heaven;
> And, as imagination bodies forth
> The forms of things unknown, the poet's pen
> Turns them to shapes, and gives to airy nothing
> A local habitation and a name.

A fine frenzy only? Imagination and instinct against intellect? The poet carried away by fantasies? No doubt the imagination is primary, and is active in a mysteriously creative way, dealing with 'things unknown', yet at the same time being part of a forming, bodying-forth process which then the writing hand has to complete by anchoring these floating forms as recognisable shapes within a human ambience. The intellectual or critical activity involved in this may be very light in a short lyric or song, or it may be a mammoth effort of concentration lasting several years as in Milton's *Paradise Lost*. The 'poet's pen', though on one level quite literal, is also a way of saying 'craftsmanship', and the craftsman, the final maker or shaper, must at least have mind enough to persuade nothing to become something, and nowhere somewhere.

To look at it from a more personal point of view: if I try to ask myself the answers to some of these questions which have been raised, since I've written both poems and critical essays, and also since my job is teaching literature, which involves a lot of close reading of literary texts, I can perhaps come up with some clues and suggestions, but of course this is only one man's view, and I'm not saying that all writers work in the same way. When I was at school I read a great deal, but it was completely uncritical. I read and enjoyed some authors who would be regarded as classics, like Dickens and Tennyson and Keats; I read a lot of books which might or might not be regarded as good literature but which I liked because they were exciting or entertaining stories, by authors like G. A. Henty, Jules Verne, Jack London, Edgar Rice Burroughs, Kipling, P. G. Wodehouse. But further down on the slippery slope I also read, usually in secret under the bedclothes, a great many cheap magazines, often American, thrillers and detective stories, horror stories, science fiction, whatever came to hand, passed round at school or otherwise obtained without parental approval. It seems to me now that this was no bad thing, despite the fact that some of the material I read had no literary value, or very little (one must remember Northrop Frye's cautionary exercise in value-judgements). My parents were angry when they discovered any of this material: I remember on one occasion, when I was about twelve or thirteen, my father found some copies of the lurid-covered American pulp magazine *Amazing Stories* and threw them on the fire (coal fire in those days). I can understand that he was trying to protect values. Yet — although I couldn't express it at the time — there must have been something that was important to me in this wide range of material from good to bad — something that fed my imagination — and I was already beginning to write, at school, stories, poems, essays. The idea of critical reading, reading selectively, making discriminations, analysing texts, only came later, when I went to university and took English and other languages, French and Russian. I mention the other languages because I think the first time when I had a sense of things being really opened out through critical analysis was not in English but in the first-year French class: we had to do Racine, and the prescribed play was *Andromaque*; we went through this play in seminar in detail, almost line by line; it should have been boring but it wasn't, in fact it was a kind of revelation, for me anyway, it was a new way of writing, apparently very stiff, full of conventional images and phrases, with very little action, but the real emotional power behind the conventions came across to me, and I found I had learned that there were different, unexpected ways of producing literary effects: Racine wasn't at all like Shakespeare but he too could write strong plays. This didn't directly affect my own writing, but it sharpened my feeling for language and style, made me think more about them, and that was valuable.

What I seem to be saying then is that although I was never tempted to 'become a critic' at the expense of creative writing, I did learn from criticism and was interested in it. But this interest came on top of the strong imaginative uncritical course of my schooldays reading, and that may be the more important thing.

But let's try to go a little deeper. What *is* a poem, is a poem itself an act of criticism, criticism of poetry or of something in life itself? Matthew Arnold said that literature was no use unless it was somehow a 'criticism of life', that's the phrase he keeps using. And a more recent American critic, Harold Bloom, argues that every poet who is trying to establish himself is engaged in a sort of life-or-death struggle with his predecessors, every poet is in a sense rewriting, redirecting the course of poetry. As an example, Thomas Carew's elegy on John Donne — itself a splendid piece of literary criticism in verse — argues that Donne too was critically altering the course of Elizabethan poetry:

> The Muses garden with Pedantique weedes
> O'rspred, was purg'd by thee; The lazie seeds
> Of servile imitation throwne away;
> And fresh invention planted, Thou didst pay
> The debts of our penurious bankrupt age . . .
> Since to the awe of thy imperious wit

Our stubborne language bends, made only fit
With her tough-thick-rib'd hoopes to gird about
Thy Giant phansie, which had prov'd too stout
For their soft melting Phrases.

The purging, the throwing, the planting, the paying, the bending, the girding all keep a vigorous enactment of the argument going forward, and the 'tough-thick-rib'd hoopes' represent in their sound, in their grammar, and in their metaphor both the potential of the language and Donne's realisation of that potential, while still announcing, Yes, and this is Thomas Carew telling you all that!

Well, that's poetry as a criticism of poetry; but what about poetry as a criticism of life? Arnold's idea has not found favour with everyone, unless you take it in a very broad and general sense. Arnold was really placing an enormous burden on poets; their job was to keep a vigorous current of moral ideas moving through poetry, so that poetry would help people how to live — it takes over, to a large extent, what religion had done in the past. Even if we don't go along with this high and serious aim for poetry, after all, why should a poem not simply celebrate life, instead of criticising it?, still, I think he is right up to a point: there is some kind of critical activity going on when you write a poem (as I suggested earlier), and the question is, what this critical activity is applied to? Is it life, or ideas, or the subject of the poem, or simply the words of the poem as it gradually evolves? It's surprisingly difficult to answer these questions. When you're writing a poem you're in a very unusual, intense state of mind, you're hardly aware of your surroundings except the immediate area of chair/table/paper etc, and once you step outside of this experience and try to look back at it and describe it later from outside, it resists analysis. All I can say is that writing a poem is a constant succession of little acts of choice between many alternatives, you have to try to find the right word, the right line-length, the right moment at which to move from one line to the next, the images that best bring out the ideas, the right moment at which either to slow down towards the end or to actually stop — and knowing when the poem is finished is the hardest thing of all. These decisions take place in a strange mixture of excitement and pleasure and acute anxiety. Once you start a poem you take on a responsibility and you hate to give it up. And this is true even though no one need ever know that you started a poem and couldn't finish it. The responsibility is an inner one, to yourself, and a novelist or a playwright feels the same thing. I think you could well call this activity a critical activity, since you're trying to judge exactly how to get the thing right, but it's obviously not the same kind of criticism as would come from a critic or a reviewer or a teacher or lecturer looking through the completed poem.

Because of the nature of this process, it is difficult to give, and then comment on, examples. There is not much you can usefully say about your own poems. But in some instances there are certainly pointers you can give. In my poem 'Resurrections', written 16-18 January 1976, I knew that I had what might have been regarded as a 'problem': how to move, but within a unity, from the public theme of the death of the Chinese Prime Minister, Chou En-lai, to the private theme of the end of a love-affair; I could not now, even if I wanted to, recall the steps towards the solution, yet it is obvious that they involved decisions about the use of place-names and personal names, the status of the register of a phrase like 'haunt off', the fairly tight-packed range of reference which might or might not be familiar to the reader:

> None of your jade suits, none of your gold-sewn princes!—
> green-shelled spoonfuls of dust like coelacanths in tombs.
> I want to be born again. Keep Tollund peat
> for roses, boots, blazes. Men of Han, princesses,
> yellowing demons and mummies, casket-crowders,
> haunt off! There's never armour made
> I'd pray to be preserved in. Don't preserve me!
> Yesterday great Chou's ashes flew
> in the wind over plain and river,
> never resting or rusting, nothing
> for an urn. Unknown he blows
> like seed, is seed,
> a little cinnamon of the millennium.
> Let them roll away the black diorite
> where millions shuffle past a husk.
> What? Christ too like Chou could not be found.
> In this strange January spring,
> so mild the blackbirds go mad
> singing in the morning above Anniesland,
> I woke, I heard them, no one at my side,
> but thought of you with the exhilaration

of that rising song where like them I scatter
and swoop in rings over the half-dark earth,
caught up in another life.

I think the problems or questions which that poem raised
while I was writing it would have been raised whether or not I
was critic as well as poet or had a job lecturing on literature.
Every writer comes up against such problems. But there
probably are some poems which I wouldn't have written if I
hadn't had some interest in criticism. In one of them, the title
itself is a giveaway: 'What is "Paradise Lost" *really* about?'
(1955):

> The bard has fired his bullet at the fox.
> The dilatory fox is full of duck.
> The gun takes brush and breakfast, quack and cluck.
> Foxes in satchels are sequestered flocks.
>
> The critic shakes the satchel with a cry.
> 'Your fur is feathers! You have bagged a bird!'
> The simple bard is bolshy when he's stirred.
> 'I felled a fox, and foxes cannot fly.'
>
> Deep in the duck the maggot faintly mauls.
> Viruses mill within the maggot's vein.
> The photomicrograph shows fields of grain.
> Down in these fields the fox's double falls.
>
> Critics can pant across this paradox.
> Critics can call the bard a blunderbuss.
> Bards who have shot their shout are boisterous.
> Bards have the fox's body in a box.

Although the poem does target some Miltonic criticism, as
well as the area of general criticism invaded by Wimsatt and
Beardsley under the banner of the so-called Intentional
Fallacy, the imagery retains sufficient ambiguity to make the
poem (I hoped) interesting to critics (even of the targeted
persuasions) while not putting off readers of poetry.

To escape the taint, if it is a taint, of writing a 'critic's poem',
while at the same time evincing interpretative literary interests,
perhaps the best method is to get down to cases, to write
concretely, from a position of knowledge and warmth, about
writers who have very distinctive qualities, and to allow the

concentrating power of poetry to say something that critical prose might not reach. I wrote a poem 'To Hugh MacDiarmid' in July 1966 which comes into this category:

> That the poet 'does not number the streaks of the tulip'
> you saw was a fallacy, yet when paradoxical Imlac
> claimed that 'to a poet nothing can be useless'
> you concurred, and out of scraps of art and life and knowledge
> you assembled that crackling auroral panorama
> that sits on your Scotland like a curly comb
> or a grinning watergaw thrown to meteorology,
> your bone to the dogs of the ages. So much to be numbered!—
> 'the red huckleberry, the sand cherry, and the nettle tree,
> the red pine and the black ash, the white grape and the yellow
> violet,
> which might have withered else in dry seasons.'
> To be forgotten is driest. Names rain things up.
> You took that hazard of naming, letting the drops
> fall on the desert of uninterest of those with 'a taste
> for Frontiniac' but not for the glass of Esk water
> or the inhuman fountain of stone that pours in a marble ear
> its endless formless message where 'schiebt ein Krug sich ein,
> so scheint es ihr, dass du sie unterbrichst.'
> And yet you let the jug of clay dip in the flow.
> A dead child or a busker or a bobbin-winder
> cries through the raised beaches and the disinterested
> eternity of the foraminifera.
> Somewhere in astonishment you would set man,
> short-range or long-range confrontation or kinship
> with all the world he changes as it changes him,
> the greater changes he grows into making now,
> the greatest like faint stars in the drift of smoke of thought.
> — Midges in cigarette-smoke! That's what you know,
> where it comes from, turning a page or writing one
> in your clear hand still, sitting by a cottage
> in a small country.

The quotations from Johnson, Thoreau, Wordsworth, and Rilke offer a tribute to MacDiarmid's own quoting habits, but an underlying consistency of imagery, carrying the reader like a travelling walkway from point to point, is me rather than MacDiarmid. The hope was therefore that it could be clearly seen as a 'Morgan poem' and not merely as a parodic acknowledgement. In August of the same year I found I was writing what was virtually a companion piece to the Mac-

Diarmid poem, though in a very different style. 'To Ian Hamilton Finlay' presents another Scottish poet/artist who despite obvious differences shared MacDiarmid's delight in moving from local to international and back, as I see links between the 'midges in cigarette-smoke' and the 'little bonfires in cold mist'. And again, although the clean-cut, chiselled construction of the poem made its tribute to Finlay's classicism (as opposed to the spread of MacDiarmid), the central 'Dover Beach' passage has a certain kind of resonance, romantic perhaps? expressionist perhaps? which is me and not Finlay:

> Maker of boats,
> earthships,
> the white cradle
> with its patchwork quilt,
> toys of wood
> painted bright as
> the zebra's muzic
> in your carousel,
> patiently cut
> space cleanly!
> There's dark earth
> underneath, not far
> the North Sea,
> a beach goes out
> greyer than Dover's
> for ignorant armies.
> Scotland is
> the little bonfires
> in cold mist,
> with stubbornness,
> the woman knits
> late by a window,
> a man repairing
> nets, a man carv-
> ing steady glass,
> hears the world,
> bends to his work.
> You give the pleasure
> of made things,
> the construction holds
> like a net, or it
> unfolds in waves
> a certain measure,
> of affection.

Native, familiar as
apples, tugs,
girls, lettres from
your moulin,
but
drinking tea
you set for Albers
his saucer of milk.

Perhaps these two poems do bring the two sides of critical and creative together. But I wouldn't be true to the facts if I didn't also say that there often is tension or clash between poet and critic or poet and teacher, if you are engaged in both activities.

I think that poetry and criticism are by no means always at loggerheads. When Keats said that poetry should come as naturally as the leaves to a tree, he really means that the finished poem should seem to the reader to have a satisfying organic naturalness about it; but his own manuscripts bear witness to the fact that Keats worked on his poems as laboriously as any other poet. In the same way, I think that criticism applied by a critic to a finished poem should not be destructive of the poem, though I know some people feel that it is destructive. Well, it may be in some cases; but good criticism should bring out and enhance the good qualities in a poem and a good poem will stand up to critical analysis, it's really quite a tough creature. Writers are wary of professional critics, because they can be wrong, or prejudiced, or imperceptive, and they can hold back a writer's reputation, even simply by neglect. But as far as the main body of the best criticism is concerned, I've tried to suggest that creative writer and critic are often closer than we think, and in fact are often to be found in the same person.

lecture given at Edinburgh University to first-
year English students, 16 November 1979

From Glasgow to Saturn

My writing has tended to penetrate a number of widely differing areas of experience rather than cultivate any one of them as central, though the Glasgow subject-matter seems to be what I most regularly return to. I was born in Glasgow and have lived most of my life there, and whatever image the city has to the outside world, to me it underlies and pervades my feeling at a deep level of identification and sympathy. At the moment it is in desperate throes of renewal, and some of the poems in this collection comment on the changes that are taking place.

Another group of poems is perhaps best described as science fiction, though I would regard these as natural extensions of the imagination in an age of science. I do not share what is sometimes called the current disillusion with science and technology. I count myself lucky to have lived at a time of discoveries of such far-reaching potential as space travel must be. The poet, I think, is entitled to set up his camp on other worlds than this, and to bring back what he can in the way of human relevance.

The present volume opens with a fair number of short lyrics and songs, and I have found myself taking increasing pleasure from lyrical expression and from attempts to explore the strength of lightness. There are of course occasions when something very different is required, as in the 'Glasgow Sonnets', which asked for density and rigid form. But I have often been struck in recent years by the extraordinary resilience of the lyric mode, and I have no doubt that somewhere in the background are the achievements of popular song, whether pop or folk or their various admixtures, which in the last decade have blown the electric horns of elfland over poetry as well as life. I would certainly want to pay tribute to the impact this music has had on me.

EM's collection From Glasgow to Saturn *(Cheadle: Carcanet Press) was a Poetry Book Society Choice in 1973. EM was asked for some notes on the volume which were printed in the* PBS Bulletin *77 (Summer 1973) p.[1]; and reprinted in* Poetry Book Society: the first twenty-five years, *edited by Eric W. White (London: Poetry Book Society, 1979), p. 51.*

'For bonfires ii' and 'Glasgow sonnet i'

Observation is important in poetry. A poet likes to keep his eyes open — and his ears. And, indeed, he wants to keep all his senses sharp and active, since poetry reflects the whole of human experience, including the most physical. On the other hand, the actual physical observation is not everything. A poet must have imagination, and part of his job is to be able to visualise, to see with his inward eye, things that he may not himself have seen, or at least not exactly as he wants to imagine them. He can describe things in his poetry either from direct observation or from imagination, and — strange as it may seem — the reader of the poem may not be able to tell the difference. But, of course, the imagination itself has to work on the poet's stored-up memories of a myriad impressions, images, pictures, which come from experience.

'For Bonfires ii' is an imagined scene overall, but built up from pieces of direct observation. The city of Glasgow, where I live, underwent great changes in the 1960s, when there was a massive demolition of slum property. I don't have a car, so I walk about the city quite a lot, and I would often stop to watch, for a minute or two, how the men on the demolition sites went about their work. When they worked behind hoardings, the contractors thoughtfully cut little windows in the hoardings because they knew watching men at work was a favourite urban hobby. The details in the poem — like the yellow helmets and the cigarette stub, the sunshine 'filtered' through half-demolished roofs or walls, the 'rags of wallpaper roses', the man throwing the rafter — are things seen, though not necessarily all on the same occasion. They are brought together in the fusing act of writing the poem.

'Glasgow Sonnet i' is even more mixed, in that it uses direct observation, imagination, and a reference to a Shelter housing report. As far as observation is concerned, writers who live in

large cities and use urban material develop — instinctively! —
a very quick, unstudied, unprying, oblique, yet intense and
unforgetful way of looking at people and things: it's like using
a very good silent automatic camera disguised as a pair of eyes.
To look too long at anyone is dangerous (in Glasgow at any
rate — I don't know about other places), and so the rapid
flickering scan is characteristic of the urban poet. The many
minute impressions are a shorthand which he can expand later
within the (slightly) less nervous world of the poem.

*these comments appeared in the schools
anthology,* Words 3, *edited by Geoffrey
Summerfield and Richard Andrews (London:
Cassell, 1983), p. 98*

'The Loch Ness monster's song',
'The first men on Mercury',
'Off course' and 'Flakes'

I began writing at school, when I was about ten or eleven, and produced not only poems but lots of long stories and essays, many of them very imaginative. I loved words — used to collect lists of words that appealed to me. And the sounds of words, as well as their meaning, made a strong impact. My poetry is of different kinds. Because of my city background — and I like cities of all sorts and sizes! — I have many poems of city life, often realistic, down-to-earth, hard-hitting, sometimes humorous, and generally about Glasgow. But the fascination of words themselves, and the interest I have in music and sound-effects, also led me to a more experimental kind of poetry, a poetry where the voice really has to be heard. Even if this poetry is printed in books, it is asking and tempting you to speak it aloud, to try out its sound, to see whether it means more when you hear it than when you read it silently. Some of these poems could be called 'performance poems', and in a sense there is nothing new about this, since from the earliest times poets have recited their work in public and been rewarded and applauded (or no doubt sometimes booed!) by a live audience.

'The Loch Ness Monster's Song' is an example of a performance piece. It absolutely demands to be read aloud, and the way the lines are set out, the spelling, the punctuation are all devised — even if it might not seem so at first glance — to help the performance. It needs a bit of practice, but it can be done, and although I have recorded the poem myself on tape, I would not want to say that there is only one way of reading it. Anyone can have a go — and enjoy it. Whether the Loch Ness Monster really exists or not — there is no clinching evidence — I imagine the creature coming to the surface of the water, looking round at the world, expressing his or her views, and sinking back into the loch at the end. I wanted to have a mixture of the bubbling, gurgling, plopping sounds of water and the deep gruff throaty sounds that a large aquatic monster might be expected to make. How much meaning comes through the sounds? A little? I leave that to you!

One of my long-standing interests has been science fiction. I enjoy writing science-fiction poems, and try to give them some 'point', so that they are not merely fantastic. In 'The First Men on Mercury', I imagine the first successful Earth expedition to the planet Mercury, and an attempt at conversation between the leader of the expedition and the first Mercurian who comes up to see what has happened. Again, to get the full effect of this poem, you ought to try reading it aloud, or of course it can be done with two voices. And the poem is not just about communication — I am sure you will find other themes and meanings. Earthman conquers the universe — or does he?

'Off Course' is one of a number of 'spacepoems' I wrote about the early rockets which were sent up by Russia and America. This one is about a disastrous moon voyage (imaginary, but related to some of the actual disasters which did take place) where the rocket goes off course and explodes, all the men inside being killed. The moment of crisis is shown by the indenting of the last seven lines: the poem itself is literally driven 'off course'. The scrambled images of the last part are meant to act out the chaotic scene of the rocket breaking up.

I suppose 'Flakes', too, is about voyages to the moon, but it is a sort of nursery rhyme as well. The unexpected images, and the jumps in the story, are like some of the effects in folk-poetry, and I liked the idea of using such techniques to talk about something as modern and scientific as a moonwalk.

from Meet and Write: A teaching anthology of contemporary poetry, *edited by Sandy and Alan Brownjohn (London: Hodder & Stoughton, 1987), pp. 37-38*

J

Concrete poetry

I became interested in concrete poetry as a means of producing economically and arrestingly certain effects which would not otherwise be possible. These effects I still consider to be within the realm of poetry, though the use made of graphic space, and the exaggeration of such visual or sonic gestalts as exist in embryo in all poems, are clearly beginning to draw the poem over into other areas — painting, sculpture, advertising, music. In my own work I don't feel that the boundary into these other areas is crossed, because I have a strong sense of solidarity with words as parts of a semantically charged flux, and in so far as I isolate or distort them I do this in obedience to imaginative commands which come through the medium of language and are not disruptive of it. This means that each of my poems has a 'point' and is not just an object of contemplation, though it is also that. I like to hear the semantic mainsheets whip and crack, but not snap. I like to extend the possibilities of humour, wit, and satire through concrete techniques and although this involves 'play', whether of words, letters, or punctuation, it must be an imaginative and therefore fundamentally serious kind of play.

I have always been interested in the plastic arts as well as in poetry. I don't find difficulty in accepting visual as well as aural impacts as legitimate targets for a poet. In all poetry which is written down or printed, a part of the effect is bound to be visual. Line-length, open or close texture, long or short words, light or heavy punctuation, use of capitals, exclamation marks, rhyme — all these produce characteristic variations of effect and induce different reactions in the viewer even before the viewer becomes in the strict sense a reader. A page of Milton's blank verse with its bristling and serried paragraphs looks quite different from a page of Wordsworth's, clear, open, light, loose, untormented. The phrasal dashes in Allen Ginsberg's long free verse lines are like white horses breaking the powerful under-swell of a poetry of big movement. The delicate cat-paw placing of words in poems by William Carlos Williams, Zukofsky, Creeley, and Ronald Johnson is halfway between being a guide to the ear and a pleasure to the eye. A more committedly visual poetry like concrete is only emphasising and developing an already existing visual component of aesthetic effect. Concrete poems are therefore not in opposition to the spirit of poetry unless we demand that poetry should be able to be read aloud, or unless they move so far into the purely graphic or the mathematical that they are no longer making their appeal through language as such. Abstract painting can often satisfy, but 'abstract poetry' can only exist in inverted commas. In poetry you get the oyster as well as the pearl, and the pursuit of purity is self-defeating. The best visual or concrete poems, as it seems to me, acknowledge this fact inversely; their anatomy may be rigid and exoskeletal, but there is something living and provocative inside.

EM was asked to contribute to the exhibition Between Poetry and Painting *at the ICA in 1965. This statement, dated July 1965, on concrete poetry was printed in the catalogue, pp. 69-71.*

Notes on simulated computer poems

Although I am interested in real computer poetry (and art and music), my special concern in these poems has been to take an ironic but not antipathetic look at the relations that will exist between computer creativity and human creativity, the challenge to the second from the first, the probability of a new approach to at least some aspects of poetry, even a deliberate emulation of the so-called blunders or digressions which at times arise (one would say) creatively within a computer context (eg there is a computer translation of Pasternak's poem 'Hops' which is not even idiomatic English but is on several counts nearer 'poetry' than the published translation by Max Hayward, and this suggests some quite far-reaching questions). My use of irony or comedy in most of these pieces was conceived as the best way of drawing attention to some of the human/electronic relationships which will have to be investigated.

'The Computer's First Christmas Card' makes use of an obvious formal grid in each line (two words each having consonant-vowel-double-consonant-y) and at the same time suggests that the machine is scanning a semantic as well as formal 'store' (all the words relating somehow to the context of Christmas cheer). It is a goal-seeking poem which misses its goal finally but in the process discovers (as a machine might) an acceptable equivalent (chrysanthemum as emblematic good-luck flower, also as a flower one might buy or give at Christmas-time).

'The Computer's Second Christmas Card' and 'The Computer's First Birthday Card' are variations on the basic approach described above. Both are goal-seeking. The first has to find the carol *Good King Wenceslas*, fails to do so because of mechanical faults (with just a touch of semantic voluntarism in the outriders on Steptoe and Son, good-class wenches, etc), and has to fall back on a straight Christmas greeting which nevertheless it gets wrong until finally corrected. Like the 'Birthday Card', it presents a true servo-mechanism which can correct itself as it proceeds. Since the message here involved a narrative and not a mere phrase, I set it out in the conventional five-letter pattern used for coded messages. The 'Birthday Card' will be self-explanatory.

'The Computer's First Code Poem, with Rhyme' is different. This is a reminder that electronic computers developed out of work in advanced cryptography during the Second World War, and it is also a metaphor for the fact that a poem itself can be regarded as a coded message. My code, though not hair-raising, is not exactly translucent. Amateur cryptographers, with or without computers, are invited to 'find the poem', which is I believe the first to have been composed in this form.

from Studio International *'Cybernetic Serendipity: the computer and the arts' issue (August 1968), p. 57*

Colour poems

The Colour Poems take up various aspects of colour: flickering or dappled effects, protective coloration, colour in living or dead metaphors. The actual colours used in the poems function at a remove from imitation and have perhaps something of the effect of metre or rhyme in ordinary poetry. An additional element may appear, as in 'Dapple', where the words are names of colours but have other meanings: a mental as well as a visual dapple.

this note did not appear with the published set of Colour Poems *(Glasgow Third Eye Centre, 1979) but was written for the Third Eye Centre's* List of Publications, *1980*

Newspoems

My 'Newspoems' are so called because they have their origin in newspapers and could be described as hidden and unintended items of 'news' which have been extracted from a page of print, isolated, and given a title. The actual process involves cutting out the new 'message', pasting it on a white sheet of paper so that it looks like a short poem, and making a photocopy of the sheet. The result comes under the general category of 'found poem' but clearly also has links with some of the collage techniques used in art and advertising. However, in so far as collage implies juxtaposition or superimposition of diverse material, this term could properly apply only to my use of a title as a creative addition to the found material. The cut-outs themselves do not involve juxtaposed elements and indeed are meant to work in the opposite direction, ie they uncover something by a process of paring away, rather as a sculptor may 'find' the form he sees buried in a mass of stone. In this process, the original piece of news is deliberately lost, and there is no intention of producing ironies between the conscious and unconscious messages of the newspaper. Ironies do abound, but these are internal to the newspoem, or come from the general contrast between each new 'message' and the idea of what a newspaper would be likely to contain.

What lies behind the newspoems is basically the now well-observed fact that much if not most human perception is misperception. Everyone will have had some such experience as misreading a headline or placard, taking from it an entirely different meaning from the one intended. The misread meaning may be quite as meaningful as the correct one, may or may not have subconscious connections with it, may come from speed of perception — something caught out of the corner of one's eye, or seen from a vehicle — or from the workings of expectation rather than objective vision. Psychologists have conducted many experiments to show how vulnerable our perceptions are to the ceaseless pattern-seeking activity of the mind. Sir Frederick Charles Bartlett in his book *The Mind at Work and Play* (1951) tells how he got members of an audience to write down what they thought they saw when a series of placards with slightly distorted graphic messages were briefly shown to them. Out of 140 people only three correctly read: 'All is not gild that glotters', only five 'The Royal Intuition'; even with the more obvious 'Fish and Chops' and 'Talcer Powdum', only 28 and 33 respectively came up with the right message. In all these misreadings the mind could not accept the simple message the optic nerve gave it, and imposed its own structure. And as Bartlett pointed out, the imposed structure was not always the verbally expected one (eg 'All is not gold that glitters' or 'Fish and Chips') but sometimes bore no verbal similarity (eg 'The Royal Baby').

My newspoems are an attempt to extend these restructuring activities into a more conscious and creative area — though 'creative' here is perhaps an evaluative rather than a descriptive term, since as I have explained I restrict myself to the actual words of newsprint, and the poems are in that sense 'found'. How exactly they *are* found is not so easy to explain. But the strange results that the process of glancing at a page of newsprint can throw up in these examples suggests an extraordinary subliminal web of meanings, and who can say that readers of the page are not being affected by meanings which their conscious mind is happily unaware of? It is not unlike the old argument as to whether photography is an art. A busy city street will have its expected intelligible range of meanings as pedestrians enter and leave shops, buses stop and start, workmen use road-drills, pigeons scatter; but the eye of the good photographer will isolate, out of the readable flux, some totally unexpected and probably unrelated collocations of persons or objects which will then seem more meaningful than all the cut-away and rejected 'meaning' of the general scene. No one else saw what he saw, though it was there to be observed. The photographer, in this sense, is like the sculptor; he pares away in order to reveal.

The whole area of found art is one that is likely to continue to be investigated, despite the sceptical noises that are often made about it. The newspoems explore one small corner of this area, sometimes employing graphic space as concrete poetry does, sometimes evolving (by luck — but what is luck?) a structurally imitative or enacting form, sometimes using distinctions of type (whether typeface, or italics, or capitals and lower-case) to bring out or underline the newly found meaning. How these graphic elements should be able to be discovered and used without alteration, in contexts utterly different from those devised by the persons making up the newspaper, remains tantalisingly beyond explanation, unless we can assume that all language, even in informative and journalistic contexts, is a tissue of ambiguous potential, waiting to be exploded and released by the ever-active human eye.

written to accompany a selection of the Newspoems *in the Preston Polytechnic magazine edited by Duncan Glen,* Graphic Lines *1, (1975), pp. 47-48*

Books I Have Read (1927-1940)

This is a list of books read between 1927 and May 1940, compiled by EM in his Letts's Pocket Diary for 1933. He noted: 'Entries begun 1933 — block of entries, ie first 6-7 pages, includes 1933 reading + remembered reading 1927-33.' The list is marked 'except poetry', but it does include some verse, mainly anthologies. In order to read as many of his favourite authors (Verne, Burroughs, Henty) as possible EM persuaded his parents to join several different libraries, in addition to those EM himself belonged to. The original list is prefixed by a system of symbols used to indicate which library a particular book had come from: School, Grant's, Argosy, Art Club, St Vincent. The diary is now in the Edwin Morgan Collection in The Mitchell Library, Glasgow (MS220/10).

Kenneth Grahame, *The Wind in the Willows*
Ian Hay, *The Right Stuff*
H. Rider Haggard, *King Solomon's Mines*
James Barrie, *Peter Pan*
Lewis Carroll, *Alice in Wonderland*
G. A. Henty, *In the Heart of the Rockies*
Jules Verne, *20,000 Leagues Under the Sea*
Percy Westerman Omnibus (3 stories)
G. A. Henty Omnibus (3 stories)
Jules Verne, *From the Earth to the Moon*
Jules Verne, *Round the Moon*
G. A. Henty, *The Cat of Bubastes*
G. A. Henty, *For the Temple*
Jules Verne, *A Journey into the Interior of the Earth*
Edgar Rice Burroughs, *At the Earth's Core*
H. Rider Haggard, *The Ghost Kings*
H. Rider Haggard, *Belshazzar Ghost Island*

H. Rider Haggard, *She and Allan*
H. Rider Haggard, *Ayesha*
H. Rider Haggard, *The Virgin of the Sun*
John Hunter, *The Mystery of the Nameless Island*
Captain Marryat, *The Settlers in Canada*
Jules Verne, *Around the World in Eighty Days*
H. G. Wells, *The Food of the Gods*
H. G. Wells, *The First Men in the Moon*
Sir Walter Scott, *The Talisman*
F. Cowley Whitehouse, *Meltonians All*
Vice-Admiral E. R. G. R. Evans, *South with Scott*
Percy Westerman, *Pat Stobart of the Golden Dawn*
Mary Proctor, *The Book of the Heavens*
Dorothy M. Stuart, *The Book of Other Lands*
G. A. Henty, *The Young Carthaginian*
Jules Verne, *The Secret of the Island*
Edgar Allan Poe, *Tales of Mystery and Imagination*

264

Victor Hugo, *Les Misérables*

Victor Hugo, *The Hunchback of Notre Dame*

Sir Gilbert Parker, *The Battle of the Strong*

Alexandre Dumas, *The Chevalier de Maison Rouge*

Grimm's Fairy Tales

Andersen's Fairy Tales

The Wonder Book of Science

The Wonder Book of the Wild

The Wonder Book of Why and What

The Wonder Book of Wonders

Conan Doyle, *The Maracot Deep and other stories*

Sir J. Hammerton ed, *The New Popular Educator*

Charles Kingsley, *Westward Ho!*

Charles Dickens, *Oliver Twist*

George Manville Fenn, *Nic Revel*

John Buchan, *Prester John*

R. M. Ballantyne, *Black Ivory*

R. M. Ballantyne, *Martin Rattler*

R. M. Ballantyne, *Coral Island*

R. L. Stevenson, *Treasure Island*

R. L. Stevenson, *Kidnapped*

R. L. Stevenson, *The Black Arrow*

W. H. G. Kingston, *Beyond the Rockies*

C. Curtis Fraser, *Round the World in 10 Days*

Herbert Strang, *1,000 Miles an Hour*

W. H. G. Kingston, *The Three Midshipmen*

Alexandre Dumas, *The Black Tulip*

Jonathan Swift, *Gulliver's Travels*

H. B. Stowe, *Uncle Tom's Cabin*

Captain Marryat, *Masterman Ready*

Captain Marryat, *Midshipman Easy*

Bulwer Lytton, *The Last Days of Pompeii*

Daniel Defoe, *Robinson Crusoe*

Herbert Reid, *Private James Fyffe*

Toxi

Angus Buchanan, *Gain*

David Lawson Johnstone, *The Paradise of the North*

Rafael Sabatini, *Bardelys the Magnificent*

The Pictorial Cabinet of Marvels

Pictorial Sport and Adventure

Edgar Rice Burroughs, *The Beasts of Tarzan*

J. Macdonald Oxley, *Diamond Rock*

Michael Poole, *The Duffer at Danby*

R. M. Ballantyne, *The Red Eric*

Herbert Hayens, *The Heart-shaped Ruby*

R. L. Stevenson, *Dr Jekyll and Mr Hyde*

H. P. Hold and R. H. Barbour, *Lost Island*

Lew Wallace, *Ben-Hur*

Alexandre Dumas, *The Three Musketeers*

H. G. Wells, *Tales of Wonder*

Ian Hay, *Pip*

Edwin Sabin, *Treasure Mountain*

Percy Westerman, *The Disappearing Dhow*

Mary Grant Bruce, *Dick Lester of Kurrajong*

A. J. Alan, *A. J. Alan's Second Book*

H. Sienkiewicz, *Quo Vadis?*

W. H. G. Kingston, *In the Eastern Seas*

Alexandre Dumas, *Twenty Years After*

Andrew Lang, *Animal Stories*

Albert Richard Wetjen, *Fiddlers' Green*

T. C. Bridges and H. Tiltman, *More Heroes of Modern Adventure*

G. A. Henty, *Both Sides of the Border*

G. A. Henty, *With the Allies to Pekin*

Charles G. D. Roberts, *In the Morning of Time*

Edgar Rice Burroughs, *Tarzan of the Apes*

Alf's Button

J. Fenimore Cooper, *The Last of the Mohicans*

Charles Dickens, *David Copperfield*

Edgar Rice Burroughs, *The Return of Tarzan*

D. Wynne Willson, *Early Closing*

H. Rider Haggard, *Child of Storm*

Roland Walker, *Deville McKeene*

H. Rider Haggard, *Nada the Lily*

Charles Dickens, *The Old Curiosity Shop*

Eugène Sue, *The Wandering Jew*

Alexandre Dumas, *The Count of Monte Cristo*

Herbert Strang, *Dan Bolton's Discovery*

H. Rider Haggard, *Finished*

H. Rider Haggard, *Montezuma's Daughter*

Jack London, *Before Adam*

Edward Woodward, *Dr Greenfingers*

Bruce Graeme, *Blackshirt Again*

Harold Avery, *Off the Wicket*

Sir Arthur Conan Doyle, *The Lost World*

Thomas Mawhinny, *English Oak and Spanish Gold*

W. B. Anderson, *Boy Trappers in the Rockies*

Baroness Orczy, *The Scarlet Pimpernel*

Charles Dickens, *A Tale of Two Cities*

Agnes and Egerton Castle, *If Youth But Knew*

C. H. Tempany, *The Eight Days' Feud*

John Sweet, *The Red House Boys*

Charles Dickens, *The Pickwick Papers*

Charles Dickens, *Master Humphrey's Clock*

H. G. Wells, *The Sleeper Awakes*

Victor Hugo, *The Toilers of the Deep*

G. A. Henty, *The Treasure of the Incas*

Charles Dickens, *Bleak House*

R. M. Ballantyne, *Philosopher Jack*

P. G. Wodehouse, *The Inimitable Jeeves*

P. G. Wodehouse, *Heavy Weather*

P. G. Wodehouse, *Meet Mr Mulliner*

Sir Arthur Conan Doyle, *Tales of Long Ago*

Charles Dickens, *Martin Chuzzlewit*

Sir Arthur Conan Doyle, *Adventures, Return, Memoirs, Case-Book and Last Bow of Sherlock Holmes* (1 vol.)

Bruce Graeme, *Alias Blackshirt*

Frank Packard, *Further Adventures of Jimmie Dale*

Sax Rohmer, *The Green Eyes of Bâst*

H. G. Wells, *The War of the Worlds*

H. Rider Haggard, *Allan and the Ice Gods*

Sax Rohmer, *The Si-Fan Mysteries*

Jack London, *White Fang*

H. Rider Haggard, *She*

Sax Rohmer, *The Yellow Claw*

Richard Marsh, *The Beetle*

H. Rider Haggard, *Cleopatra*

P. G. Wodehouse, *Mulliner Nights*

Sax Rohmer, *The Mystery of Dr Fu Manchu*

W. C. Sellar and R. J. Yeatman, *1066 and All That*

Louise Gerard, *The Golden Centipede*

'Sapper', *Ronald Standish*

Joseph Delmont, *Mistress of the Skies*

P. G. Wodehouse, *Love Among the Chickens*

Bruce Graeme, *Epilogue*

Alexandre Dumas, *The Conspirators*

Sir Walter Scott, *Rob Roy*

Neil Munro, *The New Road*

R. L. Stevenson, *The Master of Ballantrae*

R. M. Ballantyne, *The World of Ice*

Edgar Wallace, *Again the Three Just Men*

P. G. Wodehouse, *Very Good, Jeeves*

Rudyard Kipling, *The Second Jungle Book*

Charles G. D. Roberts, *The Haunters of the Silence*

P. G. Wodehouse, *Hot Water*

Charles G. D. Roberts, *Watchers of the Trails*

Edgar Wallace, *Eve's Island*

Sir Arthur Conan Doyle, *The Poison Belt*

Richmal Crompton, *Just William*

P. G. Wodehouse, *The Heart of a Goof*

Gunby Hadath, *Paying the Price*

P. G. Wodehouse, *Right Ho, Jeeves*

Kent Carr, *Playing the Game!*

Rudyard Kipling, *The Jungle Book*

Franz Sales Mayer, *A Handbook of Ornament*

'Sapper', *Bulldog Drummond*

S. R. K. Glanville, *The Egyptians*

John Buchan, *The Last Secrets*

R. M. Ballantyne, *Ungava*

R. Austin Freeman, *Dr Thorndyke's Case-Book*

Cutcliffe Hyne, *The Lost Continent*

Elsa Barker *The C.I.D. of Dexter Drake*

W. H. G. Kingston, *Manco, the Peruvian Chief*

Desmond Coke, *The Schoolboy Omnibus*

H. G. Wells, *Complete Short Stories*

Alexandre Dumas, *The Man in the Iron Mask*

E. W. Hornung, *Raffles*

Edgar Rice Burroughs, *A Fighting Man of Mars*

Various authors, *A Book of Strange Stories*

Sir Arthur Conan Doyle, *Sherlock Holmes Long Stories*

Vicente Blasco Ibáñez, *Donnica*

'Sapper', *Knock-Out*

Richmal Crompton, *More William*

P. G. Wodehouse, *Big Money*

L. M. Nesbitt, *Desert and Forest*

H. G. Wells, *The Invisible Man*

H. G. Wells, *The Island of Dr Moreau*

H. G. Wells, *In the Days of the Comet*

H. G. Wells, *Men Like Gods*

Sidney Horler, *The Murder Mask*

Frederick J. Glass, *Design and Composition*

Richmal Crompton, *William the Pirate*

Richmal Crompton, *William the Bad*

Richmal Crompton, *William the Gangster*

P. G. Wodehouse ed, *A Century of Humour*

John Bunyan, *The Pilgrim's Progress*

Alexandre Dumas, *Marguerite de Valois*

Richmal Crompton, *William the Rebel*

Richmal Crompton, *William Again*

R. Austin Freeman, *Famous Cases of Dr Thorndyke*

Edgar Allan Poe, *The Gold Bug and other stories*

R. M. Ballantyne, *The Gorilla Hunters*

E. Barrington, *Cleopatra the Laughing Queen*

A Century of Detective Stories

Rafael Sabatini ed, *A Century of Sea Stories*

Victor Hugo, *The Laughing Man*

P. G. Wodehouse, *O. Psmith, Journalist*

R. L. Stevenson, *The Bottle Imp*

G. K. Chesterton, *The Adventures of Major Brown*

J. S. Fletcher, *The Convict and the Clerics*

Ian Hay, *Natural Causes*

H. de Vere Stacpoole, *Maru*

Walter de la Mare, *All Hallows*

Rafael Sabatini, *The King's Messenger*

P. G. Wren, *Buried Treasure*

P. G. Wodehouse, *Louder and Funnier*

P. G. Wodehouse, *The Man with Two Left Feet*

Edgar Allan Poe, *The Best Known Works of Poe*

H. Rider Haggard, *Allan Quatermain*

'Sapper', *The Third Round*

J. J. Bell, *Wee Macgreegor*

Jules Verne, *Adrift in the Pacific*

Alexandre Dumas, *Chicot the Jester*

G. Davison, *Mystery of the Red-Haired Valet*

'Sapper', *The Final Count*

W. S. Berridge, *All About Fish*

H. de Vere Stacpoole, *The Cruise of the 'Kingfisher'*

Douglas Newton, *Dr Odin*

P. G. Wodehouse, *Blandings Castle*

James Ferguson, *The Table in a Roar* (Jokes)

Mark Channing, *White Python*

Rafael Sabatini, *The Sea Hawk*

Rafael Sabatini, *Captain Blood*

Rafael Sabatini, *The Chronicles of Captain Blood*

P. G. Wodehouse, *Jill the Reckless*

Paul Annixter, *Wilderness Ways*

P. G. Wodehouse, *Piccadilly Jim*

Edgar Jepson, *The Moon Gods*

H. Mortimer Batten, *Habits and Characters of British Wild Animals*

Sir J. Arthur Thomson, *The Outline of Natural History*

Sir J. Hammerton ed, *Outline of Nature in the British Isles*

Edgar Rice Burroughs, *The Gods of Mars*

Edgar Rice Burroughs, *The Chessmen of Mars*

Edgar Rice Burroughs, *Pirates of Venus*

Charles Dickens, *Little Dorrit*

Sax Rohmer, *The Devil Doctor*

Richmal Crompton, *William*

H. de Vere Stacpoole, *The Vengeance of Mynheer Van Lok*

Ernest Thompson Seton ed, *Famous Animal Stories*

'Sapper', *The Island of Terror*

Bram Stoker, *Dracula*

Various authors, *My Best Animal Story*

Ripley, *Believe it or not!*

Edgar Rice Burroughs, *A Princess of Mars*

H. G. Wells, *The History of Mr Polly*

Sir Walter Scott, *A Legend of Montrose*

Edgar Rice Burroughs, *The Cave Girl*

H. G. Wells, *Tono-Bungay*

William Thackeray, *Henry Esmond*

Edgar Rice Burroughs, *Tarzan the Terrible*

Conan Doyle, *Tales of the Ring and Camp*

Conan Doyle, *Tales of Pirates and Blue Water*

Conan Doyle, *Tales of Terror and Mystery*

Conan Doyle, *Tales of Twilight and the Unseen*

Conan Doyle, *Adventures of Medical Life*

G. K. Chesterton, *The Innocence of Father Brown*

G. K. Chesterton, *The Wisdom of Father Brown*

G. K. Chesterton, *The Incredulity of Father Brown*

G. K. Chesterton, *The Secret of Father Brown*

B. H. Clark and M. Lieber eds, *Great Short Stories of the World*

Frederick Sleath, *Green Swallows*

Naomi Mitchison ed, *An Outline for Boys and Girls and Their Parents*

R. D. Blackmore, *Lorna Doone*

Sir William Orpen, *The Outline of Art*

A. E. W. Mason, *The Three Gentlemen*

Sir Arthur Conan Doyle, *Rodney Stone*

Sir Arthur Conan Doyle, *Uncle Bernal*
Sir Arthur Conan Doyle, *Exploits of Brigadier Gerard*
Sir Arthur Conan Doyle, *Adventures of Gerard*
Arthur Upham Pope, *An Introduction to Persian Art*
J. D. Wyss, *The Swiss Family Robinson*
Charles Darwin, *A Naturalist's Voyage Round the World*
Victor Hugo, *The Outlaw of Iceland*
G. Whyte-Melville, *The Gladiators*
Dorothy Sayers ed, *Great Short Stories of Detection*
W. P. Pycraft ed, *The Standard Natural History*
W. P. Pycraft, *The Courtship of Animals*
E. Arnot Robertson, *Four Frightened People*
Stanley Weyman, *Count Hannibal*
R. Talbot Kelly, *Egypt*
James Baikie, *A Century of Excavation in the Land of the Pharaohs*
Albert Dorrington, *The Half-God*
Samuel Butler, *Erewhon*
P. G. Wodehouse, *My Man Jeeves*
Peter Cheyney, *The Gold Kimono*
Charles Kingsley, *Hypatia*
T. W. Earp, *The Modern Movement in Painting*
Talbot Mundy, *King of the Khyber Rifles*
Talbot Mundy, *Jingrim*
Talbot Mundy, *Black Light*
Talbot Mundy, *Om*
George Sim, *Vertebrate Fauna of 'Dee'*
H. Rider Haggard, *The Witch's Head*
Dashiell Hammett, *The Thin Man*
Alexandre Dumas, *Acté*
Agatha Christie, *The Mysterious Affair at Styles*
Insect Architecture
Insect Transformations
Victor Hugo, *'Ninety-Three*
H. C. Bailey, *Mr Fortune Wonders*
Gilbert White, *The Natural History of Selborne*
Ernest Bramah, *The Wallet of Kai Lung*
H. G. Wells, *A Short History of the World*
E. C. Bailey, *Mr Fortune, Please*
Henry Scherren, *Popular Natural History*
Baroness Orczy, *By the Gods Beloved*
H. Rider Haggard, *Queen Sheba's Ring*
William Goldsmith, *Animated Nature vol. 2*

Georg Ebers, *An Egyptian Princess*
Philip Henry Gosse, *Evenings at the Microscope*
Dennis Wheatley, *They Found Atlantis*
H. Rider Haggard, *Moon of Israel*
Ben Travers, *A Cuckoo in the Nest*
George Preedy, *The Rocklitz*
Agatha Christie, *The Big Four*
Rafael Sabatini, *The Nuptials of Corbal*
Sir James G. Frazer, *The Golden Bough*
Rafael Sabatini ed, *A Century of Historical Stories*
Robert Graves, *I, Claudius*
Stanley Weyman, *A Gentleman of France*
Stanley Weyman, *The Red Cockade*
Nis Petersen, *The Street of the Sandalmakers*
Rafael Sabatini, *Scaramouche*
Rafael Sabatini, *Scaramouche the Kingmaker*
H. Rider Haggard, *The Wanderer's Necklace*
Virgil Markham, *The Deadly Jest*
Agatha Christie, *Death in the Clouds*
Henry Williamson, *Salar the Salmon*
J. G. Sarasin, *Tiger-Heart*
May Sinclair, *Uncanny Stories*
Agatha Christie, *The Murder of Roger Ackroyd*
Philip Macdonald, *R.I.P.*
C. R. Maturin, *Melmoth the Wanderer*
W. Stanley Sikes, *The Missing Money-Lender*
Agatha Christie, *Why Didn't They Ask Evans?*
Edgar Rice Burroughs, *The Warlord of Mars*
Baroness Orczy, *Leatherface*
John Buchan, *The Blanket of the Dark*
Seldon Truss, *Gallows Bait*
John Ferguson, *The Man in the Dark*
William Thackeray, *English Humorists*
Sir Walter Scott, *Old Mortality*
Thomas Hardy, *Far from the Madding Crowd*
Stacey Blake, *Beyond the Blue*
Dorothy Sayers, *The Unpleasantness at the Bellona Club*
Maude Meagher, *The Green Scamander*
H. G. Wells, *The World Set Free*
Naomi Mitchison, *The Conquered*
Élie Reclus, *Primitive Folk*
Charles Kingsley, *Hereward the Wake*
Baroness Orczy, *The Laughing Cavalier*
George Preedy, *Tumult in the North*

Marjorie Bowen, *The Leopard and the Lily*

H. G. Wells, *The Wonderful Visit*

Alexandra David-Neel, *With Mystics and Magicians in Tibet*

E. A. Wallis Budge, *Tutănkhámen*

Arthur Weigall, *The Glory of the Pharaohs*

Lord Lytton, *The Last of the Barons*

P. Leslie Waterhouse, *The Story of Architecture*

S. C. Kaines Smith, *An Outline History of Painting*

J. G. Crowther, *The Progress of Science*

C. G. D. Roberts, *The Kindred of the Wild*

L. Detre, *War of Two Worlds*

Conan Doyle, *Sir Nigel*

Conan Doyle, *The White Company*

Conan Doyle, *Micah Clarke*

Conan Doyle, *The Refugees*

A Century of Creepy Stories

Jane Harrison, *Ancient Art and Ritual*

Philip Macdonald, *The Wraith*

Wonders of Animal Life

E. C. Bentley, *Trent's Last Case*

Philip Macdonald, *The Rasp*

John Ferguson, *Death Comes to Perigord*

H. G. Wells, *The Shape of Things to Come*

J. Leslie Mitchell, *Spartacus*

L. S. B. Leakey, *Stone Age Africa*

George J. Romanes, *Animal Intelligence*

H. G. Wells, *Kipps*

Dorothy Sayers, *Unnatural Death*

Ivor Brown, *H. G. Wells*

Percy J. Smith, *Lettering*

Marjorie Bowen, *The Viper of Milan*

Thea von Harbou, *Metropolis*

Hugh Walpole, *Portrait of a Man with Red Hair*

Naomi Mitchison, *When the Bough Breaks*

H. G. Wells, *The Bulpington of Blup*

Phoebe Allen, *Peeps at Architecture*

Sir Frederick Wedmore, *Painters and Painting*

Mrs Arthur Bell, *Architecture*

Algernon Blackwood, *The Willows etc.*

Henry Williamson, *Tarka the Otter*

Hal P. Trevarthen, *World D*

Georg Ebers, *Homo Sum* vol. I

Ernest Bramah, *The Secret of the League*

H. G. Wells, *The Dream*

Selected Russian Short Stories

Second Strange Stories Omnibus

Olaf Stapledon, *Last and First Men*

Ambrose Bierce, *The Eyes of the Panther*

Ambrose Bierce, *The Monk and the Hangman's Daughter*

Sir James Jeans, *The Mysterious Universe*

Julian Huxley, *Essays in Popular Science*

Great German Short Stories

Thea von Harbou, *The Girl in the Moon*

William Dwight Whitney, *The Life and Growth of Language*

Wilkie Collins, *The Moonstone*

Warwick Deeping, *The Man on the White Horse*

Margaret Mitchell, *Gone with the Wind*

E. L. Grant Watson, *Enigmas of Natural History*

Alexis Carrel, *Man, the Unknown*

Gustave Flaubert, *Salammbo*

Sir J. G. Frazer, *Aftermath*

H. G. Wells, *The Outline of History*

H. G. Wells, *Star-Begotten*

Aldous Huxley, *Brave New World*

John Galsworthy, *Man of Property*

John Galsworthy, *In Chancery*

Michael Arlen, *Man's Mortality*

Julian Duguid, *A Cloak of Monkey Fur*

Frederic Prokosch, *The Asiatics*

Charles Darwin, *The Origin of the Species*

Philip Macdonald, *The Link*

Charles Mercier, *Sanity and Insanity*

Dmitri Merejkowski, *The Forerunner*

G. K. Chesterton, *The Man who was Thursday*

Sir Leonard Woolley, *Digging up the Past*

Encyclopaedia of Modern Knowledge

J. D. Beresford, *The Hampdenshire Wonder*

Sir Thomas Browne, *Religio Medici*

H. A. L. Fisher, *A History of Europe*

Lord Lytton, *The Coming Race*

Lord Lytton, *The Haunted and the Haunters*

Eileen Power, *Medieval People*

J. B. S. Haldane, *The Inequality of Man*

Jean Henri Fabre, *Social Life in the Insect World*

John Ward, *The Sacred Beetle*

Henry James, *The Turn of the Screw*

Henry James, *The Aspern Papers*

F. Marion Crawford, *Zoroaster*

Roger Fry, *Vision and Design*

G. D. H. Cole, *Political Economics*

W. J. Perry, *The Growth of Civilization*
Olaf Stapledon, *Star Maker*
Joan Grant, *Winged Pharaoh*
J. B. S. Haldane, *Possible Worlds*
Herbert Spencer, *First Principles*
T. S. Eliot, *Sweeney Agonistes*
W. B. Yeats ed, *Oxford Book of Modern Verse*
John Dickson Carr, *It Walks By Night*
Aldous Huxley, *Crome Yellow*
Gotthold Lessing, *Laokoon*
Gotthold Lessing, *How the Ancients Represented Death*
G. B. Shaw, *Saint Joan*
Leigh Ashton ed, *Chinese Art*
Charles Baudelaire, *Les Fleurs du Mal*
Marcus B. Huish, *Japan and its Art*
Balzac, *Le Père Goriot*
Leonard Woolley, *Ur of the Chaldees*
Sigmund Freud, *Psychopathology of Everyday Life*
J. G. Crowther, *An Outline of the Universe*
R. H. Tawney, *Religion and the Rise of Capitalism*
Giovanni Boccaccio, *The Decameron*
Herbert Read, *Art and Society*
F. L. Lucas, *The Decline and Fall of the Romantic Ideal*
C. E. M. Joad, *Guide to the Philosophy of Morals and Politics*
H. G. Wells, *World Brain*
T. S. Eliot, *Murder in the Cathedral*
Jane Austen, *Pride and Prejudice*
H. G. Wells, *The New Machiavelli*
Walter Pater, *The Renaissance*
J. W. Page, *Primitive Races of Today*
Dr C. W. Kimmins, *Children's Dreams*
Michael Glenne, *Great Australian Mysteries*
Arnold Haskell, *Ballet*
Romola Nijinsky, *Nijinsky*
Peter Thoene, *Modern German Art*
Emanuel Swedenborg, *Heaven and Hell*
Curt Sachs, *World History of the Dance*
R. M. Fleming, *Ancient Tales from Many Lands*
J. W. R. Purser, *Art and Truth*
G. B. Shaw, *Complete Plays*
Laure Morgenstern, *Esthétiques d'Orient et d'Occident*
Paul-Guillaume and Munro, *La Sculpture Nègre Primitive*
Valentin Feldman, *L'Esthétique Franqise Contemporaine*
Stephen Spender, *Trial of a Judge*

Herbert Read, *Surrealism*
Jane Austen, *Emma*
Thomas Malory, *Le Morte Darthur*
M. Roberts ed, *The Faber Book of Modern Verse*
Poètes Contemporains
David Gascoyne, *Surrealism*
E. F. Carritt, *What is Beauty?*
Algernon Blackwood, *The Centaur*
William Smart, *An Introduction to the Theory of Value*
William Smart, *The Distribution of Income*
Alfred Marshall, *Economics of Industry*
Alfred Marshall, *Money, Credit and Commerce*
Clive Bell, *Art*
Marcel Proust, *Swann's Way*
Clive Bell, *Since Cézanne*
James Bridie, *The King of Nowhere*
Virginia Woolf, *The Common Reader*
A. N. Whitehead, *Science and the Modern World*
Sigmund Freud, *Totem and Taboo*
Frederick C. Benham, *Economics*
William Johnstone, *Creative Art in England*
Andre Maurois, *Ariel*
Anthony Bertram, *Design*
Epstein and Haskall, *The Sculptor Speaks*
P. Fierens, *Sculpteurs d'Aujourd'hui*
Laurence Binyon, *Painting in the Far East*
Laurence Sterne, *A Sentimental Journey*
Osbert Sitwell, *Before the Bombardment*
Clive Bell, *Civilization*
Standhal, *Le Rouge et le Noir*
R. H. Wilenski, *The Meaning of Modern Art*
G. B. Shaw, *The Intelligent Woman's Guide*
A. C. Bradley, *Shakespearian Tragedy*
Hartley Withers, *Money*
Sinclair Lewis, *Mantrap*
H. F. Rubinstein, *The English Drama*
C. J. Sisson, *The Elizabethan Dramatists*
F. S. Boas, *Tudor Drama*
Ray Lankester, *Secrets of Earth and Sea*
J. B. Priestley, *The English Novel*
G. B. Harrison, *Elizabethan England*
Herbert Read, *Collected Literary Criticism*
Flinders Petrie, *Egyptian Decorative Art*
Ernest Weekley, *The English Language*

J. R. Firth, *Speech*
C. E. M. Joad, *The Mind and its Workings*
Ernest Jones, *Psycho-Analysis*
Walter Raleigh, *The English Novel*
Archibald MacLeish, *Panic*
Auden and Isherwood, *On the Frontier*
Hermon Ould, *The Art of the Play*
Louis Golding, *The Jewish Problem*
T. S. Eliot, *Elizabethan Essays*
Anthony Trollope, *The Last Chronicle of Barset*
E. Classen, *History of the English Language*
John Bailey, *Introduction to Jane Austen*
Emily Bronte, *Wuthering Heights*
Virginia Woolf, *To the Lighthouse*
George Eliot, *Adam Bede*
Hugh Walpole, *Mr Perrin and Mr Traill*
Frank Swinnerton, *Nocturne*
C. A. Mace, *The Psychology of Study*
George Eliot, *Scenes of Clerical Life*
Oliver Goldsmith, *The Vicar of Wakefield*
Bullett ed, *The English Galaxy of Shorter Poems*
Fry, Binyon etc, *Chinese Art*
Ault ed, *A Treasury of Unfamiliar Lyrics*
Parsons ed, *The Progress of Poetry*
D. H. Lawrence, *Sons and Lovers*
Louis MacNeice, *Modern Poetry*
Peter Alexander, *Shakespeare: Life and Art*
G. B. Harrison, *Introducing Shakespeare*
Huxley, Haddon, Carr, Saunders, *We Europeans*
Peter Kropotkin, *Mutual Aid*
L. Susan Stebbing, *Thinking to Some Purpose*
Bishop Gore, *Belief in God*
C. E. M. Joad, *Why War?*
Arnold Bennett, *Literary Taste*
R. H. Mottram, *The Spanish Farm*
Ramon J. Sender, *Seven Red Sundays*
C. E. M. Joad, *Guide to Philosophy*
Ashton and Gray, *Chinese Art*
Alexandra David-Neel, *Buddhism*
E. M. Forster, *A Passage to India*
Auden and Isherwood, *The Ascent of F6*
William Saroyan, *The Daring Young Man on the Flying Trapeze*
E. M. W. Tillyard, *Milton*
Stefan Zweig, *Tolstoi*

G. M. Young, *Victorian England*
J. L. and B. Hammond, *The Bleak Age*
W. B. Maxwell, *To What Green Altar?*
T. S. Eliot, *The Family Reunion*
Alfred Einstein, *A Short History of Music*
Hugh Nicol, *Microbes by the Million*
J. Middleton Murry, *Aspects of Literature*
Raymond B. Cattell, *Psychology and the Religious Quest*
James Joyce, *A Portrait of the Artist as a Young Man*
C. E. M. Joad, *The Future of Morals*
Confucius, *The Analects*
Grant Allen, *The Evolution of the Idea of God*
Neil Gunn, *Morning Tide*
Talbot Rice, *The Background of Art*
Stephen Leacock, *Literary Lapses*
Gertrude Stein, *Picasso*
Thomas Hardy, *Under the Greenwood Tree*
Georges Duhamel, *Le Notaire du Havre*
Herbert Read, *English Prose Style*
Herbert Read, *Poetry and Anarchism*
Francis Carco, *Verotchka L'Étrangère*
Louis Chadourne, *Terre de Chanaan*
Granville-Barker and Harrison eds, *A Companion to Shakespeare Studies*
Wyndham Lewis, *The Lion and the Fox*
J. W. Mackail, *The Approach to Shakespeare*
Karl Barth, *The Church and the Political Problem of Our Day*
Arthur Symons, *William Blake*
Walter Raleigh, *Shakespeare*
Harold J. Laski, *Liberty in the Modern State*
Gerald Heard, *The Source of Civilization*
A. J. J. Ratcliff, *The Nation of Dreams*
Julian Huxley, *Essays of a Biologist*
G. Grigson ed, *New Verse*
Holbrook Jackson, *The Eighteen Nineties*
Olaf Stapledon, *Philosophy and Living*
Rosa Newmarch, *The Russian Arts*
Sheldon Cheney, *World History of Art*
Peter Kropotkin, *Russian Literature*
Petronius, *The Satyricon*
Daniel Defoe, *Roxana*
Leonid Andreyev, *And it came to pass that the king was dead*
M. Sholokhov, *The Soil Upturned*
Aylmer Maude, *Tolstoy on Art*
W. M. Patterson, *The Rhythm of Prose*
Daniel Defoe, *Moll Flanders*

Apuleius, *The Golden Ass*
Virginia Woolf, *Orlando*
T. S. Eliot, *The Idea of a Christian Society*
Walter de la Mare, *Memoirs of a Midget*
G. Wilson Knight, *The Wheel of Fire*
G. Wilson Knight, *The Burning Oracle*
Upton Sinclair, *The Wet Parade*
Izaak Walton, *The Compleat Angler*
J. W. Dunne, *An Experiment with Time*
J. W. Dunne, *The New Immortality*
N. Jarintsov, *The Russians and their Language*
P. Markov, *The Soviet Theatre*
Richard Jeffries, *The Story of my Heart*
Tolstoy, *Plays*
Maxim Gorky, *Twentysix Men and a Girl*
Maxim Gorky, *Selected Stories*
Dostoevsky, *The House of the Dead*
Berdyaef, Mauriac etc, *Communism and Christians*
Tolstoy, *Anna Karenina*
Flaubert, *Madame Bovary*
F. R. Leavis, *Revaluation*
Wyndham Lewis, *Tarr*
J. B. Priestley, *Johnson over Jordan*
Tolstoy, *Twenty-three Tales*
Tolstoy, *Essays on Life and Religion*
Oliver Lodge, *Modern Scientific Ideas*
James Rice, *Relativity*
Aldous Huxley, *Texts and Pretexts*
Pushkin, *Kapitanskaya Dochka*
Denis Saurat, *The End of Fear*
Gor'ky, *Russkiya Skazki*
Raymond Escholier, *La Peinture Française: CCC^e*
John Livingston Lowes, *The Road to Xanadu*

Mary Webb, *Precious Bane*
Leonid Andreyev, *The Life of Man*
Turgenev, *Dream Tales and Prose Poems*
Chekhov, *Selected Plays*
Oxford Book of Mystical Verse
J. M. Richards, *An Introduction to Modern Architecture*
I. A. Richards, *Principles of Literary Criticism*
Virginia Woolf, *The Waves*
Osbert Sitwell, *Triple Fugue*
Stalin, *Dialectical and Historical Materialism*
I. A. Richards, *Practical Criticism*
A. N. Whitehead, *Religion in the Making*
J. A. Herbert, *Illuminated Manuscripts*
Oxford Book of Russian Verse
William McDougall, *The Frontiers of Psychology*
Joseph Gregor, *Masks of the World*
S. F. Robinson, *Celtic Illuminative Art*
Dilys Powell, *Descent from Parnassus*
Oxford Book of Carols
Oxford Book of Spanish Verse
T. S. Eliot, *Selected Essays*
Konody and Wilenski, *Italian Painting*
Montaigne, *Selections*
James Feibleman, *In Praise of Comedy*
MacNicol ed, *Hindu Scriptures*
Tolstoy, *A Confession*
Tolstoy, *What I Believe*
Westermarck, *Christianity and Morals*
Charles Fort, *Lo!*
P. D. Ouspensky, *A New Model of the Universe*
A. E. Taylor, *Socrates*
J. B. Rhine, *New Frontiers of the Mind*

Index

273